+HV6018 .M43 1990

Y0-EER-282
/Measuring crime : large-scale, long t...
HV6018 .M43 1990 C.1 STACKS 1990

Measuring crime

HV
6018
M43
1990

	DATE DUE	

AUDREY COHEN COLLEGE LIBRARY
345 HUDSON STREET
NEW YORK, NY 10014

SUNY Series in Critical Issues in Criminal Justice
Donald J. Newman, Gilbert Geis, and
Terence P. Thornberry, editors

MEASURING CRIME

LARGE-SCALE, LONG-RANGE EFFORTS

edited by

Doris Layton MacKenzie, Phyllis Jo Baunach,
and Roy R. Roberg

State University of New York Press

Published by
State University of New York Press, Albany

©1990 State University of New York

All rights reserved

Printed in the United States of America

No part of this book may be used or reproduced
in any manner whatsoever without written permission
except in the case of brief quotations embodied in
critical articles and reviews.

For information, address State University of New York
Press, State University Plaza, Albany, N.Y., 12246

Library of Congress Cataloging-in-Publication Data

Measuring crime: large-scale, long-range efforts/edited by Doris
　Layton MacKenzie, Phyllis Jo Baunach, and Roy R. Roberg.
　　p. cm.—(SUNY series in critical issues in criminal justice)
　Bibliography: p.
　Includes index.
　ISBN 0-7914-0144-8.—ISBN 0-7914-0145-6 (pbk.)
　　1. Criminal statistics—United States. 2. Criminal justice.
Administration of—United States—Data processing. I. MacKenzie,
Doris L. II. Baunach, Phyllis Jo. III. Roberg, Roy R. IV. Series.
HV6018M43 1990
364′072073—dc19　　　　　　　　　　　　　　　　　　　　　89-30043
　　　　　　　　　　　　　　　　　　　　　　　　　　　　　CIP

10 9 8 7 6 5 4 3 2 1

Contents

Acknowledgments	1
Foreword: Jack B. Parker	3
Preface: Steven R. Schlesinger	5
1. The Challenge of Measuring Crime Doris Layton MacKenzie and Phyllis Jo Baunach	9

PART I DATA COLLECTION AND SAMPLING

2. Limits and Use of the Uniform Crime Reports Victoria W. Schneider and Brian Wiersema	21
3. The Future of the Uniform Crime Reporting Program: Its Scope and Promise Yoshio Akiyama and Harvey M. Rosenthal	49
4. The National Crime Survey, 1973-1986: Strengths and Limitations of a Very Large Data Set James Garofalo	75
5. The Current and Future National Crime Survey James P. Lynch	97
6. State Prisons and Inmates: The Census and Survey Phyllis Jo Baunach	119

PART II MEASUREMENT AND ANALYSIS

7. Using Archival Data for The Secondary Analysis of Criminal Justice Issues Michael W. Traugott	145

CONTENTS

8. The Use of Microcomputers with Large Data Bases 157
   Edgar Barry Moser

9. Nationwide Homicide Data Sets: An Evaluation of the Uniform Crime Reports and the National Center for Health Statistics Data 175
   Marc Riedel

PART III   THE PAST AND THE FUTURE

10. Measurement in Criminology and Criminal Justice: A Brief 20-Year Retrospective 209
    Robert M. Figlio

11. Alternative Futures in Measuring Crime 223
    Benjamin H. Renshaw III

Notes 237

References 249

Contributors 267

Index 271

Acknowledgments

This book would not have been possible without the help of many people, foremost of whom are the members of the Departments of Experimental Statistics and Criminal Justice, Louisiana State University who contributed their time to the symposium from which this book grew: Patrick R. Anderson, William G. Archambeault, David C. Blouin, Steven M. Buco, Binshan Lin, Marc Lor, Graden (Pete) McCool, Edgar Barry Moser, Roy Sorbet, George S. Tracy, L. Thomas Winfree, Jr., Patricia Wozniak, Raytai Wu. In particular, thanks are given to Kenneth L. Koonce who created an atmosphere of teamwork which fosters such cooperative activities. Without his support and encouragement this book would not have been possible.

Thanks are also given to others who helped with the symposium and the resulting book: To Alma Jean Williams for her careful typing and editing of many of the chapters; to the conference participants in particular, Lynne Goodstein, for their stimulating discussions and active participation in the symposium; and to the Office of Short Courses and Conferences, Division of Continuing Education, LSU who helped with the organization of the symposium.

Foreword

This is one of the most important books on crime measurement to come forth for some time. *Measuring Crime: Large-Scale, Long-Range Efforts* helps us to take stock of our present knowledge about measuring crime, and it gives us direction in our future efforts. One of the unfortunate impediments to knowledge is that too many people already know too much that is not true. Certainly there is no dearth of "experts" or people with opinions about the cause and eradication of crime. Even criminologists can not always be comfortable with our theoretical and statistical interpretations. This book gives us a reliable baseline from which to understand the present and future use of large data set measurement of crime.

The work of a single author on this topic would not have been as authoritative as this multiple effort. It is difficult to imagine an individual possessing the breadth and depth of knowledge necessary to compare with the collective expertise of this distinguished group of authors. The idea for this work grew out of a symposium dealing with large data sets held recently at Louisiana State University. It immediately became apparent to those in attendance that we were being given an unusual opportunity to explore and evaluate the "state of the art" in large scale, long range measurement of crime. It also became apparent that this was an opportunity that should be shared with everyone interested in the topic.

The magnitude of crime presents many problems to the researcher, but these can be overcome by the development of advanced methodology and statistical techniques. The creation and effective utilization of large data bases offers excellent opportunities for such advancement.

This effort should aid its readers in more intelligent use of existing large data bases through a clear explanation of the values, strengths, and weaknesses of the large scale measurements.

Crime measurement has been in existence long enough to have a history, as described in this work. By now we have a good understanding of what data has value and what has little to offer. Through the revision of data collection instruments, reporting, and survey techniques, large data sets will become more valuable to the criminologist, government officials, and the practitioner. The sophistication of newer generation microcomputing will make analysis of large scale data bases more usable by a much wider audience. Greater benefit from secondary analysis will also be possible. We are on the threshold of an exciting new era in measuring crime. Perhaps we will no longer have to continue to beat the theoretical and analytical dead horses of the past.

JACK B. PARKER

Preface:
Creating Statistics for Policy and Policies for Statistics

The management of a statistical enterprise requires simultaneous concern for two political and technical imperatives: first, the continuous effort to collect and publish statistics that inform policy by contributing to public decision making, and second, the quieter, internal decisions about data elements, methodological components, technological options, and presentation in publications. If a statistical agency is to be successful in the first objective of providing empirical data in support of executive and legislative branch decisions, early prescient choices with relation to data to be collected are the undergirding of future policy relevance. Since the time span from initial conception to final analytic results is necessarily lengthy for the large scale data sets discussed in this volume, the effective statistical manager must anticipate the issues that will be in the criminal justice policy arena in future years. This requires the design of new statistical efforts and the redesign of existing surveys to enhance their utility.

As these words are written in September 1988, two massive redesign efforts begun in the late 1970s have concluded. Both the Uniform Crime Reports (UCR) and the National Crime Survey (NCS), following multi-year and multi-million-dollar evaluations, have been redesigned in terms of the anticipated policy requirements of elected and analytic consumers. The evaluation and assessment of these two preeminent national indicators of crime and victimization in American society were conducted during years of intense budget scrutiny and competition within the Department of Justice; thus, these statistical programs—and others related to corrections, adjudication, system transactions and criminal histories—were subject to the same intense cost/benefit examination as operational criminal justice programs. While all of the enhancements that might have been possible in a more beneficent budget environment have not been made, enough valuable improvements have been made to carry the measurement of crime into the twenty-first century.

Critical to the continued success of these and other large-scale, long-range data series is acceptance and recognition of the need for multiple national indicators of both crime and the response of this nation's system for the administration of justice. Multiple and composite indicators of economic conditions are as ingrained in the policy institutions of this nation as the desire for economic well being. Effective national intelligence on crime requires the same multiplicity of indicators; at a minimum, there is the need for a thermometer of information from victims of crime, and a barometer of information from local law enforcement. The experience of the past five and a half years convinces me that such acceptance will never be as complete as in the economic field. To assure it, the academic and research community must function in political conjunction with those advocating this cause in the Washington political environment. The advocates must understand the data concerns of those whose careers evolve from publications of analyses; the research community must appreciate the constraints on those in the Federal government who administer these statistical enterprises.

One reality of effective advocacy for large national surveys and series ignored by the vast majority of the academic constituency is the absolute necessity for a national statistical program to have an intergovernmental component. The Bureau of Justice Statistics funds a variety of Federal-state networks for improvement of criminal histories, for state implementation of uniform crime reporting, and for state policy analysis in support of the nation's Governors and state legislatures. Such an intergovernmental program builds the legislative support essential to continuation of national scope data sets. A national statistical program cannot mature and prosper with statistical efforts conducted solely by Federal statistical agencies; the intergovernmental component is essential to the survival of a national statistical agency in the field of law and justice.

So, what of the future of the major statistical programs of which this volume treats? With the culmination of the NCS and UCR redesigns, the future support of both series within the Federal government seems assured if the increased analytic potential of both series is demonstrated by a stream of policy-relevant publications from both BJS and the FBI. Given the extraordinary focus on corrections issues and the criminal/substance abuse history of offenders, the future of correctional and self-report statistical programs also appears secure. Yet the operational environment within the Department of Justice, and the macro-budget situation within the nation as a whole, means that we must continually demonstrate the benefits for national criminal justice policy of the numbers we generate. For me that means that the analytic community—in which I include a continuum from police crime analysis units through major nonprofit agencies to university research—must mine the resources of these national data sets. It also means that Federal statistical agencies must be open to the views from this community concerning policies to improve these statistical series. In this way, policies for the management of statistical enterprises lead to statistics informing national policy.

STEVEN R. SCHLESINGER

1

The Challenge of Measuring Crime

Doris Layton MacKenzie and Phyllis Jo Baunach

Modern day criminology and criminal justice research are characterized by the use of sophisticated social science research techniques. These techniques help us to understand criminal events, criminal behavior, and the functioning of the criminal justice system. Progress has been made in recent years in the study of crime. However, as frequently happens, the more we know the more complex the issues become. This complexity has arisen in both our understanding of the issues (for example, criminal careers are not the same for all offenders), and our knowledge of the research process. By the latter we mean the mechanisms for measuring crime or the techniques which characterize social science research. These are the procedures that give us the information used to address the issues. The process of measuring crime (e.g., criminal events, criminal behavior, and system activity) is the focus of this book.

Today many of the research efforts aimed at understanding crime are large-scale. That is, they include numerous observations, individuals or cases, each with a large number of variables. Additionally, researchers have stressed the need to collect data over time in longitudinal or trend studies. These large-scale, long-range efforts often employ advanced social science research methodology.

At various stages throughout the criminal justice process an enormous amount of empirical data are collected. Victimization surveys attempt to measure the criminal event as closely as possible to its occurrence. Police files record police activity, reported crimes, and arrests of offenders. Other data are collected from the courts and from corrections, the final stage of criminal justice processing. Suffice it to say there is a plethora of data that comprise large, and frequently complex data bases.

1. Data Collection and Sampling

This book is divided into three sections. The five chapters in Part I discuss and critically evaluate three major Federal data collection efforts: (1) the

Federal Bureau of Investigation's (FBI) Uniform Crime Reporting (UCR) Program; (2) the National Crime Survey (NCS) of the Bureau of Justice Statistics (BJS); and (3) the Survey of Inmates of Adult State Correctional Facilities and the Census of State Adult Correctional Facilities in BJS' National Prisoner Statistics Program.

These data bases are particularly important because the information and data from them are so widely disseminated. They are major sources of information about crime, criminal behavior, and criminal processing in the U.S. Statistics produced from such data collection efforts can and do have a major impact on criminal justice policy. Furthermore, the data bases provide an extensive amount of information for researchers to use in secondary analyses.

An open forum for discussion of criminal justice data bases is important for many reasons. For one thing, such discussions act as feedback mechanisms to improve the data bases themselves. Second, there is an advantage in educating consumers who will use the information produced. Such forums will also facilitate the use of the data in secondary analyses.

To use large data bases for research purposes, or to critically evaluate the information derived from these data sets, researchers and policy-makers must understand the data collection procedures. Understanding the procedures allows recognition of the strengths and weaknesses of the data bases. For the meaning of terms to be clear and unambiguous the operational definitions of concepts must be understood. Perhaps one of the best examples of the importance of understanding operational definitions lies in discussions of crime trends. Commonly appearing in newspapers are headlines such as: "U.S. Crime Decreasing." Anyone using this information must ask how the "crime" referred to is defined and measured (i.e., operationalized). Omitting drug offenses from the definition of "crime," for instance, limits knowledge about changes in the level of criminal activity and could affect manpower planning by agencies such as the Drug Enforcement Administration. The point is that knowledgeable use of the information produced from a data collection effort requires an explicit understanding of the methodology.

Similarly, to appropriately use the information produced from data bases, it is necessary to understand some of the limitations. Some analyses, such as extensive analyses of rape from victimization surveys, are impossible because of low base rates. Other analyses may be limited because of the research methodology or technique. For example, some analyses of NCS data may be biased due to problems in sampling transients. Information about incest or family violence may not be reported in interview settings because of the sensitive nature of the inquiry.

In summary, sharing information from large data sets is beneficial to a variety of different users. However, these data sets are not without fault. Some criticisms can be addressed in future redesigns of a data base. Alternatively, open discussions of strengths and limitations make users aware of the issues and facilitates and improves secondary data analyses.

The data collection efforts described in Part I of this book represent different stages in criminal justice processing and different types of data collection efforts. The methodology varies from inmate self-reports to police records. The NCS is a national survey of a probability sample of U.S. households. Respondents are interviewed regarding victimizations they have suffered. The UCR makes use of police reports of crimes and arrests sent to the FBI by local law enforcement agencies. The Survey of Inmates and Census of Prisons collect data from the final stage of criminal processing—prison records and inmates. The Census obtains information regarding state adult correctional facilities through the use of mailed questionnaires. The Survey involves interviews with a representative sample of inmates in these facilities.

The data collection procedures and sampling techniques for these data bases are described in Part I. The strengths and weaknesses of the data sets are reviewed from the perspectives of both the technique in general (archival data, surveys) and each specific data collection effort. For example, missing data takes on different meanings depending upon the data base or the technique examined. On one hand, data may be 'missing' if the technique is not conducive to supplying such information. Such is the case with the UCR and reports of trends in crime in the U.S. As is frequently noted, such statistics omit information on unreported crime. On the other hand, missing data may refer to data that are not reported to the FBI from specific law enforcement districts or for some months. Since one of the goals of the UCR is a complete record of reported crime in the U.S. such missing data must be estimated through an imputation process. How the data are or should be imputed by the FBI is currently under discussion.

Issues related to missing data for surveys such as the NCS are very different from UCR issues. The goal of such a sample survey is to collect information from a representative sample of the U.S. so that victimizations for the whole U.S. can be estimated. Issues of importance to the NCS relate to sampling methodology and the use of the responses to estimate the population's characteristics. The problems and the method of examining missing data differs substantially from the UCR. This short discussion of issues related to missing data using different techniques, demonstrates both the importance of examining the data sets and the variability in data sets in terms of the issues involved.

Two of the data bases reviewed in Part I, the NCS and the UCR, have recently been formally evaluated. Individuals with varied experience and expertise, including, among others, practitioners, researchers, and representatives of government agencies provided input to the evaluations. In the evaluations, the strengths and weaknesses of each data base and possible methods for correcting the problems were examined. Furthermore, recommendations were made for cost efficient changes to address the problems identified. As a result of the committees' recommendations some changes have already been made in the research procedures, while others are anticipated.

Chapters on the UCR by Victoria W. Schneider and Brian Wiersema, and on the NCS by James Garofalo review the development of each respective data base, and discuss the limitations and problems that have been identified in each. Subsequent chapters by Yoshio Akiyama and Harvey M. Rosenthal (on the UCR) and James P. Lynch (on the NCS) describe proposed changes in the data bases that would address these problems. The authors describe the planned redesigns of the data bases and the rationale for the changes.

The oldest and most widely used method of measuring crime in the U.S. has been the UCR. Originally developed as an index of the crime rate, this data base has been criticized by both practitioners and researchers. Despite its problems the UCR has provided valuable information about reported crime. In Chapter 2, Schneider and Wiersema review some of the major files developed from the UCR. The offenses known to the police are, perhaps, the most well known of the more than seventy files available from the UCR data file collections. The authors note that there are limitations to a data set which is developed with little theoretical guidance. Flawed operational definitions, lack of clarity and unstandardized data collection policies are just a few of the issues that must be considered if reported crimes are to be validly and reliably measured. In addition, the validity of estimates for infrequently reporting agencies has been questioned. Schneider and Wiersema review the UCR program of the FBI as it is today, and they discuss criticisms of the UCR and the difficulties presented by its current format.

The FBI listened to the experts' critiques of the UCR and addressed some of the concerns. First, a full evaluation of the program was done. Second, changes were made that could be incorporated in a redesign of the program. Two of the major changes recommended by the evaluation were to: (1) implement incident level reporting; and (2) sample more completely from jurisdictions to obtain information for in-depth analyses. In Chapter 3, Akiyama and Rosenthal review the development of the UCR program, concerns about the program, and the planned redesign. The enhanced UCR program will address some of the problems which led to the criticism of the old UCR.

In addition to the UCR, with its focus on reported crimes committed by offenders, the NCS provides an overview of crimes from the victims' standpoint. As with reported crimes, these surveys pose measurement problems. Frequently these problems are different from those involved in the measurement of reported crimes. As pointed out in Chapter 4 by Garofalo, the methodological issues of sampling, interview techniques, low base rates, and definitions of crime are just some of the difficulties presented by crime surveys. Some issues, such as definitions of crime, overlap with the difficulties inherent in reconciling the measurement of crime with reported crimes, and other relatively new problems, are related to the survey technique. In this context, Garofalo discusses the strengths and limitations of surveys in general and in the NCS in particular.

The NCS has been recently evaluated and revised for future data collection efforts. In Chapter 5, Lynch discusses the criticisms directed at the NCS from both the academic community and practitioners, the formation of a Crime Survey Research Consortium (CSRC) to address these criticisms, and the planned redesign of the survey to correct some of the identified deficiencies.

The third set of data collection efforts, the Survey of Inmates and Census of Prisons, conducted by BJS have also undergone revisions in recent years. In Chapter 6, Phyllis Jo Baunach outlines the development of the Survey and Census, their purpose and some of the limitations.

The close ties between theory and/or policy issues and the design of a survey or census becomes clear in Baunach's discussion of the rationale for inclusion of specific variables. Items about inmates' military service, family information, or drug and alcohol use relate to current national interest in these topics to enhance our understanding of correlates of criminal behavior. For instance, interest in prior military service on the 1979 inmate survey was to determine whether large numbers of veterans from the Vietnam era are in prisons, and if they had become drug dependent while in the service. Interest in the history of inmates' drug use stems from our current concern about the complex drug-crime linkage, and the development of adequate policies and programs to handle these issues. Items focussing on the family and child care stem from concern about children whose lives are affected by a parent's incarceration.

Baunach's criticisms of the survey revolve around its utility; since the sample includes incarcerated inmates the results cannot be generalized to all offenders. In addition, as with all self-report studies, the validity of self-report data can be questioned.

2. Measurement and Analysis

The chapters in Part II of this book relate to issues of measurement and analysis in research with large data bases: (1) secondary data analysis; (2) microcomputers; and (3) the reliability and validity of data.

A large amount of time and energy is expended on the development of large data bases. In order to encourage the maximum use of the data, some of the agencies responsible for the data collection make the data available to other researchers. In fact, with the realization of the great costs involved in original data collection efforts, the National Institute of Justice (NIJ), U.S.

Department of Justice, now requires all grantees to submit machine readable copies and descriptions of all data collected in NIJ funded projects. To guarantee compliance, data sets must be received by NIJ before the work of the grant is considered completed. The Social Science Division of the National Science Foundation has a similar policy, but data need not be submitted until two years after a grant is completed. The goal of these efforts is to maximize the use of the data for secondary analyses. Furthermore, to improve the quality and, therefore, facilitate use of the data sets, NIJ has contracted for technical services to review and edit these data sets before they are archived.

Thus, after a study is completed, the original researcher submits the data with complete documentation describing the contents. The technical support staff review and edit the documentation, access the data, and discuss problems with the researcher, as necessary. The data are then archived with documentation, and at this point they are available for other researchers to use. Possibly in the future, preparation of "good," useable, and well-documented data sets might be regarded as equal to a scientific publication; use of such a data set and the resulting citations might, similarly, add to the prestige and professional standing of the scientist who originally collected and archived the data.

Reports of results of large Federal data collections frequently limit presentations of statistics. In fact, there is often a wealth of information left untouched. Agencies have encouraged use of the data bases by scheduling workshops to help users understand the data sets and by making the data available in public-use archives. Some agencies, such as NIJ, have grant programs specifically developed to encourage use of previously collected data. This is a financially less risky method for agencies to support new researchers who are just getting started.

There are numerous advantages to secondary data analysis, as described in Chapter 7 by Michael Traugott. Secondary data analyses often use data that are of a complexity, size and quality that are well beyond what an individual researcher could collect. Such analyses provide a cost-effective way to maximize the amount of knowledge that results from the initial investment. There are also advantages in secondary data analysis from the perspective of scientific research: the ability or inability to replicate the original research findings permit a secondary researcher either to validate or to identify flaws in the original research.

Frequently, documentation is one of the major stumbling blocks for the researcher using secondary data. Documentation refers to the code book which should give a complete description of the operationalization of each variable. The code book may be incomplete or difficult to interpret. But equally as important for new users are both a knowledge of the difficulties that might be encountered using data bases, and a critical evaluation of these data bases. This kind of information is often hard to obtain. Conceptual descriptions of the strengths and weaknesses, advantages and disadvantages, and/or problems in using specific large data sets as given in the earlier chapters are critical. Such information, in Traugott's opinion, should aid consumers and users of the data bases to critically evaluate the information produced.

Other problems with secondary data analyses relate to the distribution of data sets and users' technical needs. The size of the data set may prohibit its use by certain researchers. For this reason, archive centers, such as the National Archive of Criminal Justice Data, have been developed to help with documentation, counseling, distribution, and technical advice.

There are other difficulties in using archival data for secondary analyses. For example, considering the size of many of these data sets, the technical aspects can be overwhelming to researchers at locations which are limited in computer facilities and in technical help. The use of microcomputers may have the greatest impact on this problem, and is explored in Chapter 8 by Edgar Barry Moser. The new capabilities and low cost of microcomputers will allow many more researchers to take advantage of secondary data analysis. Additionally, microcomputers will facilitate the exchange of information from archive to user or from user to user. Conceivably in the future, data archives will distribute subsets of large data bases, including only the specific information requested, on diskettes rather than on large data tapes.

Even though microcomputers may simplify the use of large data bases, there are still problems related to the complexity and size of the data bases. The structure of the data (flat or hierarchical) may have to be maintained in microcomputers. Before purchase, software must be evaluated to insure its adequacy. If the capacity to upload or download from the mainframe to microcomputer is important, then software with this capability must be available.

The final chapter in Part II addresses issues of reliability and validity. In Chapter 9, Marc Riedel compares the data available on homicide from two different sources: (1) the UCR, including the Supplementary Homicide Reports (SHR), and (2) the National Center for Health Statistics Data (NCHS). The difficulty in measuring crime becomes obvious when data sets are compared. Few problems might be expected in the reporting of homicide, which is presumably a clearly defined and well-reported crime. Yet Riedel's comparison of the data from the SHR in the UCR and the NCHS demonstrates that this is not the case. Because these two sources of homicide reporting are available, it was possible for Riedel to compare the two to determine problems of coverage and changes in what is or is not reported. Even the definition of homicide is unclear. One can only speculate that these difficulties are even more severe for less serious, less well-documented, or less clearly defined crimes. How such problems affect research results is an interesting question; in Riedel's opinion there is a possibility that the conclusions could be seriously affected.

3. The Past and The Future

The use of large-scale, long-range data bases in the past and in the future is the topic of Part III. A brief review of how crime has been measured in the last 20 years, from the initial reports of the President's Commission on Law Enforcement and Administration of Justice in 1967 until the present, is Robert M. Figlio's topic in Chapter 10. He warns that it is possible to be overwhelmed to the point of inertia when confronting the problems of measuring crime. In his opinion the difficulties of today are not due to a lack of accomplishments, but rather, result from the substantial advances made in criminal justice research. Despite the difficulties which he spells out, there is a "new criminology" which has developed over the past twenty years. This new criminology is characterized by the development of advanced research methodology and statistical techniques.

According to Figlio, these "large-scale, long-range efforts" must continue to effectively attack the problem of crime. In addition, Figlio contends that theoretical perspectives must be challenged to insure critical analysis of all policy-relevant issues. There is a close link between the way in which crime is measured and the theoretical perspective of the measurers; this link should not be forgotten when examining the process of measuring crime.

In Chapter 11, Benjamin H. Renshaw looks at the future of large-scale data collection efforts. As has been shown throughout this book, the process of collecting data is no easy task. Each method carries certain difficulties and is flawed. For this reason, it is imperative that we continue using multiple methods in our attempts to understand crime and criminal behavior. Today data is collected from victimization surveys, self-report and longitudinal studies, among others, and these are used to augment the official records of reported crime. Yet, despite the flaws characteristic of each data collection method, there are some surprising consistencies among the methods. Thus, one of the advantages of the use of a multiplicity of methods has been to give us more confidence in our conclusions. Renshaw discusses some of these findings and reiterates a theme found throughout this book—in the future, widespread understanding, dissemination, and use of these data bases will be imperative if we are to make progress in understanding and attacking the problem of crime.

4. Summary

The process of measuring crime and the characteristics of criminal behavior are, and will continue to be, a challenge. The challenge involves the development of complex research methodology, statistical theory and computer technology. But the challenge does not stop with advances in these technologies. A knowledgeable clientele, ie., researchers and practitioners, who can utilize and evaluate the process is critical. The close tie between process and theory necessitates interactions among policy-makers, researchers and theoreticians. Maximum benefits from large-scale, long-range efforts to measure crime will accrue if various groups become involved. Involvement may be at the development stage, when the decision is made as to what information to obtain; after data are collected, when researchers use the data in initial and secondary data analyses; or later, when critical and informed evaluations are made of the research. In addition, the challenge encompasses the development of data bases that are useful to decision-makers. Secondary data analyses can provide invaluable information in the development of policies and programs. After all, the purpose of all this measurement is to deal with the crime problem. A significant aspect of the challenge, then, is to continue to develop the mechanisms of measuring crime, to involve numerous people in this process, and to inform an even larger number of people about the procedures and utility of large-scale, long-range data bases.

Part I

Data Collection and Sampling

2

Limits and Use of the Uniform Crime Reports

Victoria W. Schneider and Brian Wiersema

1. Introduction

The oldest continuing series in the United States for recording crimes known to the police at the national level is the Federal Bureau of Investigation's (FBI) Uniform Crime Reporting (UCR) Program. Until the advent of national victimization surveys in the early 1970s, the UCR provided the only frequently updated and comprehensive national estimates of crime for law enforcement agencies, researchers, government policy-makers, and the media. These groups have made the UCR the most widely consulted data source for assessing the magnitude, patterns and trends of crime in the United States.

At the same time, there has been considerable dissatisfaction with the UCR. National victimization surveys, and in particular the National Crime Survey, represented one response to this dissatisfaction. This has led to important research on the effectiveness and utility of Uniform Crime Report data in measuring the incidence of crime in the United States. Many criticisms have been leveled against the UCR as a result not only of this research, but also of the experiences of the UCR's various user constituencies. Police administrators as well as researchers have pressed for a better UCR, especially one that would provide immediately useful information for policing. In response, the Federal Bureau of Investigation and the Bureau of Justice Statistics have recently undertaken steps to redesign the UCR Program.

Improvements obviously will take time. The following chapter in this volume discusses the long-term future of the UCR Program including plans to correct some of the weaknesses perceived. Because these improvements will require cooperation and some resource investment by local police agencies, changes are unlikely to be implemented on a large scale for a number of years. It seems therefore reasonable to assume that, as a practical matter, the current UCR will retain its position as a national data source for some time to come. Whatever the future impact of a revised UCR, the current UCR's longevity and accessibility will likely help it continue as an important and heavily used resource in attempts to measure crime. For these reasons, the present chapter reviews the content and major limitations of the current UCR and offers information and techniques for facilitating further research.

Our initial aim is to provide an appreciation of the care and caution needed to make the best use of the data by briefly reviewing the highlights of past research. Like many widely-used data sources, the UCR has been a frequently misused source of crime data. Indeed, applications of these data have sometimes gone beyond the UCR's purpose and design. In other cases the data have simply been misinterpreted. Understanding the pitfalls and shortcomings of the UCR, the subject of a considerable body of research, remains a fundamental issue in the appropriate use of the data.

Our second objective will be a description of the currently available machine-readable UCR data sets, several of which are surprisingly underutilized and unexplored. Advances in both knowledge about the UCR and its potential uses have been made possible by the relatively recent availability of these data in a machine-readable form. Many potential users seem to be unaware of the wealth of data that is only available in computer-accessible versions. There are many advantages to using UCR computer files rather than the printed volumes, but one of the main reasons is the access they provide to detailed characteristics at the most basic levels of official reporting. In any case, using the data with a computer allows a flexibility in analyses that is impossible with the FBI's printed report.

Finally, we offer some suggestions for the management and use of computer-readable UCR data by way of a demonstration. We use, as our example, agency-level data from the 1980 UCR to create a state-level data set that contains estimates of crimes that local police agencies "knew about" but failed to report to the FBI, a process known as imputation and upon which many of the figures in the FBI's annual publication, *Crime in the United States*, rely. Interesting in itself, this exercise also illustrates some important techniques for accessing and analyzing the data. In all, we intend to show the usefulness as well as the limitations of the Uniform Crime Reports in the spirit of encouraging additional interest in, and development of, these data.

1.1. An Historical Perspective

Since the 1930s the Uniform Crime Reporting Program has been the nation's primary source of data on arrests and reported crimes. Through the years the Uniform Crime Reports have been the subject of great debate. The purpose of this section is to describe some of the major problematic aspects of the Uniform Crime Reports. This section begins with a brief history and is followed by a discussion of three general topics: limitations of reporting, methodological problems, and questions of interpretation. Much of what we have to say is not new and has been said before at greater length and detail by many others. Nonetheless, it is important, particularly for those who may not be well-acquainted with the UCR, to understand what it is and how it came to be. Even more important is an understanding of what it is *not* so that one can avoid misuse and misinterpretation. Far from discouraging all use of the UCR (as some critics have suggested), an awareness of its limitations as a measure of crime can prevent serious errors and allow the pursuit of new and profitable research.

During the 1920s the International Association of Chiefs of Police formed a committee on Uniform Crime Reports in an effort to promote national crime statistics. This committee was charged with developing a viable system of uniform police statistics. In 1929 the committee finalized a plan for crime reporting after extensive evaluation of record-keeping practices used at that time. From surveys of local police departments a list of seven crimes was chosen to serve as an index of the fluctuating crime rate in the United States. The Crime Index, as it is called today, includes murder and non-negligent manslaughter, forcible rape, robbery, aggravated assault, larceny-theft, burglary, and motor vehicle theft. In 1979, by a congressional mandate, arson was added as the eighth index crime. To deal with the problem of differences among state statutes defining criminal activities and in order to provide nationwide criminal statistics, an attempt to create and use "uniform" offense classifications was incorporated into the system. According to the UCR's instructions to law enforcement agencies, they are directed to use the FBI's definitions of crime when completing reports and submitting data, rather than classifications defined by local law or custom (Federal Bureau of Investigation, 1984).

The UCR program began in 1930 with 400 participating law enforcement agencies. Since its inception the UCR program has been based on voluntary reporting by local police departments.[1] Mead (1929: 76), in an early comment on the newly-created Uniform Crime Reports, observed:

> statistics on the number of offenses known to police form the best available means of measuring the extent of crime at a given time, and the changes from time to time in the prevalence of the more serious offenses against persons and against property.

The National Commission of Law Observance and Enforcement, also known as the Wickersham Commission, endorsed the UCR Program in 1931: "the best index of the number and nature of offenses is police statistics showing offenses known to police" (National Commission of Law Observance and Enforcement, 1931: 25). Today there are over 16,000 agencies participating in the UCR Program.

1.2. The Current UCR

The UCR collects data on five general reporting forms: offenses known to police; property stolen and recovered; supplementary homicide report; age, sex, race, and ethnic origin of persons arrested; and police employees (Wolfgang, 1962: 708). Each form is completed monthly by local police agencies and forwarded either directly to the FBI or through state-level UCR programs (Federal Bureau of Investigation, 1984: 1-2). In general, the Uniform Crime Reports do not gather any data on offenses committed in violation of Federal law, many white collar crimes, rules governing commerce and industry, and laws concerned with unemployment and social security benefits (Shulman, 1966; Wolfgang, 1968). The latter categories involve violations of laws but are normally handled by administrative agencies like the National Labor Relations Board or the Securities and Exchange Commission. Data are not collected for other types of illegal activities. For example, there is little information on drug offenses; data on arrests for such incidents and types and amounts of drugs seized are not included in the current UCR.

Instructions to police agencies on reporting procedures are transmitted by various means, but the central document is the *Uniform Crime Reporting Handbook* (Federal Bureau of Investigation, 1984). This document provides guidelines and definitions for classifying offenses according to the UCR system. Police departments that participate in the program are asked to categorize, count, and report monthly totals of each of the requested items. The FBI performs several consistency checks and has established some provisions for auditing data returns. Quality control over the data is mainly limited by the voluntary nature of UCR, although many states have mandated local UCR participation in recent years. After the FBI performs its edit-checks, the data are released.

Since 1958 the Uniform Crime Reports have been published annually as *Crime in the United States* (CIUS). More recently, the FBI has begun to publish special reports from time to time on such topics as population-at-risk rates (Federal Bureau of Investigation, 1985) and age- and race-specific arrest rates for selected offenses (Federal Bureau of Investigation, 1984 and 1986).

2. Problematic Issues

UCR publications provide the major source of information for officially reported crime, yet there has been dissatisfaction with the amount and type of information they offer (see, for example, Skogan, 1975). Particularly, as the methodology of social science research improved, critics pushed for better techniques for collecting crime data (Maltz, 1977: 34). The introduction of national victimization surveys has permitted quantification of some of the UCR's defects. In fact, much of the systematic research on the UCR's shortcomings we owe to the National Crime Survey (NCS). Comparisons with the NCS have helped social scientists to identify and categorize the UCR's methodological difficulties into three general areas: limitations of reporting, methodological problems, and questions of interpretation. The next section reviews some implications of the reporting-based limitations of the UCR.

2.1. Limitations of Reporting

There are many reasons why crimes are not recorded by the UCR system. As Skogan (1975) has explained, official crime reports are first initiated by the public, namely victims, their relatives, neighbors, or bystanders. They must first be aware that an incident has occurred and that it is something of which the police need to be aware. Second, crimes can occur but such events can remain unknown. For example, one can easily imagine instances of larceny, shoplifting, or employee theft that may happen often, but remain undetected by the authorities. Awareness that such events have occurred may only come later through a company's inventory shrinkage analysis.

Once a crime is reported to police, some record of that crime must be made by them before it will be counted as "known to the police" (Dodge and Turner, 1971). Citizens fail to report crimes for several reasons. They may think the police can do very little about the crime, or they may have a generally negative view of police as incompetent or uninterested, or they may not know the correct procedures involved in reporting a crime. Overall, non-reporters have little confidence in the ability of the police to handle criminal matters or in the willingness of police to believe their complaints are legitimate (Skogan, 1975: 20-22).

Turner (1972) found that the likelihood of reporting a personal crime of violence such as assault, rape, or robbery was dependent upon the relationship between the victim and the offender. More cases were reported when the offender and victim were strangers. A NCS pilot study in Dayton and San Jose (Law Enforcement Assistance Administration, 1974) estimated that 60 percent of robberies were not reported to the police. Skogan (1976) discovered that less than half of all personal robberies and burglaries were reported to the police.

According to the Bureau of Justice Statistics (1984: 17-18) one-third of all personal crimes were reported to the police in 1982. The public generally reported serious or costly crimes more often. Thus, forcible entry burglaries, aggravated assaults, and robberies with injuries had high police reporting rates. Conversely, only 27 percent of all non-contact personal and household larcenies were reported. In 1982, the most important reason given for non-reporting of crimes by victims was that the offense was not important enough to warrant police attention.

Much crime in the United States is committed against businesses that also fail to report relevant incidents. This is particularly true for shoplifting, employee theft, passing bad checks, and even burglary (Reiss, 1967; 1969). Many business owners and managers neglect reporting crimes to police because the property is insured. When losses are not covered by an insurance policy, a person fails to report because there is no personal gain to be achieved. Even when people have insurance they may not report losses because of fear of cancellation, non-renewal, or a rate increase in their policy (Reiss, 1969: 131-143).

Many police, like citizens, also fail to report crimes. Unwritten departmental policies may dictate that certain violations be overlooked. For example, minor drug users may be ignored, assuming such arrests may frighten away the upper-level dealers in which police are especially interested (Skolnick, 1966). According to Skogan (1975), police loathe filing crime reports. An officer's decision to report a crime is, in one sense, judicial. In some instances the officer must weigh what the complainant states against the statements of the alleged offender. Wolfgang (1968), in his study of the New York City police, found a 20 to 90 percent underreporting of criminal events in files. He stated that commanders were pressured to reduce crime, and did so by down-grading offenses.

Black (1970) looked at a sample of 554 cases from a larger number of incidents recorded in Boston, Chicago, and Washington, D.C. during the summer of 1966. He found that a number of factors influenced a police officer's decision to formally report a crime. When the relational distance between participants in a dispute was small, the likelihood of the case being pursued in court was also small. Thus, the officer was not likely to file a report. Police tended to defer resolution of incidents to the complainants who, in many instances, only mobilized police as a warning mechanism for another party. Police were more likely to file a formal crime report when the complainant was deferential to them and was a member of the middle or upper class. In cases where juveniles were involved, police often deferred to adults at the scene and did not make formal reports of the incidents.

Maltz (1975: 180) stated that the probability of an incident being formally recorded by a police officer depended upon the training of the officer, the description given by the victim and witnesses, results of a police investigation, the definition of the crime given in the *Uniform Crime Reporting Handbook* (Hoover, 1966), and the administrative and political pressures placed on the responding officer. Shulman (1966: 487-88) focused on the limitations of police as a crime-reporting agency in terms of their law enforcement powers. Police have a very restrictive role in law enforcement due to constraints imposed by the laws of arrest, the constitution, and other civil liberties. They are primarily a "peace preservation body," and most of their contacts with the public center around peace-keeping duties rather than law enforcement.

In summary, official crime statistics are determined by citizen and police decisions to report crime. In turn, such decisions help shape community views on how much and what kinds of crime are committed by whom. Although the UCR does not claim to account for non-reported crime, the fact that significant amounts of crime may not be represented by the UCR is a fundamental issue in its measurement. Use (or rather, misuse) of the UCR as if it included non-reported crime would obviously bias results because measurement validity for this purpose is poor. A less obvious problem results when one acknowledges the presence of the unreported component, but assumes "constancy between reported and unreported crimes and (or) between Index and other offenses" (Poggio, Kennedy, Chaiken, and Carlson, 1985: 27). Estimating the magnitude and variation of citizen non-reporting is a challenge both for future research with victimization surveys, and for development of the new UCR. We turn now to questions about the data which arise after the decision to report and record an incident has been made.

2.2. Methodological Problems

There are internal validity issues associated with the UCR as well as the external ones just mentioned. These focus on the procedures by which reported incidents are classified by police for UCR submission. Given that an incident results in its recording by police, the methods for categorizing it as a UCR crime become important. UCR classification methods have been criticized as vague, imprecise, and subject to varying interpretation. If consistency in offense classification is not rigorously maintained, the resulting data will suffer from low reliability and, hence, low validity.

Although the recording system may appear at first to be rather straightforward, the UCR actually requires its reporting agencies to engage in a fairly complex decision process when considering each incident report. First, UCR crime definitions may vary in subtle ways with the jurisdiction's normal (legal) definitions of crimes, and it may be difficult for the agency to distinguish the differences. Second, each offense definition usually requires the UCR coder to ascertain the simultaneous presence of a number of component conditions, i.e., necessary factors, which together constitute a sufficient basis for classification. Third, the procedure for "scoring" or counting offenses is complex, involving the use of a "hierarchy" which requires that only the most serious offense committed during an incident is counted, even if there are (in the eyes of the police agency) multiple offenses.[2] Content analysis research has found that the more complexity that is involved in an individual's mental process of classifying an event, the more unreliable that decision is likely to be (see, e.g., Holsti, 1968: 657-659). Complex definitions can lead to variation in classification decisions and adversely affect reliability and validity.

In 1982 the Federal Bureau of Investigation and the Bureau of Justice Statistics jointly sponsored a review conducted by Abt Associates, Inc. of the present UCR Program. The review included evaluations of the original and current UCR Programs, and recommendations for modifying and enhancing the system. We will disuss two areas of methodological limitations in the UCR noted in the Abt study: (1) flaws in operational definitions and (2) lack of comparability in the face of jurisdictional variation.

2.2.1. FLAWS IN OPERATIONAL DEFINITIONS

The *Final Report of the UCR Study* (Poggio, et al., 1985) described several problems with the operational definitions utilized by the current UCR system. Some users have complained about what they see as overgeneralized crime categories and the UCR's lack of detailed information or disaggregated data for each offense. Data collection for the UCR is based on crime categories that are fairly broad; crimes which may have important differences, but have similar definitions, are counted together in the current UCR. Some index crime definitions have been criticized as encompassing different types of incidents. A prime example is larceny-theft which groups together such incidents as petty larceny and shoplifting with non-forcible thefts from persons, like pocket-picking or some purse-snatchings. Also, thefts involving large monetary losses are not distinguished from those involving small dollar values. Auto theft, too, is a heterogeneous classification in the UCR system. Incidents of joy-riding can be counted the same as thefts by professional car thieves. The difficulty lies in the inability to identify salient differentiating factors because such details are simply not collected in the current system.

Other complaints about the paucity of information are directed at data which would describe characteristics of specific crimes. For example, linking property stolen in one jurisdiction with property recovered in another is impossible in the current UCR. Homicide data lack information on circumstances like child abuse or self-defense. Similar criticisms were levied against data collected on robbery and burglary incidents. For example, data on victim-offender relationship and circumstance of robbery are not collected and burglaries committed in residences, residential outbuildings, and commercial establishments are not differentiated (Poggio, et al., 1985: 29-3l; Beattie, 1960: 56-57). Also, definitions of juvenile offenses were characterized as too broad and unclear. Ethnic origin information is simplistically based on the particular individual's last name. Categories like Japanese, Chinese, and Pacific Islander are omitted from the UCR forms (Poggio, et al., 1985: 3l-32). Ethnicity is divided into "hispanic" and "non-hispanic," which does not represent a precise definition of ethnic origin.

Overall, data collection for each type of crime does not contain in-depth information on events surrounding its commission. Demographics on victims and offenders, geographical location, time of day, and day of week for each reported criminal incident are missing from the UCR. Attempted acts are included in crime counts with completed acts; no distinctions between the two are made in the current system (Wolfgang, 1962). The lack of detailed information in the current UCR has led those working on its redesign to identify the kinds of information users would find desirable and it also serves as a guide to those who may wish to use existing data.

An important point when working with existing data is realizing that UCR crime classifications are complex and not always completely defined or precise. As Skogan (1975: 18) has pointed out, measurement "involves the application of definitions to delineate aspects of the empirical system which are of interest ... matching selected attributes of those phenomena to symbols." Reliable measurement means that, if independent coders were to consider the same event, the process of applying definitions would result in the same classification. In the case of UCR data, there are thousands of "coders" in law enforcement observing a range of relatively similar events and attempting to apply the definitions provided by the UCR Program. Imprecise or complex definitions which lead observers to varying conclusions in similar circumstances are an undeniable source of measurement error.[3]

To illustrate this point, consider the rule for classifying burglaries, which requires the coder to make at least three decisions about each candidate for a UCR burglary classification. First, there must be an unlawful entry, or an attempted unlawful entry involved. Second, the object entered must be a "structure." Third, an intent to commit a felony or a theft must be evident. Since a UCR definition of lawful versus unlawful entry is not provided, one assumes that the unlawfulness of the event is defined by state or local laws governing the reporting police agency. If this is true, behavior considered unlawful in one jurisdiction may not be illegal in another, which contributes to the problems in data comparability discussed in the next section (2.2.2). In guiding the coder around the "structure" question the UCR provides a list, but not an exhaustive list, of acceptable structures. Rather than actually defining the concept, police are instructed:

> Whenever the question arises as to whether a type of structure comes within the purview of the burglary definition, the law enforcement officer should look to the nature of the crime and be guided by the examples set forth (in the UCR Handbook). If a question remains, contact the Uniform Crime Reporting Program (Federal Bureau of Investigation, 1984: 20).

The examples tell us that tents, trailers, and mobile homes that are impermanently fixed and used for recreational purposes do not constitute structures. However, "any housetrailer or other mobile unit that is permanently fixed as an office, residence, or storehouse should be considered a structure" (Federal Bureau of Investigation, 1984: 20). A special set of directions (the "Hotel Rule") applies to scoring UCR burglaries of such structures as hotels, motels, and lodging houses. The final test for coding a burglary is evidence of intent to commit a felony or a theft. Again, the UCR Handbook is not clear as to which authority's definitions of "felony" or "theft" to use or what criteria determine "intent." Granted that definitions of crimes are legal constructions which are often difficult to understand, there seems to be considerable complexity, not to mention ambiguity, in many UCR offense classification instructions.

One may argue that police officers, who must interpret legal definitions all the time, are fairly well equipped to interpret UCR classification instructions, particularly if they have received the FBI's training in UCR reporting. They are also in the best position as first-hand observers to examine the facts of the incidents they investigate and match their characteristics according to the UCR's definitions. However, many UCR classifications are completed not by the investigating police officers but by records personnel who may or may not have a background in law enforcement and, in any case, must interpret the incident reports second-hand. Accurately classifying these reports depends on the sufficiency of available information, background and training of the coding personnel, and the ability to consistently apply ambiguous and complex decision rules provided by the UCR. If the definitions of UCR crimes are open to various interpretation *within* a jurisdiction, the problems are compounded when comparing data *across* jurisdictions.

2.2.2. JURISDICTIONAL VARIATION AND COMPARABILITY

Many researchers and policy-makers want to use UCR data for comparing jurisdictions or groups of jurisdictions according to population size or some other characteristic(s). The endeavor may be limited, however, by the difficulty police departments face in distinguishing UCR crime definitions from those they use daily in enforcing their jurisdiction's laws. Some researchers believe that jurisdictional variation has led to a data set in which the units of observation are not comparable.

Certainly there is considerable variation in the legal definitions of crimes across states. Every state has its own system of criminal law and procedure. Even within states, governmental jurisdictions can have local ordinances which define minor violations variously (Beattie, 1960: 51). For example, in California a theft from an auto is classified as a burglary, while the UCR classification system says such an incident should be categorized a theft.

There is evidence to suggest that local practices which are at variance with UCR procedures do sometimes influence how data are recorded for UCR purposes. Seidman and Couzens claim that "administrative changes are common (within police departments) and tend to have a substantial impact on the statistics" (1974: 463). They relate the case of Chicago's larceny figures which changed from 10,000 per year to 30,000 per year at about the same time Superintendent O.W. Wilson instituted changes in bookkeeping practices. Seidman and Couzens investigated the relationship with a time-series analysis of larcenies reported by the District of Columbia Metropolitan Police Department. They inferred from their results that changes in internal administrative procedures affect levels of reported crime (Seidman and Couzens, 1974). Decker (1977: 48) also notes that differing administrative policies governing data collection may contribute to a low-level of reliability in the UCR. Observers seem to agree that jurisdictional differences in classifying offenses escalate the difficulties in comparing UCR data across municipalities (Poggio et al., 1985). To date, however, there have been few attempts to quantify this source of measurement error, and no systematic study describes the error associated with jurisdictional variation among the present set of participating police agencies.

How much the existence of jurisdictional variation affects the classification of UCR events remains an empirical question. According to the FBI, jurisdictions are supposed to pay attention only to UCR definitions of crime and ignore prevailing local practices and crime definitions, should they diverge from the UCR's. The problem, as we have noted, is that "offense definitions provided by the FBI lack clarity" (Robison, 1966: 1043), and these ambiguities may instead encourage a police agency to rely on its own set of definitions and criteria for reporting. One response of the FBI to limit differences in interpretation has been its provision of authoritative resources, including UCR training personnel, to local police agencies. The UCR Program has also established edit-check procedures which, it is claimed, reduces some of the classification error. Even so, *Crime in the United States* (CIUS) routinely cautions its readers to exercise care in comparing jurisdictions, and to take into consideration demographic and other differences among units.

In any case, the degree to which jurisdictional variation is a significant problem remains the subject of further research. The fact that uniform application of Uniform Crime Reporting procedures is being questioned has led those involved in the UCR redesign effort to call for better procedures to measure data quality. Random audits of police records and recording practices have been proposed as one such method. Auditing records, in addition to improving on-going "quality control" efforts, would help in identifying and estimating the amount of error associated with differences in jurisdictional procedures and crime definitions.

2.3. Questions of Interpretation

A final criticism of the Uniform Crime Reports concerns the lack of direction or guidance provided by an underlying criminological theory (Poggio et al., 1985; Wolfgang, 1962). Critics have claimed that there is an absence of a formal research design, procedures for hypothesis testing, and a precise relationship between conceptualization and operationalization, and that the use of UCR data is limited to the interpretations that can be drawn from their analysis.

Kitsuse (1962) and Wheeler (1967) investigated the procedures by which the UCR were formulated. In their opinion, the inability to use and interpret the UCR is a consequence of an assumed underlying conception of crime and not due to any technical difficulties in data collection or definitions. Data on criminal incidents "are records of responses to the actions of criminals. [These] statistics reflect passive responses of officials to the active behavior of criminals" (Wheeler, 1967: 317).

In essence, the question is whether the UCR data can be interpreted as a measure of criminal behavior in the United States. Many researchers have criticized the UCR as more a measure of police activity, not criminal behavior (Kitsuse and Cicourel, 1963; Biderman and Reiss, 1967a, 1967b; Wolfgang, 1962). The Abt study observed that, within the range of opinion regarding the appropriate role and interpretation of UCR data, some of their respondents "thought the UCR should be viewed as reports of citizen contacts with police rather than as an accurate indicator of crime itself" (Poggio et al., 1985: 27).

To sum up, consistent interpretation is hindered by the variability of criminal statutes, community values, and police actions throughout the United States. UCR user proclivities also affect how the data are interpreted. For example, despite the FBI's caveats against comparing counts from one jurisdiction to another, many find it simply irresistible. Another example is the tendency by some to take the Crime Index at face value without regard to issues such as the relative seriousness of its component crimes. Perhaps because its user audience is diverse and the kinds of data are limited, little consensus has been achieved on how the UCR is interpreted. Within even one of these user groups, scholars, there is little consensus on its most appropriate meaning. One hope for an improved UCR—one based on unit-record reporting—is that it would have the flexibility the current UCR lacks to adjust to the different needs of law enforcement officials, government decisionmakers, researchers, and the media.

We have tried to review the shortcomings and criticisms of the UCR with the intention of pointing out some of the pitfalls surrounding its use. So much has been written about the UCR's problems that many potential users have drawn the (erroneous, in our view) conclusion that the UCR is virtually useless and should be abandoned altogether. We draw a different conclusion. We believe that awareness of the UCR's problems and limitations is crucial, not to deter all use, but to enable appropriate and careful research with the existing data. Despite the laudable efforts to redesign and improve the UCR Program for the future, the product of these labors is still several years from realization. More to the point, there is a tremendous amount of data, spanning many years, that has been accumulated under the current system and is currently available to researchers and others.

Finally, we think it bears repeating that flawed as it may be, the UCR has not been replaced by the National Crime Survey; the two data collection systems are, we think, rightly viewed as complementary, not competitive, sources of crime data.[4] They are different lenses on the picture of crime and each provides a unique and important view that can enrich our knowledge of this phenomenon. Our focus should be on what we can still learn from UCR data, not on how little they can tell us.

In this spirit, we turn our attention to the UCR data resources available for research. The point we wish to make in the next section is that the UCR is a very large and varied collection of data which requires a computer to take full advantage. In contrast to the data available in UCR publications, there are computer-readable versions of the data that are much more detailed and hold a great deal of potential which has yet to be exploited. Our intent is to promote research by providing a descriptive introduction and means for organizing the publicly archived, machine-readable UCR data collection.

3. Available Computer-Readable Data Sets

Although the UCR reports go back to the 1930s, the UCR has only recently become available in computer-readable form. The FBI began recording individual police agency reports on magnetic tape in the early 1960s with the first relatively complete data year being 1967 (Pierce, Bowers, Baird and Heck, 1981). Prior to the 1960s, the data had been tabulated and recorded in printed form only. Nevertheless, machine-readable UCR data for the post-1966 era did not become generally available until 1981 when the first data sets were released through the Inter-university Consortium for Political and Social Research (ICPSR) of the University of Michigan.[5] Previously, the FBI magnetic tapes were in formats suited to their organization's internal needs, but were difficult for researchers to access and manipulate.[6] This, more than anything, prevented widespread use of computerized UCR data sets during the 1960s and 1970s.

Fortunately, access to computer-readable UCR data has improved considerably in the last several years. A number of researchers, who acquired

UCR data sets directly from the FBI, reformatted and transformed the data into easier-to-use versions. Copies of these files are now available from public data archives such as ICPSR. In addition, the data archives themselves have been consistently and systematically purchasing, reformatting, and disseminating data from master tapes provided by the FBI.

There are at least two immediate consequences of the relatively recent availability of machine-readable UCR data. First, the computer data have not yet been subjected to a great deal of scrutiny; certainly not to the same degree as those found in CIUS. Due to printing constraints, the FBI's UCR publications must summarize many of the details originally solicited from police departments. Data stored on magnetic tape do not suffer from this kind of limitation. In fact, much of the UCR data that are available on tape are not typically reported in UCR publications; there are many more variables and cases available in the computer files than have ever been presented in Government Printing Office documents. For example, the FBI publishes annual counts of offenses known to police, offenses cleared by arrest, persons arrested, and law enforcement personnel. However, these printed versions do not include information for any jurisdictions with populations less than 12,000. Also, the printed UCRs do not provide details which are collected for specific offenses. The computer-readable versions provide offense breakdowns such as the number of robberies and assaults committed with guns, cutting instruments, and/or other weapons.

A second consequence is that a large increase in the number and types of analyses has been made possible simply by the flexibility machine-readable data provide. Data may be aggregated, subsetted, recoded, transformed, or merged with other data in ways that were previously impractical, if not impossible. For instance, one of the strengths of the UCR is that it is designed to collect data by place of occurrence. Geographical aggregations of victimization survey responses are difficult in part because they are oriented to place of residence, and although there is probably a large portion of overlap, the UCR may be more appropriate for use with other geographically-based data.[7] Analysis of crime and expenditures on the police is a good example because both crime and expenditures are measured in the same units of observation: local governmental agencies. This type of analysis is facilitated by the availability of both machine-readable UCR and expenditure data such as the County and City Data Book files and other Census Bureau data files which can be merged together.

An indirect but useful method for arguing that the analytical opportunities have expanded is to summarize a variety of UCR computer files currently available for research. For convenience, we describe data sets available from the National Archive of Criminal Justice Data sponsored by the Bureau of Justice Statistics, and maintained by ICPSR. Of course, data may also be purchased directly from the FBI,[8] and data archives other than ICPSR maintain UCR collections as well. We begin by describing the master data files and conclude with some of the more specialized collections. In all, more than 70 UCR computer-readable data files are represented by these summaries. More detailed information about the following collections may be found in the codebooks and other printed documents that have been created for use with the machine-readable files.[9]

3.1. Return A: Offenses Known to the Police

We will begin with Return A (Offenses Known to the Police) because it is the most well-known component of the UCR. To many, the UCR starts and ends here because it is the source of most information in the FBI's annual UCR publication. In fact, it is only one of five major data parts in the UCR Program (the others are described below). It contains monthly data on the number of "Part I" (crime index) offenses reported to police agencies, and the number of offenses cleared by arrest (or other exceptional means).[10] Each agency is identified by a number of variables: a state code, city number, SMSA core-city code, population group number, and a set of three associated population and place codes used to distinguish data for agencies that overlap county boundaries. Annual totals for each monthly variable are available, as are variables summarizing the number of months of data each agency has reported.

The machine-readable version of Return A has many details which are not presented in the printed volume. For example, the monthly figures for each crime type, offense characteristics such as weapon-specific robbery and assault, counts of simple assault, and type of vehicle for motor vehicle thefts are in the computer-readable data files. ICPSR releases these data in annual files. These annual files contain 1420 variables for over 15,000 agencies. Data are presently available for 1976-1986 (with data for other years to be added).

3.2. Supplement to Return A: Property Stolen and Recovered

This part of the UCR data collection is one of the most under-utilized and least known. The machine-readable files have monthly data on the nature of crime and the value and type of property stolen and recovered incident to each crime. The Supplement to the Return A form requires that a value be assigned to each piece of property stolen and recovered for each Part I crime type except aggravated assault. Determination of property values was the responsibility of each investigating police officer. These data were originally compiled by the FBI from monthly agency reports and contain the same agency identification variables as the Return A data set (see above).

The *Supplement to Return A* files have monthly offense figures for robbery according to place of occurrence, such as highway, commercial house, gas station, or others; burglary according to time and place of occurrence, resident night or day, or non-resident night or day; larceny according to amount in dollars taken and type, such as pocket-picking, purse-snatching, bicycle, or others. Stolen property is described differently for each offense type. Auto thefts are divided into stolen and recovered locally, stolen and recovered other, or stolen other and recovered locally. Other stolen property is divided by type: currency, jewelry, clothing, office equipment, firearms, household goods, and several other categories.

ICPSR releases this part of the UCR collection in annual files. These files contain 1130 variables for approximately 16,000 cases (agencies). Data are available from 1976 through 1986.

3.3. Supplementary Homicide Report

These UCR files receive a great deal of attention from criminal justice researchers. In contrast to other types of UCR data, which are collected as monthly counts by each agency, the Supplementary Homicide Report (SHR) acquires data on each homicidal incident reported to police. The SHR is also the only continuing national instrument that includes information on offender characteristics, victim-offender relationship, and circumstances surrounding the homicide. Since the SHR is treated at length in another chapter, we will confine our discussion to the available computer-readable files. Due to scholarly interest and the disaggregated nature of the SHR, separate data sets are available in which cases can represent victims, offenders, or incidents.

The master SHR files, as distributed by the FBI, contain detailed information on each criminal homicide, i.e., murders, non-negligent killings (also called non-negligent manslaughters), negligent killings and justifiable homicides. The structure of the FBI's SHR files is hierarchical, with varying numbers of victim and offender records per incident present. The complex structure of the files has led to the creation of various "rectangular" versions of the data.[11]

The unit of observation in the ICPSR version of the master files is the homicide "incident."[12] Data on the victim(s), offender(s), the relationship between these individuals, weapons used, and the circumstances involved are available for each incident. Information is also present regarding the agency reporting each incident, including the same identification variables that are available in the "Return A" files (see section 3.1 above). Each incident may have more than one victim and offender (up to a maximum of ten victims and eleven offenders). Homicides are collected and categorized in a six-level situation code which is keyed to each victim. In situations where two or more victims were killed by a single offender, the offender data are linked to each victim. The occurrence of this situation does not result in multiple counting of offenders since the situation code and count variables indicate the number of offenders included. Presently, ICPSR has incident-level SHR data available for the years 1976 through 1986. Each file has 152 variables.

3.4. Law Enforcement Officers Killed and Assaulted

These data are released by the ICPSR under the title, *Police Employee (LEOKA) Data*. These files contain police employment data, such as the total number of employees by sex, numbers of officers according to patrol type (one- vs. two-person vehicles) and shift (day or evening). Detailed data on monthly assaults on police are classified as with or without injury and further subdivided into firearm, knife, other weapon, or hands or feet. There is also information on the circumstances surrounding officers killed in disturbance calls, burglary and robbery calls, calls for services, arrests and attempted arrests. All of these figures are reported on a monthly basis.

These data were originally compiled by the FBI from the Return A and Law Enforcement employees Reports, which were completed by participating agencies. The data files are very large; approximately 2256 variables for 16,000 cases. Annual files are available for the years 1976 through 1986.

3.5 Age, Sex, Race, and Ethnic Origin of Persons Arrested

Due to their massive size, the annual Age, Sex, Race, and Ethnic Origin of Persons Arrested files are not yet generally available from the public data archives. We mention them here because they comprise the fifth major UCR data component. Users are interested in these data because they include information on the number of persons arrested each month by local law enforcement in each gender, race, and age group for every offense classification.[13] Because such detailed information is requested from each agency each month, the master tapes have been quite unwieldy and expensive to convert to archivable formats and are therefore not currently available from ICPSR. Nevertheless, ambitious "data crunchers" with an interest in arrest activity are encouraged to acquire these data directly from the FBI.

3.6. Other Related Data Collections

The ICPSR also has five other UCR data collections available for public use. In contrast to the preceding files, which were obtained directly from the FBI, the following data sets were processed and assembled by various researchers who drew upon UCR sources (printed and machine-readable) for specific analytical purposes and later submitted their files to ICPSR for archiving. Consequently, there is a fair amount of "overlap" among these files and the files described above. They differ mainly by unit of observation, structural organization, or by the addition of variables from other sources. The availability of UCR data sets in a variety of aggregations and content offers the advantage of reducing data preparation for particular uses. Section 4, which follows, will underscore the importance and effort involved in data preparation and management.

3.6.1. UCR, 1966-1976: Data Aggregated by Standard Metropolitan Statistical Areas. The unit of observation in this data file is a Standard Metropolitan Statistical Area (SMSA) component county. Data on each index crime are available for 2609 cases (counties) which represent 291 SMSAs. Each case has 160 variables. This file was prepared by the Hoover Institution for Economic Studies of the Criminal Justice System, Stanford University.

3.6.2. UCR, 1958-1969, and County and City Data Books, 1962, 1967, and 1972: Merged Data. This file contains selected variables and cases from the UCR, annually for the years 1958-1969 as well as from the County and City Data Books, 1962, 1967, and 1972. Data are reported for all U.S. cities with a population of 75,000 or more in 1960. The UCR data include the number of homicides, forcible rapes, robberies, aggravated assaults, burglaries, larcenies over $50, and motor vehicle thefts. The County and City Data Book information focuses on population characteristics and city finances. There are 162 variables for 172 cases (cities). The file was prepared by Alvin Jacobson during a summer ICPSR workshop on the Quantitative Analysis of Crime and Justice in 1978.

3.6.3. UCR: National Time Series Community-Level DataBase, 1967-1980. (Pierce, Bowers, Baird and Heck, 1981). This collection includes monthly criminal offense and clearance data for only those police agencies that submitted ten or more monthly reports in every year from 1967 through 1980. This criterion resulted in 3328 agencies (which the original investigators interpreted as representing "communities"). Of particular interest are monthly weapon-specific robbery and assault counts; types of rape, burglary, larceny, and motor vehicle theft; and clearances by arrest of adults and juveniles for each offense sub-type. Each agency is identified by the FBI's "ORI Code," geographic region, state, population size and group, and frequency of reporting. Variable definitions were consistent over the study period with the exception of some manslaughter, robbery, and larceny classifications. The ICPSR has derived a comparable robbery measure and the remaining problems with manslaughter and larceny are noted in the ICPSR codebook which documents the data collection. There are 1210 variables for each yearly data file.

3.6.4. Trends in American Homicide. 1968-1978: Victim-Level Supplementary Homicide Reports (Riedel and Zahn, 1987). The investigators for this study, under a grant from the National Institute of Justice, acquired Supplementary Homicide Report data from the FBI for 1968 through 1978 and transformed them from agency-based data to victim-based data. Variables include information on the reporting agency, the circumstances of the incident, and characteristics of the victim and offender. Within these categories are variables pertaining to population and city size, victim's and offender's age, race, and sex as well as the number of victims and offenders involved in the incident. Information about the incident includes the type of weapon used and the circumstances surrounding the incident. During the time period for which these data were compiled two major changes occurred in FBI coding of the Supplementary Homicide Reports. Consistent coding exists within the time periods, 1968-1972, 1973-1975, and 1976-1978, but not between them. The data are released in annual files with 37 variables in each and varying numbers of cases (victims).

3.6.5. UCR: Supplementary Homicide Reports, 1976-1983 (Fox and Pierce, 1987). These investigators have reformatted and restructured SHR data into three separate data files. An incident file contains one record per incident, an offender file has one record per offender, and a victim file is organized with one record per victim. Victim and offender characteristics may be found in their respective files. Information concerning the location and type of incident as well as relationship, weapon, and circumstances are found in the incident file.

In reviewing the UCR data available for use, we have organized them into two main groups: data from the UCR master tapes and data compiled in specialized collections. Master tape data are provided in annual files which include the monthly UCR submissions of individual police agencies across the country. There are separate files for *Return A, Supplement to Return A, Supplementary Homicide Report, Police Employee-LEOKA,* and *Age, Sex, and Race of Persons of Arrested* data. The first relatively complete data year available in machine-readable form is 1967 and the end point of the collection is updated each year. As of this writing, 1987 files had just been released by the FBI. The second group of files consists of specialized UCR collections which have been compiled and archived by independent researchers who needed UCR data in formats and aggregations other than what were typically available from the FBI. Using these data, rather than the master tape files, may be more efficient if the data requirements coincide with the available files.

The UCR collection available in data archives is extensive and growing and presents opportunities for useful, new research. What may not be clearly evident is that the files are large, unwieldy, and sometimes difficult to use. Because of this and because little attention is generally paid to the topics of data preparation and management, we believe it would be useful to provide some guidance to the potential data user. The next section of the chapter discusses management and utilization issues surrounding work with the data.

4. Managing and Using UCR Data

Data restructuring and management is an important issue to consider; it is central, in fact, to planning statistical analyses. It assumes even more importance when data sets as large as the UCR are to be used. Although once the exclusive province of computer programmers and other trained technicians, many data management tasks no longer require access to high-priced skills and abilities, thanks to the availability of easy-to-use, integrated software packages.[14] In fact, as more non-technically oriented people manage their own data, the advantages of exercising direct control in shaping data should become more apparent. Our point is that profitable analysis derives from appropriate data preparation, and understanding data preparation is as important to analysis as interpreting the statistical output. This is particularly true of UCR data because a fair amount of "preparation" has already been done by the time they are released by an archive.

As with most archival databases, UCR files are structured so that every possible data element can be stored and retrieved as efficiently as possible by even the most basic computing environments. It is a "lowest common denominator" approach with at least three advantages. First, it is designed for flexibility in disseminating data across differing computing installations without completely re-processing every data set for each request. Second, UCR files are built to include every variable available at the lowest possible level or unit of observation. It is not an archive's role to evaluate and select which variables and at what level of aggregation the data should be analyzed, so all available information is preserved. Third, it provides a degree of continuity and stability since the data are stored and distributed in known and predictable formats that are usable over the long-term, despite inevitable improvements in computing technology. Maintaining the data in standard formats and storage modes encourages exchangeability and standard methods for accessing the data. Thus, the formats of archived data address needs for storage efficiency, standardization, and flexibility.

In practice, end-users of the data frequently find that archival formats are neither efficient nor desirable for the particular analyses they contemplate. The files may be too large and cumbersome for the analytical software. The variables might not be in the form necessary for particular statistical routines. The analysis might dictate use of only a portion of the available cases. The unit of observation, too, might need to be manipulated. Our experience, as data managers who interact quite frequently with researchers and analysts, suggests that these users often find out "too late," after they have already expended a fair amount of effort in a project, that it requires extensive, perhaps excessive, data preparation relative to their goals. In the next section we outline the process and techniques typically used in preparing

UCR data for analysis. This is followed by their application in a "case study" in which the process of preparation and analysis of a computer-readable UCR data set is described.

4.1. Data Preparation

The first step in getting data ready for analysis is to determine how they may be accessed. In particular, the way in which data are stored will determine the appropriate method used to read them. Frequently, the user will want to convert the data to a format that will be easier to manipulate in subsequent operations. For example, UCR data are distributed by ICPSR in OSIRIS[15] format accompanied by SPSS^X "control cards"[16] on magnetic tapes.[17] Certain popular software packages have made it convenient to access OSIRIS data by providing routines specifically designed for this format. Due to the massive size of some UCR files it might be especially wise to use one of these direct conversion routines which interpret the OSIRIS "Type 1" dictionary.[18] SAS[19] has a procedure called "CONVERT" which accomplishes this by creating a SAS data set while preserving variable label and missing data code information from the OSIRIS version (SAS Institute, 1985b: 843). Likewise, SPSS^X has an OSIRIS-to-SPSS interface (see the "GET OSIRIS" subcommand, SPSS Inc., 1986: 301). Other statistical packages may have similar built-in programs and there may also be stand-alone programs that have been specifically designed to transfer data from one proprietary format to another. We mention the SPSS^X and SAS routines only because these packages are popular and relatively widespread across academic and research institutions. Data distributed by ICPSR can, of course, be accessed by other means that do not require the use of SAS, SPSS^X, or OSIRIS.[20]

Once the technique for reading the data has been chosen, the primary data management strategy should be the reduction of the data set to a usable size as early in the processing sequence as possible. This means that one should first decide what variables and cases will be needed and what form or structure will be most desirable for analyzing the data. If, for example, the researcher is interested in performing a time-series analysis, a desirable structure would likely have the cases representing months rather than, say, law enforcement agencies. Perhaps a regional or state-level analysis is planned. In this situation, the data must be reorganized so that cases represent geographic entities. Whatever format is chosen, the data will be easier to store and use once irrelevant observations and variables (if any) are removed from the working file. Most often these decisions will involve either aggregating, subsetting, or recoding the data in some way.

When data are aggregated, they are summarized by a new, hierarchically higher, unit of observation. For example, information about local police agencies may be combined to represent states. Monthly data could be combined to represent years, and so on. The key idea is that observations which share a common characteristic (such as location) are grouped together so that a summary statistic can be calculated for each group. A new file is created in which the summary statistic for each group in the original file becomes a case in the new file. A common method of summarization is summation. Values of original observations are added together within each aggregation group and the sums are output as observations in the resulting file. Other methods of summarization are frequently available as well. One could create an aggregated file based on descriptive statistics such as minimums, maximums, means, or standard deviations within groups just as easily as a file based on stratum sums.

Subsetting data is conceptually simpler than aggregation. Here one wants to filter out variables and/or cases that satisfy (or fail to satisfy) some criterion. Unlike aggregation, the cases which are retained after filtering have the same interpretation as before filtering. A file of homicide victims results in a file of homicide victims after subsetting. There may be fewer variables or fewer cases in the resulting file, but the cases represent homicide victims nonetheless. Sampling is, essentially, a method of subsetting cases. The primary motivation for subsetting UCR data is to create a more manageable data set, one that not only is easier to manipulate, but also does not consume computing resources unnecessarily.

Many important decisions that will later affect interpretation of the data are made during the data preparation phase, including the determination of how the data are aggregated, subsetted or otherwise reorganized. Another, perhaps more basic, operation in preparing data for analysis, and one with which researchers are more familiar, is the recoding of variables. We will not describe recoding methods here since good introductions are available elsewhere (see, for example, Helwig, 1985: 17-22), except to say that it is essential to keep good records of the steps undertaken in recoding. Documenting all variables and cases including important recodes, so that their meanings will be clear and precise even after time has passed, cannot be stressed enough. If one of the goals of science is reproducibility of results, careful and complete data documentation is fundamental.

4.2. Using UCR Data to Estimate Crime

The preceding section was meant to introduce data users to some of the techniques that are typically used to prepare data for analysis. We turn now to applying some of these techniques in a demonstration using UCR data. We use as our example agency-level data from the 1980 UCR to create a state-level file that contains estimates of crimes that local police agencies "knew about," but failed to report to the FBI, a process known as imputation and upon which many of the figures in the FBI's annual publication, *Crime in the United States*, are based. Our purpose is two-fold. First, it is necessary to provide a more detailed description of the imputation procedure than that which is currently available in FBI publications. Our second goal will become apparent in the process of the first; we illustrate useful techniques for dealing with the preeminent UCR data set, the Return A (Offenses Known to the Police) files (U.S. Department of Justice, 1984).

4.2.1. A BRIEF INTRODUCTION TO IMPUTATION

Estimation, from the point of view of the FBI, describes the total number of crimes as if every police agency had consistently submitted complete UCRs to the FBI. Note that this type of estimation differs from other kinds of crime estimation. It is not intended to represent crimes that for one reason or another have not been recorded by the police. Instead it attempts to account for locally recorded crimes that are not reported to the UCR Program.

Submitting crime reports to the UCR Program is not compulsory, and varying levels of police agency participation exist.[21] The FBI attempts to compensate for this by estimating or "imputing" crime counts for agencies that report infrequently (Federal Bureau of Investigation, 1981: 3). Such estimates are incorporated as aggregate figures in the crime index presented by the FBI in its annual publication (CIUS). These crime statistics, compiled at the national, regional, state and metropolitan area levels, are the sum of the crime counts from fully reporting jurisdiction, plus estimates of crime in jurisdictions that submitted less than complete reports. UCR crime estimates are prominent[22] in CIUS and are likely the figures most frequently used to describe the picture of crime.

An important issue in estimating crimes known to the police (but whose UCR returns have not been forwarded to the FBI) is determining the imputation method used by the FBI.[23] Because the UCR's current imputation method has not yet been described by the FBI with a high degree of precision, users of this large data base are left with two options for estimating the nation's reported crime as a whole: (a) produce estimates "close" to the FBI's using the limited information available, or (b) design their own imputation methods. As it stands, the only machine-readable version of the data currently distributed by the FBI are "agency-level," and do not include imputed values; the data appear exactly as they were reported to the UCR Program (after error correction) by individual police agencies. If an agency failed to submit a return or if its crime and clearance activity was reported through another agency, "missing data" codes were entered.

An examination of "missing data" on the 1980 *Return A* tape suggests that the FBI imputed crime counts for nearly 2,500 law enforcement agencies representing over thirteen million residents in 1980. Frequency of reporting varied positively with agency size and urbanization. Smaller agencies or those outside of metropolitan areas were more likely to report less frequently than larger jurisdictions or those within metro areas. It can be argued then that crime imputation is not a trivial matter even though the vast majority of police departments fully participate in the UCR Program.

4.2.2. IMPUTATION METHODOLOGY

The FBI described the main features of crime estimation in a recent introduction to CIUS:

> [o]ffense estimation occurs within each of three areas: Standard Metropolitan Statistical Areas, "other cities," and rural areas. Assuming that non-reporting areas have the same proportionate crime experience as those which did not submit complete data, estimates are based on the reported crime experience of similar areas within a state (Federal Bureau of Investigation, 1981: 3).

Three general groups among UCR contributing agencies are distinguished: 1) agencies reporting for the full twelve months; 2) agencies reporting at least three but less than twelve months; and 3) agencies reporting less than three months. For the latter two groups, data were imputed using different methods for each.

First, counts for agencies that reported between three and eleven months are inflated using simple extrapolation. The equation is: $y = x(12/r)$ where x is the total number of crimes actually reported, r is the number of monthly reports submitted, and y is the 12-month estimate of the agency's crime. The FBI usually follows this procedure unless there is some reason to believe that a particular jurisdiction has an artificially inflated count which might have occurred as a result of an unusual event, such as a riot or a mass murder. When this happens, the amount of crime attributed to an unusual occurrence is subtracted from the count, while the number of reporting months remains unchanged. The purpose of this procedure is to reduce any over-estimation that could result by multiplying the derived factor by an unusually high crime count.

The FBI uses a different procedure to impute data for agencies that submit less than three monthly reports. These agencies are identified according to their jurisdiction's population size and type of governing authority (city or county) within each state to produce estimation strata. A value is then assigned that is equal to the mean number of crimes known for the other twelve-month reporting agencies that fall into the same stratum. Group codes are based on population estimates of reporting agencies:

1. cities with population 250,000 or over;

2. cities between 100,000 and 249,999;

3. cities between 50,000 and 99,999;

4. cities between 25,000 and 44,999;

5. cities between 10,000 and 24,999;

6. cities between 2,500 and 49,999

7. cities under 2,500;

8. rural counties (outside SMSAs); and

9. suburban counties (within SMSAs).

To avoid the potential problem of overestimating crimes by double counting, two sets of agencies are removed from the algorithm. First, it is necessary to exclude agencies which reported for less than three months and which had no associated population values because the data were coded such that population (but not population group) was listed only once among jurisdictions with overlapping boundaries. Second, all agencies whose counts were "covered" by other agencies are excluded.

The FBI indicates, with the "covered-by" code, cases in which a law enforcement agency submits crime counts for another agency. An agency may be "covered by" another because it is convenient. This may happen when a very small agency doesn't have the volume of incidents to justify preparing their own returns. In other cases it may be necessity rather than convenience that leads agencies to report for others. For example, budgetary constraints in a jurisdiction may lead to a situation in which another agency assumes policing responsibilities for the financially strapped jurisdiction and includes that area's offense counts with its own. When imputing missing data, agencies whose counts are included in another agency's returns are excluded from the algorithm-because double-counting would otherwise result. Except for the "covered-by" indication, these agencies appear in the data file exactly like agencies whose crime counts are missing because no returns were submitted.

After the data have been properly filtered and the imputed values assigned according to the procedures relevant to each agency's level of reporting, aggregate estimates for larger geographic areas can be produced by adding together the offense counts for the areas of interest. Actual reported values are used for agencies that reported all twelve months and estimated counts are inserted for the less frequent reporters.

4.2.3. REPRODUCING PUBLISHED FIGURES

In an earlier work, we attempted to reproduce the estimates that were published in the 1980 CIUS using the method just described (Schneider and Wiersema, 1985). We found that the resulting offense estimates erred within one percentage point of comparable CIUS figures for 40 of 51 state-level observations. In the other states (with two exceptions), the reproduced estimates were within 7.5 percent from the published estimates. Data coding inconsistencies and the mis-identification of comparable agencies were responsible for large errors in estimates for Vermont and Connecticut (the two exceptions). Clearly, either the imputation procedures or the raw data employed were not identical to that used by the FBI (although fairly close approximations were possible in many cases). There were some indications that the data, rather than the procedures, may have been responsible for the discrepancies.[24]

Since we are unaware of any other research analyzing the composition (much less the validity) of UCR estimates, we conclude that efforts to present a complete picture of "crimes known to the police" in the face of incomplete UCR data require validation and improvement. According to Poggio et al. (1985: 172) improving future UCR estimates will require "using more stratification information."[25] Preliminary evidence from the Schneider and Wiersema (1985) study seems to point to a different conclusion, however. Imputation, as currently conceived, depends on the number and type of comparable agencies that submit complete reports; as more stratification information is employed, the number of agencies with complete data that are "comparable" will decrease. Improvements may require other factors such as the use of longitudinal information and/or more sophisticated cross-sectional methods.[26]

4.2.4. REVIEWING THE EXAMPLE

This exercise in crime imputation demonstrates several concepts involved in using UCR data for analysis. First, for what is regarded as a well-known source of offense data, some UCR technical methods are not easy to ascertain. The method we employed needs confirmation and validation. Second, we needed to do a fair amount of data preparation for this analysis and the procedures with which this was done directed its interpretation. We did some subsetting to remove cases that were represented by other cases (i.e., agencies "covered by" other agencies). This was accomplished by using the Covered-by Code variable as a "filter" when assigning mean values to target cases (those with "real" missing data caused by failure to submit a monthly return). We also did two kinds of recodes. It was initially necessary to calculate a variable that contained the mean number of crimes for agencies within different population groups in each state. Then we recoded the existing crime index variables using a replacement function. Missing values in one variable were "replaced" by the values of another variable, in this case, the stratum mean variable. Finally, we sorted the data by state and aggregated by summation to create a file with states, instead of agencies, as the units of analysis. This file resulted in offense totals that included estimates for non-reporters for each state. In comparing our estimates with those published by the FBI we found that certain cases we estimated diverged considerably from the published figures, but that a sizable majority conformed within two or three percentage points. We concluded that following the method as currently stated in FBI publications will approximate, but will not exactly reproduce, the published UCR estimates. Depending on the level of precision desired, users may wish to invent their own imputation algorithms to create estimates of complete UCR reporting.

5. Summary

The purpose of this chapter was to describe problems with the current Uniform Crime Reporting Program, which range from limitations in reporting practices to deficiencies in methodological development. Tracing the history of the UCR Program showed that interest in a comprehensive system of collecting crime statistics began in the early 1920s. While the UCR Program has expanded from 400 participating law enforcement agencies in 1930 to more than 16,000 today, concern over the official measurement of crime has also escalated. A reporting-based system depends on citizens and police alike to record crime events. The reasons why such events go unrecorded have been the subject of a long tradition of scholarship that indicates the UCR, if interpreted as an accurate measure of crime, will lead to seriously biased results. Understanding the UCR's strengths as well as its weaknesses, however, can lead to more useful findings.

The UCR has been criticized for lack of direction or guidance provided by underlying criminological theory, which is particularly evident in operational definitions of the Program. Not only are specific crime definitions too vague or general, but the data are not collected at a level of disaggregation that would allow analysis of detailed offense characteristics. It is difficult to compare data across jurisdictions due to varied interpretations of UCR definitions based on differing systems of criminal law and procedure and administrative policies governing the data collection. Then, too, because participation in the UCR Program is not mandatory, varying levels of police agency reporting exist.

We described some of the currently available machine-readable UCR data sets, several of which are surprisingly under-utilized and unexplored. Advances in both knowledge about the UCR and its potential uses have been made possible by the relatively recent availability of these data in a machine-readable form. Many potential users seem to be unaware of the wealth of data that is available only in the magnetic tape versions. We also mentioned some of the advantages of using UCR computer files rather than the printed volumes. Using computerized UCR data provides access to detailed characteristics at the most basic levels of official reporting and allows a flexibility in analyses previously impossible with the FBI's printed reports.

Finally, we offered some suggestions for the management and use of computer-readable UCR data by way of a demonstration. We used, as our example, agency-level data from the 1980 UCR to estimate crimes that local police agencies for one reason or another failed to report to the FBI; a process known as imputation. In an attempt to describe the picture of recorded crime for the nation as a whole, the FBI produces estimates for infrequently reporting police agencies. The method with which this is done needs validation, if not improvement. The exercise illustrated some important techniques for accessing and analyzing the data and, in particular, demonstrated the close relationship between preparing the data for analysis and the analysis itself.

In all, we intended to show the usefulness as well as the limitations of the Uniform Crime Reports in the spirit of encouraging additional interest in, and development of, these data. For some purposes, like analyses of small geographical areas, the UCR is a more appropriate data source than the NCS. Despite the volume of work already done, much basic research, particularly of measurement reliability and validity, still needs to be done. Finally, we note that many have drawn the erroneous conclusion that the UCR is virtually useless and should be abandoned altogether. Although it has serious flaws, the UCR's unique qualities lead us to conclude that the focus should be on what we can still learn from this valuable source of data. We believe that awareness of the UCR's problems and limitations is crucial, not to deter use, but to enable careful, appropriate, and useful research with the existing data.

3

The Future of the Uniform Crime Reporting Program: Its Scope and Promise

Yoshio Akiyama and Harvey M. Rosenthal

The Uniform Crime Reporting (UCR) Program, despite its limitations, has been used synonymously with the term "crime statistics" for many years. From the time of its inception to the present, the Program has undergone limited modifications. Changes have been made with respect to population coverage, data quality, and meeting the needs of the various user groups. People began to see that computerized incident-based reporting would increase UCR's utility markedly. An enhanced data base was also viewed as a step that will result from such an incident-based system offering researchers, decision-makers, and other consumers of crime statistics a refined tool for measuring criminal activity.

The purpose of this paper is to discuss the various modifications that have occurred in the UCR Program over the past several years. The planned changes in the Program to better meet the informational needs of consumers and researchers are also described.

1. The Development of the UCR Program

Prior to and during the period that the UCR Program was developed in the 1920s, the need for a crime information system with well-defined objectives was established. The International Association of Chiefs of Police (IACP) had expressed the importance of obtaining nationwide data on "the nature and extent of the crime problem" (FBI, 1939). Consequently, the IACP's Committee on Uniform Crime Records was given the task of developing a viable crime data collection system. In translating the aforementioned information needs into an operational data collection mechanism, the Technical Staff of the Committee on Uniform Crime Records had to resolve a number of problems pertaining to the eventual form such a system would take.

The nature of the concerns centered around the structure of the data base, the source of the data, crime measures to be used, geographical uniformity of crime definitions, rules for scoring and counting offenses, the mode of data collection, etc. The history of the development of the UCR Program prior to 1930 indicates that the Committee on Uniform Crime Records addressed these issues through expert experience and the conduct of extensive research. As a result of its efforts and support of the IACP, the concept of a UCR System was developed and documented in the manual, "Uniform Crime Reporting" (1929). This blueprint for the collection of crime statistics was adopted by the IACP in the same year.

The system developed by the Committee possessed unique characteristics that became synonymous with the UCR Program. The UCR was conceived as a program whereby law enforcement agencies voluntarily participated in the data collection effort. It was decided that police records or offenses known to the police constituted the best measure of crimes committed. Clearance counts (the number of crimes disposed of by arrests) were viewed to represent a measure of the efficiency of law enforcement agencies in combatting crime. The compilation of data regarding offenses known to the police and clearances were categorized as Part I offenses. From this category of offenses emerged the concept of the Crime Index. The Crime Index, the totality of reported crime, was considered to be a gauge of crime movement, fluctuations, and trends. Characteristics of persons arrested, charges placed against them, and their final dispositions, although not implemented at that time, were also recommended to become part of the original UCR data base.

In order to insure uniformity and consistency of the data contributed by participating agencies, rules and guidelines for classifying and scoring offenses were devised. An examination of the criminal statutes in different states eventually led to the development of a uniform set of offense definitions and a hierarchical ordering of the crime categories in terms of severity. The Committee on Uniform Crime Records began data collection under this model in January of 1930. Later that year, the Bureau of Investigation of the U. S. Department of Justice, the predecessor of the Federal Bureau of Investigation, was assigned by the Attorney General (who was authorized through an act of Congress) to function as a repository for crime data collected under the aegis of the UCR Program.

Since its inception, the fundamental characteristics of the UCR Program have remained largely unchanged. These characteristics include the voluntary nature of the Program, data collection through summary reports, the use of police records as the data source, counting of offenses known to the police, the use of seven (or eight) offense classes designated as Index crimes as a crime indicator, crime definitions, the mode of classification, scoring, etc. Although the UCR has remained virtually intact when compared with its original design as delineated in the "Uniform Crime Reporting" manual prepared by the Committee on Uniform Crime Records, there have been certain important changes during its years of operation. The following are some of the most significant modifications that have been adopted:

1. Arrest data extracted from fingerprint cards was stopped (1952).

2. Statutory rape was dropped from the Part I offenses (1952).

3. Larcenies below $50 were eliminated from the Index crimes, although such data collection continued (1958).

4. Manslaughter by negligence was excluded from the Index offenses (1958).

5. The UCR Program decided to use current population estimates rather than the preceding decennial census figures (1958).

6. The UCR semiannual publication was replaced by an annual report (1958).

7. Computerization of UCR data storage commenced (1960).

8. Introduction of the careers in crime program to the UCR publication "Crime in the United States" (1963).

9. The introduction of UCR form changes and modifications of the hierarchy rule with respect to gambling and simple assault (1964).

10. Discontinuation of the collection of traffic data (1972).

11. Larcenies below $50 were added back into the Index offenses (1974).

12. Arson was added as a Part I offense (1982).

2. Critiques of the UCR Program

Since the UCR commenced, a number of shortcomings inherent in the design and methodology of the Program have been addressed by various students of this data collection system. Most criticism has focused on the fundamental aspects of the Program. Some of the more common concerns include:

> The compactness or the lack of comprehensiveness of the UCR data base mitigates against an in-depth understanding of crime or using UCR statistics as a basis for decision-making.

Reported crimes are not necessarily representative of the crimes committed. In particular, since reported crimes could be affected by the reporting practices of citizens, some viewed that reported crimes do not constitute a valid basis for ascertaining long-range trends or levels of crime.

UCR data are not conducive to direct means of data quality control or error structure analysis. Some critics suggested through episodic means, the possibility of politically motivated manipulation of data at various stages of data flow.

The Crime Index is not a valid indicator and is too crude to measure what it was designed to measure. The adoption of seriousness weights were suggested, for example, to overcome these difficulties.

The data base, and therefore, UCR publications, lack utility with respect to law enforcement operations at the agency level.

In 1958, the report, "Uniform Crime Reporting—Report of the Consultant Committee" was prepared by Lejins, Chute and Schrotel (1958). Prior to the recently completed Abt Associates, Inc. study (1984), this was the most comprehensive evaluation of the UCR Program. The Committee's efforts yielded twenty-two recommendations designed to improve the UCR Program; a number of these were adopted.

During the nearly three decades since the Lejins, et al. evaluative study was implemented, the data collection environment has greatly improved. First, the utilization of computer technology has strongly impacted all phases of the UCR work effort, including the facilitation of both data processing and data analysis. In addition, computerization has been instrumental in generating sophisticated police record systems from which crime statistics can be derived. "The Uniform Crime Reporting Study: 1984 Survey of Law Enforcement Agencies," (Chaiken and Akiyama, 1984), conducted as an adjunct to the "Blueprint for the Future of the Uniform Crime Reporting Program" (Poggio, et al., 1985) examined this issue with both UCR contributing and non-contributing law enforcement agencies. Secondly, statistical sampling has become widely accepted as a means of obtaining statistical information. If sampling techniques are used, more extensive and flexible data collection programs and surveys are feasible. Thirdly, state UCR programs that started to develop in the 1960s have increased in number, and have begun to fulfill the data needs of the respective states. Some of these states designed their data bases and systems specifically for their local crime analysis needs, maintaining the National UCR Program data elements as a sub-database of their programs.

The National UCR Program should not be just a collection of fifty states' UCR publications. Rather, it should serve multiple purposes, such as to give a national perspective. During the course of UCR history, user groups have expanded and there is a need for more comprehensive data. At the same time, in spite of a number of attempts to increase their utility to the law enforcement community, the UCR data base has not been considered by the contributing law enforcement agencies to be very useful for their administrative or operational purposes.

The nature of crime has changed since the 1920s and 1930s. Crimes such as those related to high technology and the sale and use of drugs are viewed neither as variations of traditional crimes nor as offenses that will fade away with time. On the contrary, the changing nature of crime is viewed as real, and perhaps has best been described by Tully (1986), "What probably will fade away are the traditional crimes of armed robbery and perhaps burglary." These changes in the nature and configuration of crime dictate that certain enhancement efforts have to be made with respect to the National UCR Program. This will require a review of its goals, limitations, user groups, data sources, factors related to data quality, publications, relationship with other information systems, data collection mechanisms, and so on. On a number of occasions, the IACP, with the support of other groups, has suggested that such a study be conducted. In their opinion, such a study would result in a set of recommendations for modernizing the UCR Program to better meet the needs of the law enforcement community and other decision-makers in the 21st century.

3. The 1982 UCR Evaluation and Redesign Effort

With the concurrence of the FBI, the Bureau of Justice Statistics (BJS), also of the U.S. Department of Justice, agreed to fund a comprehensive three-phase evaluative study and redesign effort. In September 1982, a grant was awarded to Abt Associates, Inc. of Cambridge, Massachusetts, an independent contractor, to conduct a multi-year evaluation of the National UCR Program.

The first two phases were designed to ascertain what, if any, changes should be implemented in the current Program. The third phase would focus on implementing the recommended changes. Overseeing the research project was the FBI/BJS Task Force and a Steering Committee comprised of an eclectic group of respected individuals representing a variety of fields.

An examination of the historical development of the Program was conducted during the initial phase of the study of 1982. During this phase, every aspect of the UCR, including goals and objectives, user groups, data elements, modes of reporting, quality control procedures, and publications and user services, were reviewed.

During the second phase of the redesign study, launched with a conference in early 1984, a number of alternative directions for the future of the Program were investigated. Findings of the first phase of the study were reviewed and possible adjustments to the Program were explored. The result was a set of recommended changes that should be considered during phase two of the evaluation (Abt Associates, 1984). In order to bring the perspective of the law enforcement community to the enhanced UCR Program and to better understand the state of the art with respect to law enforcement record keeping, a survey of law enforcement agencies was conducted (Chaiken and Akiyama, 1984).

4. Blueprint for the Future

At the conclusion of this evaluative study, Abt Associates, Inc. (1985) prepared a report "Blueprint for the Future of the Uniform Crime Reporting Program." In this report, conceptual recommendations were made in regard to the future scope of the UCR. The "Blueprint" incorporated input from law enforcement agencies, data users, state UCR Program administrators, criminologists and other interest groups. Since the report sets the direction that the UCR should take to better fulfill its mission, the major recommendations proposed in the document are described below, and implications for the future are explained.

4.1 Method of Reporting

The single most important recommendation in the Blueprint is that of "unit-record reporting," synonymously called "incident-based reporting." With few exceptions, the current National UCR Program is based on summary data from local law enforcement agencies and it could be called a "summary data collection" program. The counts of reported crimes, clearances, arrests, etc., are processed and maintained monthly for each data contributing agency. In an incident-based reporting system, on the other hand, agencies submit designated characteristics and information pertaining to each prescribed crime or arrest incident rather than submitting aggregate monthly statistics. At present, the Supplementary Homicide Report (SHR) of the National UCR Program, wherein each murder incident is reported according to the SHR-specified format combined with relevant narratives, is the closest to an incident-based reporting system.

The Blueprint recommended that the entire UCR system be converted to incident-based reporting instead of the current summary reporting system. All local law enforcement agencies would submit reports on each individual criminal incident, clearance, arrest, etc. Incident-based reporting pertains to the format of the data submitted but not to the content of that data. In this sense, the term incident-based reporting is generic. Different types of incident-based reporting have been tried and implemented by a number of state UCR programs. The "Law Enforcement Agency Survey" mentioned earlier, found that even state UCR programs that do not have an incident-based reporting program tend to support the concept.

4.1.1 Incident-Based Reporting

The advantages associated with incident-based reporting relate to 1) crime analysis, 2) data gathering and 3) data processing. Incident-based reporting improves the data structure for data analysis. A structure using individual incidents allows cross tabulations among any number of variables. Incident-based reporting also allows a linkage and structure among data elements. This is not feasible under a summary-data-reporting system unless each report form is designed to represent a multi-dimensional matrix. Since such a form requires a large amount of space and complicated entries, only marginal totals in a matrix are reported in most summary data reporting systems, as is the case with the current UCR Program.

Given a set of variables, conditional distributions can be computed under an incident-based reporting program. This greatly increases the flexibility of the data for research purposes. For example, a researcher can examine questions such as whether a higher robbery clearance rate (higher than that for total robberies) is associated with more "serious" types of robberies, or if there are different age peaks in arrest rates for different racial groups, or if the average monetary loss associated with juvenile larceny arrestees differs from that associated with adult larceny arrestees.

Unlike the current UCR Program, analyses involving time, such as the time from the date of the offense to unfounding, clearance, arrest, or recovery of a stolen item are feasible only under an incident-based reporting system. These increased analytic capabilities are strictly the result of structural refinements of the data and have nothing to do with the expansion of data categories or breakdowns within a category. If additional data elements are incorporated into the UCR Program's data base, as will be described later, the system's capability to respond to crime-analytic data requirements will be multiplied.

With respect to data processing, it has been suggested that the accuracy and quality of the data will be greatly improved under an incident-based reporting system. With its many rows and columns, and numerous "corresponding" totals on different forms, summary reporting forms open chances for mistakes in entering, sorting, or adding. Fewer arithmetic errors are expected if data are submitted in an incident-based reporting system, because no tallying, counting, or sorting is required. One has only to choose a correct code or transcribe a number (such as dollar loss or date) into an appropriate blank. It is anticipated in the Blueprint that automated data submission necessitated by an incident-based reporting system will be a primary factor in UCR data quality improvement. The level of data accuracy resulting from automated retrieval and codification under an incident-based system was viewed to be much higher than the quality of data manually tallied and counted. The inclusion of identification numbers associated with each offense and arrest is expected to facilitate the data checking and reviewing to test data quality.

4.1.2 GENERAL IMPLEMENTATION ISSUES

There is increased flexibility in data collection procedures and system modifications in incident-based reporting. For example, collection of data needed for a specific purpose does not require extensive form redesign, and changes in crime classifications or subcategories can be achieved rather expeditiously when compared to a summary data system. Even larger scale modifications in the UCR data base would be practical under an incident-based reporting system. It was estimated in the Blueprint that, except for the increased workload required at the time of implementation, incident-based reporting does not generate an unbearable burden on UCR contributing agencies if necessary software development is supported by the generic model. Also, some agencies indicated that incident-based reporting is simpler and less time consuming than summary data reporting.

For other recommendations in the Blueprint to be adopted, incident-based reporting must be implemented. While this concept is strictly an issue associated with the mode of data collection, and is unrelated to problems with data elements, definitions, analysis, etc., it is a prerequisite for their solution. The structural refinements of UCR data mentioned earlier are considered to be the primary benefits which will be achieved in transformating the UCR from a summary data reporting system to incident-based reporting. In this sense, although the recommended change to incident-based reporting is mechanical, its implications are far-reaching, encompassing the problem of the analytic capability and the ultimate utility of UCR data.

A few caveats are relevant at this juncture. First, incident-based reporting will change the traditional concept of data editing within the UCR Program. For example, under incident-based reporting, UCR would not be concerned with a problem such as: To what extent can the number of unfounded crimes exceed the number of crimes reported? Or, is it possible to report a negative number of actual crimes in a given month? Or, how much discrepancy should the Program allow between the figures on the Return A form and those on the Return A Supplement? Due to the greater complexity in the structure of data under incident-based reporting, it is expected that reviewing and editing need to be far more extensive than the current scheme of data quality control.

Secondly, under the proposed National Incident-Based Reporting System (NIBRS), classification is done at the agency level. It can be argued that if the UCR Program can relieve contributing agencies from committing arithmetic errors through the implementation of incident-based reporting, then it can also relieve their errors at the classification stage. In 1976, SEARCH (System for Electronic Analysis and Retrieval of Criminal Histories) Group conducted a field test of a system that was called Attribute Based Crime Reporting (ABCR). This system was founded upon the philosophy that contributing agencies should provide sufficient fundamental characteristics associated with individual crimes (instead of classifying incidents at the time of reporting using UCR standards and guidelines) so that a computer can classify each incident into an appropriate crime category. This approach was rejected in the Blueprint because of the bulk of decisions to be made by the computer, and because of the possible discrepancies remaining between the correct UCR classifications and computer-generated classifications. In order to implement an ABCR-type of reporting system, fundamental factors constituting each crime need to be defined accurately and explicitly so that they provide a sufficient basis for classification. For example, what factor distinguishes an aggravated assault from a simple assault? In terms of the degree of injury, or type of weapon used? A conceptual study such as the Blueprint does not address these questions. The national UCR Program has a firm commitment to the proposed concept of incident-based reporting with agencies classifying crimes. Great effort is being expended to insure that this mode of data collection is realized in the future.

4.1.3 Implementing the National Incident-Based Reporting System in the UCR

In the Blueprint, the incident-based reporting system was proposed to be implemented in two levels: Level I and Level II. The Level I incident-based reporting system is the easier of the two to implement. In brief, it is virtually a direct translation of the current UCR Program with its data base converted into an incident-based reporting mode. All agencies, unless chosen in the more comprehensive Level II program (to be discussed later), would contribute their crime and arrest data in the Level I mode.

The Level I component was to continue to collect virtually the same data elements in incident-based reporting fashion, as under the current UCR, with the following modifications:

1. From the current Part I offenses, eliminate the negligent manslaughter category.

2. Broaden the rape category to include all forcible sexual offenses.

3. Report all Part I crimes (except murder) so that attempts are distinguished from completed offenses.

4. The UCR Hierarchy Rule dictates that criminal events that occurred in a continuous series within a criminal incident are represented by an offense that is most serious in terms of the prescribed hierarchy. In order to describe the multiple offense situation, it was recommended that all distinct offense categories be reported ignoring the Hierarchy Rule. However, it was suggested that the Hierarchy Rule be retained to determine the most serious offense category committed for each victim. Furthermore, the Rule is also applicable within a given offense category in the selection of the most serious subcategory.

Although the Hierarchy Rule has been vigorously debated, there is no evidence that the amount of multiple offenses distorts the resulting statistics when the Hierarchy Rule is applied. On the contrary, the 1984 Oregon UCR study (Kincaid, 1984) indicated that its impact is nominal (with the Hierarchy Rule, 1.2 percent of the Part I crimes are lost).

5. Redefine aggravated assault more explicitly by introducing the weapon and injury in its definition. The meaning of a simple assault, for example, will then be clearer.

6. Redesign the Supplementary Homicide Report (SHR) to include more comprehensive data such as homicide location, time, geographic area, etc.

7. Distinguish crimes against residents of a jurisdiction from nonresidents. This recommendation is based upon the situation existing in some jurisdictions where there is a large influx of nonresidents (commuters, daytime business populations), tourists, and seasonal workers thus requiring a certain adjustment in the crime rate.

8. Distinguish among crimes committed against businesses, individuals, and other entities.

9. Collect property loss and recovery, whenever applicable, in terms of exact dollars instead of reporting in interval values.

10. Associate an incident number with each offense and use such numbers as a link to other unit records.

The Level I component, then, is an incident-based reporting system that retains the basic characteristics and data elements of the current UCR Program with minor modifications. These modifications pertain to clarifications, refinements, or linkage capabilities of the data. The Blueprint is a conceptual framework for an enhanced UCR Program. It was promulgated and accepted as a statement of the general direction that should be taken by the UCR in the future. Therefore, during the course of implementation, it is expected that the Level I proposal could undergo certain changes, additions, or deletions.

The main thrust of the second enhancement phase or Level II, is to collect from selected agencies, more comprehensive data than those collected in Level I. Users of UCR data have repeatedly noted that the current UCR data base does not possess sufficient detail, nor is it extensive enough to conduct in-depth crime analyses. Therefore, the Level II component is viewed as a means of providing more detailed data than the Level I component, encompassing all crime categories (e.g., Part II crimes), a refined breakdown of victim characteristics, and other information related to individual crime incidents. Since data collection and processing at Level II involves a greater workload for local agencies, as well as the National UCR Program, it was proposed in the Blueprint that Level II be implemented on a sample basis. The Blueprint recommends that all agencies covering jurisdictional populations of over 100,000 (there are approximately 300 such city police departments and county sheriff's departments), and other randomly selected agencies (at least an additional 300 agencies) participate in Level II. Random sampling should be stratified by geographical location, the degree of urbanization (e.g., SMA vs non-SMA), and the population size of the agency. The above mentioned sample size was proposed in order to provide usable information for national and regional crime analyses. For effective analysis at the state level, a larger sample would be required.

Although Level II was developed as a random sample program, it should be noted that current UCR data collection is performed (in a majority of the states) through state UCR programs. An individual state may choose to participate exclusively in the Level II component through its state UCR program. If an already operational state UCR program contains all the Level II data elements, there is little reason to have a dichotomy of a few selected Level II agencies and the remaining contributing agencies falling under the rubric of Level I. It should be observed that Level I and Level II data bases are compatible. The coexistence of Level I agencies and Level II-selected agencies does not create confusion within a state. However, if a potentially more beneficial program (i.e., Level II), is feasible in a given state, it is reasonable to choose the option of total statewide participation in Level II rather than maintaining the 2-component option of Levels I and II.

Care has to be exercised under the conditions described above so that no particular state or locality unduly impacts the national estimates generated through the Level II program. When the random selection process is combined with voluntary participation in the Level II component, over- or under-representation of crime data can result. A statistical scheme is required to avoid this aberration.

When Level II data correspond with Level I data (e.g., both Level I and Level II programs generate Part I crime totals), a national total is obtained by combining the two sets of figures. No estimation is necessary except for the portion of data that was submitted incomplete. In this case, Level II data will be used for breaking the totals down. For data elements (such as UCR Part II crimes) where the Level I component does not generate the corresponding Level I agency total, the Level II data would be used exclusively to arrive at an estimate.

As mentioned earlier, the primary reason for implementing Level II is to create a comprehensive data base amenable to in-depth crime analysis, something beyond straight counting or descriptive statistics. Therefore, data coverage must exceed the compactness of Level I data. Automation in agency record keeping is a prerequisite for Level II participation due to the increased amount of data reporting. The data elements shown in Table I are reported in NIBRS.

Table 1. Offenses Reported in the National Incident-Based Reporting System

Group A Offenses
—Arson
    Structures—Single Occupancy Dwellings
    Structures—Other Dwellings
    Structures—Storage
    Structures—Industrial/Manufacturing
    Structures—Other Commercial/Business
    Structures—Community/Public
    Structures—Other
    Mobile-Motor Vehicles
    Mobile-Other Mobile Property
    Other Property
—Assault Offenses
    Aggravated Assault
    Simple Assault
    Intimidation
—Bribery
—Burglary/Breaking and Entering
—Counterfeiting/Forgery
—Destruction/Damage/Vandalism of Property (Except "Arson")
—Drug/Narcotic Offenses (Except "Driving Under the Influence")
    Drugs/Narcotic Violations
    Drug Equipment Violations

Table 1—Continued

—Embezzlement
—Extortion/Blackmail
—Fraud Offenses (Except "Conterfeiting/Forgery" and "Bad Checks")
    False Pretenses/Swindle/Confidence Game
    Credit Card/Automatic Teller Machine Fraud
    Impersonation
    Welfare Fraud
    Wire Fraud
—Gambling Offenses
    Betting/Wagering
    Operating/Promoting/Assisting Gambling
    Gambling Equipment Violations
    Sports Tampering
—Homicide Offenses
    Murder and Nonnegligent Manslaughter
    Negligent Manslaughter
    Justifiable Homicide
—Kidnaping/Abduction
—Larceny/Theft Offenses
    Pocket-picking
    Purse-snatching
    Shoplifting
    Theft from Building
    Theft from Coin-Operated Machine or Device
    Theft from Motor Vehicle (Except "Theft of Motor Vehicle Parts or Accessories")
    Theft of Motor Vehicle Parts or Accessories
    All Other Larceny
—Motor Vehicle Theft
—Pornography/Obscene Material
—Prostitution Offenses
    Prostitution
    Assisting or Promoting Prostitution
—Robbery
—Sex Offenses, Forcible
    Forcible Rape (Except "Statutory Rape")
    Forcible Sodomy
    Sexual Assault with an Object
    Forcible Fondling
—Sex Offenses, Nonforcible (Except "Prostitution Offenses")
    Incest
    Statutory Rape
—Stolen Property Offenses
—Weapons/Law Violations

Group B Offenses
—Bad Checks (Except "Counterfeited Checks" or "Forged Checks")

Table 1—Concluded

—Curfew/Loitering/Vagrancy Violations
—Disorderly Conduct
—Driving Under the Influence
—Drunkenness (Except for "Driving Under the Influence")
—Family Offenses, Nonviolent
—Liquor Law Violations (Except for "Driving Under the Influence" and "Drunkenness")
—Peeping Tom
—Runaway (Persons under 18)
—Trespass of Real Property
—All Other Offenses

4.2 Data Verification and Quality Control

The lack of information pertaining to data quality has been mentioned by many as one of the major problems in the UCR Program. Data verification of the current UCR Program is indirect in that instead of direct data auditing, "symptoms" associated with the deterioration of the quality of incoming data are detected through "reasonableness" criteria, established within the UCR Program or through deviations from statistically established benchmarks. Through indirect examination and data editing procedures, the UCR Program has tried to achieve data quality control. Symptoms of possible deterioration in data quality or sudden shifts in the level of crime are pursued and questioned. The reported experience of these agencies are compared with certain benchmarks that are deemed to represent the aggregate experience of agencies having similar demographic characteristics, degree of urbanization, or simply equivalent jurisdictional populations, or through historical norms established by an agency's past reporting patterns. A number of quality control procedures (such as Kalman filter application) were explored for this purpose. An interval estimation model was formulated to statistically generate an allowable amount of variation in reported crime from one period to another. Needless to say, in many situations, errors in UCR data reporting are mechanical, and therefore, are easily rectifiable as in the case of arithmetic errors or non-compatible totals on different UCR forms. It has to be remembered, however, that except for evidence of the existence of mechanical errors, the presence of error symptoms are not necessarily indicative that actual errors are present. For this reason, UCR discrepancies in reported data are currently resolved through agency inquiries rather than institutionalized audits.

During the mid 1970s, the IACP developed "The IACP-UCR Audit/Evaluation Manual" (IACP, 1976), that directly identified errors involved in crime reporting. The manual addressed four stages of examination, (1) examination of initial complaint calls through the review of telephone tapes, (2) reviewing accuracy in agencies' complaint cards or incident reports, (3) counting errors in the classification and scoring process, and (4) reviewing the tallying process to check whether registers of incidents were accurately counted. Although the IACP's auditing scheme is not currently used, the Blueprint recommendations in data quality control are rooted in the IACP's model.

4.2.1 RECOMMENDED CHANGES

The Blueprint recognized the need for more than indirect data editing that examines only the reported figures but not how these figures have been generated. The Blueprint calls for the implementation of a direct, on-going, anonymous auditing scheme based on a sample of agencies. The model would directly examine data accuracy at the agency level and is aimed at establishing the extent to which reported offenses, arrests, clearances, and other data should be adjusted to depict the correct crime picture. Therefore, the primary objective of the proposed auditing process is the establishment of a system for making proper longitudinal comparisons. It is anticipated that the implementation of an auditing system based on random sampling would serve as an incentive for agencies to submit their data with a high level of accuracy.

The Blueprint recommends the following modifications of the procedures set forth in the IACP manual:

1. The review of telephone tapes should be limited to the minimum necessary because this process is costly.

2. Rather than checking different sets of samples at each stage, crime incident samples should be followed through all stages whenever possible.

3. The auditing of tally forms is not necessary under an incident-based system.

4. Auditing should identify both unreported clearances and false clearance reports. (The IACP audit approach does not detect unreported clearances.)

5. Audits of arrest data should be performed. (The IACP audit methodology does not address this.)

It is apparent that auditing has utility for the UCR Program. The results of an audit could be statistically aggregated to provide error estimates and adjustment factors for data users, help document typical errors in reporting in order to emphasize their prevalence in UCR training, and aid in providing data integrity to the UCR Program. Historically, challenges to UCR data quality have come more often from case studies rather than statistical or analytical ones. They cited possible incidents of data distortion arising from politically motivated pressures or from an agency's capriciousness in adjusting its data to make it more palatable for local consumption. To what extent such incidents may have impacted UCR data has not been established. If implemented, an auditing approach that estimates the degree of accuracy from a global perspective has value.

4.2.2 IMPLEMENTATION ISSUES IN QUALITY CONTROL

A sample design related to auditing, as described above, may be quite different from that needed to select agencies for the enhanced new UCR Program. The stratification scheme used, based on geographic location, level of urbanization, and jurisdictional population would not be as effective for auditing as for estimating crime. Factors such as the degree of automation, the type of record keeping systems, or the emphasis placed on crime data by the agency, etc., may divide agencies into more homogeneous strata. Since the level of over-reporting and under-reporting is unknown at the present time, a number of design problems will be confronted at the implementation stage.

As the UCR Program continues to function on a voluntary data submission basis, the term "auditing" in the strict sense of the word (as applied to UCR) is a misnomer. A review and examination of an agency's data must be predicated upon an agreement between the particular agency selected and the UCR Program. It should be noted that of all UCR contributing agencies that participated in the UCR Law Enforcement Agency Survey, 26 percent disagreed with the idea of auditing even when conducted on a confidential basis. Furthermore, 32 percent were neither for or against the practice.

A serious impediment to auditing to ascertain the necessity of statistical adjustments is that a sample size of at least several hundred agencies would be required. Considering the current fiscal constraints, implementing such a requirement would be difficult. It is, therefore, anticipated that the national UCR Program will initially designate a group within the Program to assist agencies in the development of self-verification procedures, to set standards of data quality, visit agencies requiring the development and implementation of data assurance devices, and to work extensively with the quality control assurance personnel of the individual state programs. A second phase in the development of an enhanced data quality control system should include the implementation of the above mentioned statistical sampling approach, or a related system dedicated to the quantitative analysis of the structure and configuration of errors.

As a part of UCR quality assurance, the Blueprint also recommended the development of a code of professional standards in UCR data reporting and improved feedback to agencies through self-administered proficiency tests and other means. Unquestionably, the future UCR Program will place strong emphasis on the assurance of data quality through a combination of such means. State involvement and initiative in the the quality assurance process is vital, particularly because it is expected that National UCR data will be derived from comprehensive state crime statistics data bases that vary from state to state.

4.3 The UCR and Other Crime Data Sources

The relationship of the UCR Program with other sources of crime data, particularly the National Crime Survey (NCS) program and the statewide Offender-Based Transaction Statistics (OBTS) programs, were addressed in the Blueprint. NCS collects data on crimes committed, victim characterizations, and citizens' perceptions of crime and the criminal justice system; UCR starts from where a crime is reported and indicates the law enforcement reaction to reported crime through unfounding, clearances, and arrests; and OBTS follows the UCR data component by tracing the criminal justice system arrests, charges, and dispositions. Strong emphasis was placed on the necessity of resolving the compatibility problem between UCR and NCS crime trends and statistics.

4.3.1 THE UCR AND THE NCS

With aspect to the often mentioned UCR-NCS data discrepancies or lack of comparability, there are certain changes that UCR can institute to mitigate the currently prevailing dilemma. As mentioned earlier, distinguishing commercial victimizations from personal or household victimizations, making a clearer distinction between aggravated and simple assault, providing more comprehensive victim information, and distinguishing burglary with theft from those without theft, are some of the means of increasing the level of comparability between the two programs. The recently completed NCS redesign study also suggested a number of ways of reducing UCR-NCS statistical discrepancies.

Data reconciliation between the two Justice Department programs was further addressed from the perspective of data presentation. Typical recommendations delineated in the Blueprint are the preparation of joint UCR-NCS press releases and the documentation of the sources of differences (statistically dividing the differences into well-defined parts). Other suggestions for remediating the UCR-NCS presentational discrepancy problem involve the use of different denominators in the computation of rates (e.g., UCR has presented victimization rates using different population-at-risk rates, including rates per household or per registered automobile, etc.), counting only victims at age twelve and over as is done in the NCS program, or generating UCR statistics based on census tracks.

4.3.2 THE UCR AND OTHER DATA SOURCES

Basic recommendations contained in the Blueprint that relate to correcting the discrepancies between UCR data and other crime data systems include:
1. The UCR, the NCS, and the OBTS systems should remain independent programs rather than merging into a single integrated information system. They should be complementary to each other without compromising their intrinsic nature in order to achieve tangential comparability.
2. Whenever feasible, an attempt should be made to structure, modify, or augment mutual data bases for higher data comparability and ultimate analytic comparability.
3. With respect to the future design of the UCR Program, an attempt should be made to achieve maximum linkage with the state OBTS Programs so that police records and prosecutive or judicial data have common units of count as well as statistical compatibility.

There is no immediate or simple solution suggested in the Blueprint with respect to the compatibility of data sources. It is evident, however, that a clearer understanding of the differences between the UCR, NCS, and OBTS is certainly one of the priorities of the enhanced UCR Program along with the development of satisfactory ways of structuring the UCR data elements to minimize the perceived discrepancies.

4.4 User Services and Publications

A number of ways to increase the utility of the UCR publications were proposed in the Blueprint. These recommendations revolve around increased interpretive analyses, clearer and conscious efforts to direct each publication or report on a particular group of users, more explicit documentation of UCR methodologically oriented matters, and direct services to UCR contributing agencies. With respect to periodic publications, the following six series were proposed:
1. An annual publication containing descriptive statistics and graphics focusing on global crime issues.
2. Quarterly press releases of crime counts and trends.
3. Data source-book-type of publications listing statistics for individual agencies.
4. Annual compilations of crime data to be forwarded to individual UCR contributing agencies. A specific law enforcement agency will receive

compilations of aggregated crime experiences of a well-defined group of agencies similar to that agency.

5. Publications of substantive crime research findings.
6. Documentation of methodological and technical issues relating to UCR estimation procedures, quality control models, analytical models, etc.

In 1986, the UCR Program implemented a broad-based release series of publications. These releases not only address new trends and volume figures based on the most recent data available, they also focus on findings that are considered to be of public interest. The Program generates publications dealing with time series data for specific topics incorporating updated historical data. For example, age-specific arrest rates, race-specific arrest rates, and population-at-risk rates have been documented for periods covering over two decades of UCR data. These publications contain only statistical tabulations without textual explanations since they are designed to provide a starting point for research rather than present UCR research findings.

The Blueprint does not emphasize the way different data are presented. For example, at present, the annual publication "Crime in the United States" uses different sets of data for different purposes. Some figures are estimates, some represent data from all agencies that submitted complete 12-month reports, some percentage change figures are based on "comparable" agencies that have "admissible" data for both of the periods under consideration, etc. While incident-based reporting is not amenable to the estimation of crimes, clearances, and arrests on an agency level, complete estimation of data, describing error ranges, is feasible on a stratum level. Complete estimated data for each stratum can then be used as a building block for higher aggregations and certain data requirements below the stratum level will be achieved by applying actual distributions to estimated totals. Future UCR publications, therefore, will not present different totals in different tables.

Another important enhancement will be the elimination of less useful presentations from the current publications along with the addition of new ideas.

Direct user services are one of the most important aspects of UCR activities. These activities encompass special data compilations provided in the format requested, communication of already published data by telephone or written correspondence, assistance for correctly using historical UCR data in analysis, clarification in the use of UCR data tapes, etc. User services under an enhanced UCR Program will focus on: more expeditious services through increased automation of the UCR data retrieval system; and more self-explanatory data presentations so that users do not have to learn and retain all rules and exceptions to them, that are applicable only to the UCR Program. This is partially related to the "one-number-for-each-item-of-information" problem mentioned earlier. While historical changes and new breakdowns would always necessitate a certain level of UCR knowledge for analysis, some of the confusion arising from using different methodologies in the statistical summaries could be minimized.

4.5 The UCR as a Crime Index

As mentioned in the introductory portion of this article, the validity of the Crime Index has been questioned throughout the history of the UCR Program. Although, under the enhanced UCR Program, the Index may cover more than seven (or eight) crime categories, one grand total and several subtotals grouped by criminal types may substitute for the traditional Index and be used as a crime indicator. In this sense, the Index will be just a sum of crime counts. The criticisms of the UCR Crime Index are multifaceted whether viewed as a traditional UCR Index or as total(s) or crime counts. A general criticism is that the scope of Index crimes does not focus on the concept of crime. Futhermore, it has been noted that reported crimes do not measure all crimes committed, and the statistical method of Index construction (sum of all crime counts) is too simplistic.

One of the most serious criticisms leveled at the Crime Index is the lack of a viable weighting scheme for different seriousness levels of crime. The Blueprint however, rejected the notion of a weighted crime Index as an alternative to the currently used Crime Index. Moreover, the Blueprint also discouraged the concept of one Crime Index being used as a gauge of all crime movements. While a one-figure Index could be a handy and appealing way to looking at complex crime situations, it has been suggested that such an approach has too many weaknesses when carefully scrutinized. In spite of theoretical advantages that the weighted Crime Index has over the current Index, it also shares the same drawback when it is used as a single indicator of the "reality" of crime.

5. The Redesigned and Enhanced UCR

Publication of the "Blueprint for the Future of the Uniform Crime Reporting Program" in 1985 marked the end of the second phase of the UCR redesign effort. This publication directed attention to the issue of operationalizing and instituting the recommendations made. Since the Blueprint is conceptual in nature, implementation of the recommended changes and enhancements to the UCR Program will require a great deal of effort and commitment.

In order to maximize the utility and acceptance of the views expressed in the document, the joint BJS/FBI Task Force closely guided and monitored the course of the study which led to the publication of the Blueprint. It should be noted that although the Blueprint advocated a number of changes to the Program, the most basic UCR concepts, including the voluntary nature of the program and the use of data from the police record systems, were left intact. Therefore, not all the criticisms that have been directed at the UCR over the course of its history have been quelled. Nevertheless, instituting the fundamental change suggested—transforming UCR from a summary-based program to an incident-based system—will greatly increase the utility of the Program to the entire user audience.

The Blueprint recommendations were generally well received by the law enforcement community, getting endorsements from the IACP, and the National Sheriffs Association (NSA). Without this support, the UCR evaluation that culminated in the release of the Blueprint would not have any chance of eventually leading to changes in the programs.

Views in regard to the Blueprint recommendations were solicited from a broad spectrum of UCR data users. Based on the number of responses, it was considered that the enhancement plan contained in the Blueprint was acceptable, at least in principle, to the majority of the respondents. Two-thirds of the comments on the Blueprint came from members of the law enforcement community, the group that will be most affected by revisions to the Program. Among this group, there was a high level of support for the report's recommendations. Some concerns were, however, articulated. The primary reservations pertained to costs to departments in terms of dollars and personnel; disruptions to record keeping systems; and benefits to contributing agencies vis-a-vis other UCR data users. Responses from outside the law enforcement community indicated support for the enhancement approach advocated in the Blueprint.

One of the initial steps taken by the FBI in the implementation process was to award a contract for the development of refined offense definitions and data elements for the enhanced UCR system. This involved:

(a) revising the definitions of a number of Part I offenses;

(b) deciding which additional Part II offenses should be reported;

(c) refining definitions for both new and current Part II offenses; and

(d) developing data elements to meet the requirements of incident-based reporting as opposed to the current summary reporting system.

Imperative to the success of any research and development effort is a demonstration or feasibility test under real world conditions. In the belief that the state UCR programs will play an even more important role under the redesigned UCR than they currently do, it was decided that the redesign demonstration project would be conducted under the aegis of a state program.

While the data elements were being prepared, the BJS and the FBI jointly reviewed the 41 state UCR programs in order to choose a site for conducting a pilot test of the enhanced Program. In light of its well-established incident-based system, the South Carolina Law Enforcement Division (SLED) was selected. In March 1986, the SLED agreed to serve as the site for the pilot test. Six months later, the demonstration project was funded. South Carolina selected nine law enforcement agencies to participate in the test. Actual data collection began in April 1987 and continued through October 1987.

In accepting the role of demonstration site, SLED agreed to modify its system in accordance with the requirements of the enhanced Program and collect both offense and arrest data consistent with the revised Part I and Part II offense definitions. To aid SLED in conducting the pilot project, data elements and offense definitions that were developed by the private contractor were placed at the disposal of the SLED staff. In addition, the Technical Services Division of the FBI devised "Automated Data Capture Specifications," enabling the State's data processing procedures to incorporate the updated system; contained in the specifications were proposed data entry screens to show linkages between files.

The implementation guidelines used in South Carolina will continue to be refined. This will be accomplished through internal study by the FBI, through input from the Uniform Crime Records Committee of the IACP, the UCR Committee of the NSA, the state UCR programs, and individual law enforcement jurisdictions. It is anticipated that the guidelines for the redesigned UCR Program will be finalized and ready for use nationwide in July 1988.

As noted earlier, the redesigned UCR will require the collection of data on each single incident and arrest within twenty-two offense categories. It is expected that the pilot test will result in system modifications. However, the changes should eventually result in a reduction of reporting requirements. With respect to data collection, the object of the redesign is to capture information that is currently being gathered by contributing agencies, and not to require them to collect data not currently available in law enforcement records. For each reported offense, data elements will also be gathered. Incident, victim, clearance, arrest, and offender descriptors will be included.

During the course of the development of the prototype redesign Program, it became apparent that the two-level system recommended in the Blueprint had to be modified. A considerable number of law enforcement administrators at both the state and local level indicated the collection of data on all crime categories can be more easily accomplished than can the extraction of information pertaining to particular offenses. While Level I will continue to to be an option, it appears that most contributing law enforcement agencies will choose to move directly to Level II upon implementation. Consequently, the implementation of Level II will develop on census participation rather than on random sampling as proposed in the Blueprint. Furthermore, since virtually all agencies will opt for Level II involvement, there is no longer any reason to refer to the concept of levels. For all practical purposes, then, the redesigned Program will have only one level of participation.

During Fiscal Year 1987, the BJS made monetary awards to thirteen states (Alabama, Arkansas, California, Delaware, the District of Columbia, Iowa, Kentucky, Maine, Massachusetts, Minnesota, Montana, New York, and Wisconsin) to begin implementing the enhanced UCR Program. South Carolina, as the initial demonstration site, continued to be funded. Invitations to apply for funding during Fiscal Year 1988 were issued to the remaining states. The FBI and the BJS have announced that periodic meetings will be held with the selected states for purposes of coordinating necessary implementation activities and discussing problems experienced by the funded states.

6. The UCR and Policy Decisions

In conjunction with crime analysis and publications, the utility of the UCR and its function must be examined. This will help clarify the scope and objectives of the Program. The UCR is a statistical program in that aggregate characterizations of crime are the principal outputs of the systems. As such, its utility in investigative line functions or case intelligence must be carefully assessed. The timeliness and comprehensiveness of the data, even with the expanded incident-based system, would be far below what would be necessary for investigative activities.

As a statistical information source, the utility of the UCR Program has to be examined from the perspective of how well it meets the informational needs of those individuals and organizations who rely on the Program's output. This is particularly true if vast resources are to be expended. For a long time, the UCR Program has been data collection oriented. UCR tried to gather as much complete information as was possible. The Program's existence was largely justified by steadily increasing its population and data coverage. As a result, UCR went from 400 contributing agencies to the current 16,000. Now that the 21st century is approaching and the data base is being expanded, UCR must justify its existence also by its product-the product being statistical information.

Statistical information is most useful when someone wants or needs to know it. Data collection can be justified when it meets expressed societal needs. Amassing large quantities of data without having a specific need or orientation is not cost efficient nor beneficial. With respect to the need for UCR data analysis and research, former Director William Webster pointed out that UCR Staff should not be guardians of historical data. Their analytical work products must be problem or need-oriented. Any research effort should focus on providing the kind of data analysis enlightened users need for decision-making. Having a Task Force to guide the UCR redesign effort was important because the enhanced Program was specifically developed to better meet the needs of various user groups.

In order to appropriately address the problem of data utility, the UCR must differentiate between administrative data and statistical data. Data collected for administrative purposes must be accurate and complete in that it must represent a particular fact that doesn't allow errors. For example, when an individual contacts his bank and requests the balance in his checking account, he wants to know the one figure that represents the correct amount in his account. Likewise, when a law enforcement agency contacts the National Crime Information Center (NCIC), they want to know if a particular automobile is stolen. Administrative data is thus individually oriented and demands absolute accuracy. They are gathered for the operation of a certain program.

The significance of statistical data is, on the other hand, slightly different from administrative data. What is sought in statistical data is not a particular value or item of individual information. The utility of this data is in the overall picture that the data as a whole can convey. With a statistical information system, accuracy and completeness are obviously important. However, the focus of demands on data accuracy are different from administrative data. When data are aggregated and analyzed, certain facts or truths are expected to be contained in the data. Data elements must, therefore, be chosen to make it possible. The data must be accurate if the statistical findings are to be valid and reliable but the data may be very different from what is needed in administration data sets. Statistical data are used to determine certain policy decisions rather than to find facts on individual items.

Often, confusion arises from not distinguishing between statistical and administrative data sets. If UCR data is looked at in terms of administrative data, its utility is small. It is neither accurate, complete, nor timely. UCR data's utility is statistical. As a corollary to the fact that UCR is a statistical system, it must be observed that the ultimate benefit of UCR data does not always come directly from the UCR Program. This paradox arises because the UCR data is funnelled through decision-makers who take the information, digest it, and make decisions that will ultimately impact the criminal justice community and the public-at-large.

In the UCR system, law enforcement agencies send data to UCR, but useful statistical information may not be sent back or communicated directly to the data contributors. Instead, the statistics go to people who have to use the data for decision-making and these decisions influence a broader spectrum of people than just the original contributors. The decision-makers include police chiefs, city mayors, state revenue sharing personnel, governors, etc., and on a national basis, the data could be utilized by the President or his crime task force committee members. These are the people who set crime and law enforcement priorities. Their decisions are the outcome of the UCR system with UCR statistics acting merely as a catalyst to that outcome.

It must be clearly understood that the UCR Program is only one part of a total criminal justice data system in this cycle of chain reactions: data reporting, data analysis, and decision-making. A major goal of the UCR Program is to provide viable crime information to facilitate this decision-making process.

In the final analysis, it should be clearly understood that the UCR Program alone cannot provide all the information necessary to meet the needs of decision-makers. UCR data must be used in conjunction with data from other segments of criminal justice research as well. Only by using relevant data from these sources, can a meaningful picture of the criminal justice system be obtained. State data, national data, juvenile data, rehabilitation data, and so forth, are all necessary components to obtain a unified picture of the status of crime and criminal justice. The new UCR system should be thought of as a comprehensive part of a systemic outlook of criminal justice. The UCR Program is a link in the chain which feeds the needs of data users who are also utilizing other kinds of information to meet their decision-making responsibilities.

7. Summary

The major recommendations in the Blueprint have been discussed and analyzed in this paper. These recommendations have been accepted, in principle, as a reasonable set of goals for the future UCR Program. A concrete prototype was developed (FBI, 1987) to realize proposed objectives. The Program is currently being tested to identify its problems and assess its viability. The national UCR Program will remain a voluntary data reporting program. However, since a number of states are under laws mandating local agencies to submit UCR data to a designated state agency, UCR may not be viewed by contributing agencies as a voluntary program. Yet from the perspective of the national UCR Program, data submission is voluntary and based on the cooperation of law enforcement agencies. There is strong historical evidence from the UCR program that a data collection system of this magnitude can be successfully conducted on a voluntary basis, and therefore, this aspect of the data submission has not received any substantial challenge during the UCR evaluative study. Secondly, the national UCR Program will continue to be based solely on local and state police records, that is reported crimes, clearances, arrests, and other data associated with criminal incidents in police records will constitute the UCR data base.

The FBI will continue to function as the administrator and coordinator of the national UCR Program. Along with IACP and the NSA advisory boards, the FBI will develop a series of new UCR publications, conduct crime analyses, provide technical assistance, supply crime information to its wide user audience, and set UCR standards and crime definitions. The FBI will also, in conjunction with state UCR Programs, direct the data quality assurance efforts. The NIBRS will be capable of providing more structured and comprehensive data in the conduct of substantive crime analyses.

While it is realized that a change to the enhanced UCR Program at the national level will be a long and difficult endeavor, every effort will be made to insure the state's Programs and local agencies receive assistance when necessary. Success in the implementation process will only come about with hard work and strong commitment. However, to law enforcement communities, legislators, and other individuals interested in the nature and level of crime in America, the work should be worth the effort. The NIBRS will provide more information on crime, in greater depth, and with increased precision than ever before. Crucial in combatting crime is the ability to accurately identify when and where it occurs, its nature, and the characteristics of its perpetrators and victims. The NIBRS will provide the law enforcement community, legislators, and other interested parties, with this information.

4

The National Crime Survey, 1973-1986: Strengths and Limitations of a Very Large Data Set

James Garofalo

The National Crime Survey (NCS) is the only national database in the United States that allows case-level analyses of victims and their victimizations in a variety of crime categories. It is also the only national indicator of the level of crime that attempts to record crimes that do not come to the attention of the police. These two characteristics make the NCS a potential information gold mine for researchers interested in the causes, trends, processes, and outcomes of crime.

Use of the NCS by researchers has been strongly encouraged by the sponsors of the data collection program: the Bureau of Justice Statistics (BJS) of the U.S. Department of Justice and its predecessor federal agencies. BJS has supported workshops for users of the NCS, issued requests for proposals to analyze the data and to design data collection supplements, disseminated reports and bulletins on NCS findings, and supported preparation and dissemination of the raw data tapes through the National Criminal Justice Archives at the University of Michigan.

Given the great potential of the NCS and the encouragement of BJS, there is not much need to offer a "sales pitch" for national victimization surveys. The NCS, in many ways, is a "self-selling" product. Since the data started to become available in the mid-1970s, researchers have applied them to a variety of substantive issues (for examples, see references in Chapters 5 and 6 of Sparks, 1982, and in Gottfredson, 1986).

My experience has been that interest in the NCS is widespread but that new users often do not recognize the limitations of the data. A good sense of what can and cannot (or should not) be done with the NCS usually develops through "mucking about" with the data over a period of time. But trial-and-error is not very efficient, especially with a data set as large and complex as the NCS. Thus, the emphasis in this chapter is on the limitations of the NCS.

However, that emphasis is not meant to discourage its use; in fact, I have used the data extensively for a number of years and plan to continue doing so. Rather, the emphasis is meant to encourage efficient and realistic use of the NCS.

1. What is the National Crime Survey?

The NCS program is a continuing survey of a probability sample of U.S. households. The program is sponsored by the BJS; the sampling, interviewing, and data preparation are performed by the Bureau of the Census. The program began in 1972, and data are available for every year since 1973.

1.1 The Sample

The NCS sample is very large. Currently, interviews are conducted in about 100,000 households containing more than 200,000 eligible individual respondents every year.

The sampling procedure selects housing units through a multi-stage clustering design. Ideally, when a housing unit enters the sample, all of its occupants who are twelve years or older are interviewed seven times, once every six months. At each interview, respondents are asked about certain kinds of victimizations they may have suffered during the six months preceding the month of the interview.

The first interview in the series of seven is not used in producing estimates of victimization because of a problem called "forward telescoping." Respondents have a tendency to recall victimizations that occurred more than six months ago as happening within the last six months. The second and later interviews are "bounded," which means that the interviewer has a summary of information from the previous interview and can help the respondent to avoid forward telescoping. The first interview is not used because it is "unbounded".

After the occupants of a housing unit have been interviewed seven times, that unit is dropped from the sample and a new housing unit enters the sample. The process is referred to as a "rotating panel design."

As one might expect, there are departures from the ideal procedures that have just been described. For example, when the occupants of a sampled housing unit move during the series of interviews, the NCS does not try to follow them to their new address, which would be extremely costly with a national sample. Rather, the series of interviews continues with the new occupants of the housing unit, if there are any. Although the initial interview with these new occupants is "unbounded," it is still used to make estimates from the survey.

The primary sample of housing units is drawn using information from the decennial census. Over time, old housing units are demolished and new ones are constructed. The Census Bureau continually brings some of the newly-constructed housing units into the NCS sample. In jurisdictions that issue building permits, the permits are sampled; in other jurisdictions, the Bureau relies on visual inspection of small-area samples.

1.2 The Procedures

The basic NCS procedure is to conduct a face-to-face interview with each member of a sampled housing unit who is twelve years or older. One knowledgeable adult is designated as the "household respondent" and is asked about crimes that are deemed to affect the household as a whole: burglary, vehicle theft, and larceny of property from in and around the home. Each household member twelve and older is questioned about personal victimizations: rape, robbery, assault, larcenies involving victim-offender contact, and larcenies that occur away from the home but do not involve direct victim-offender contact.

There are exceptions to the face-to-face, individual interview procedure. Until very recently, twelve and thirteen year old household members were interviewed by proxy rather than directly; a knowledgeable adult was asked about victimizations suffered by these youngsters. Proxy interviews are also allowed for household members who are incapacitated and for ones who are temporarily away and not expected to return during the field interview period.

The NCS interviewers have always been allowed to use some telephone interviews—for example, to contact a household member who was rarely at home and who preferred to be interviewed by phone. Since 1980, telephone interviewing has expanded and become systematic. The initial interview in the series of seven is still conducted in person, but all but one of the subsequent interviews are conducted by telephone (if a phone is available and if the respondents consent to telephone interviews).

The protocol for asking about victimizations during the interview involves a two-stage process. First, the respondent is asked a series of screen questions. These questions are framed in non-technical language and are meant to determine whether or not (and how many times) the respondent suffered some kind of victimization during the preceding six months. Second, after all the screening questions have been asked, the interviewer uses an incident report to question the respondent about each victimization detected in the screening procedure. In the incident report, details are collected about time and place of occurrence, offender characteristics, weapon use, victim injury and loss, reporting to the police, and so forth. The information in the incident report determines the type of crime category into which the victimization is placed.

1.3 Caveats

This brief introduction cannot do justice to the complexity of the NCS program. Details about the sampling procedures, the panel rotation scheme, the interview process, weighting and estimation techniques, and other design considerations would consume more pages than are allotted for this chapter.

More extensive, but still relatively concise, descriptions of NCS methodology can be found in an appendix to the annual NCS report (e.g., BJS, 1987) and in the introduction to the NCS data tape documentation produced by the National Criminal Justice Archives (ICPSR, 1987). For readers interested in the most in-depth treatment available, the Census Bureau maintains a large volume on *Survey Documentation*.

2. Characteristics of the NCS Data Set

2.1 Structure and Size

The NCS data tapes are initially arrayed in a hierarchical file structure. The primary case is the household. The next level in the file, after the listing of household characteristics, consists of records on each household victimization uncovered. Then there are records for each household member eligible to be interviewed. For each person, individual characteristics are listed, and these are followed by a record for each personal victimization reported by the person.

Although software for handling hierarchical files is becoming more common, many users prefer to work with flat files (each case having the same record length and containing the same variables in the same locations). An example is a file of personal victimizations that occurred during a given year, in which each case contains the characteristics of the person victimized and detailed information about the event. In this example, people who suffered more than one victimization during the year would be represented by more than one case.

The situation becomes fairly complex when one wants to generate rates of victimization for a given year from the data tapes. Recall that respondents are asked about victimizations that occurred in the six months preceding the month of the interview. Since field interviews take place every month, 17 months of interviews are needed to get information about the victimizations that occurred in a given year. For example, for information on all of the victimizations occurring in Year X, one would need to use all of the interviews from February through December of Year X as well as the interviews from January through June of Year X + 1.

In addition to being complex, the NCS data sets are very large, in terms of both the numbers of cases and the numbers of variables per case. Currently, about 8,000 household interviews (nearly 17,000 individual interviews) are conducted each month. To produce annual rates of household or personal victimizations, as described in the preceding paragraph, requires analysis of about 135,000 household cases or about 280,000 individual cases.

Of course, smaller numbers are involved in analyses of flat files containing a case for each household or personal victimization that occurred in a given year. Still, the data sets are by no means tiny. For example, the 1985 file contains records for more than 20,000 victimizations. Furthermore, each victimization record contains hundreds of variables on the tapes distributed by the Criminal Justice Archives.

Analysis of the NCS data is not something that can be undertaken lightly. On the other hand, the size and complexity of the data sets should not be an absolute deterrent to potential users. The staff at the Criminal Justice Archives can be very helpful to users of the data, and under certain conditions, they can supply abbreviated data sets that are limited to just what the user needs (e.g., a file of robbery victimizations for a given year).

2.2 Scope of the NCS

Data from the national survey of households is available from 1973 through the current year. When the program began, there was a parallel survey of a national sample of commercial establishments. The commercial survey covered only robbery and burglary. In response to (a) criticisms of the design and usefulness of the commercial survey (see Penick and Owens, 1976: 59-61), and (b) pressure to contain costs, the commercial survey was dropped from the NCS program in 1977. Thus, national data on commercial robbery and burglary victimizations cover only 1973 through 1976.

A set of city surveys, with both household and commercial components, was also conducted in the early years of the NCS program. A total of 39 surveys were conducted in 26 cities (13 were surveyed twice) during the period, 1973 through 1976 (Garofalo and Hindelang, 1977: 15-17). In addition to victimization data, the city surveys collected attitude data from persons sixteen years of age or older in a random half of the sampled households (see Garofalo, 1977).

Because the commercial and city surveys were discontinued a number of years ago, this chapter uses the term NCS to refer solely to the on-going, national survey of households.

2.2.1 PERSONS COVERED

As noted earlier, only persons twelve or older in the sample households are eligible for the NCS and no attempt is made to collect victimization information about younger household members.

There are also a few categories of people that the Census Bureau does not try to sample for the NCS:

> Crew members of merchant vessels, Armed Forces personnel living in military barracks, and institutionalized persons, such as correctional facility inmates, ... United States citizens living abroad and foreign visitors to this country ... (BJS, 1987: 105).

On the other hand, the Census Bureau does go beyond houses, apartments, and other common housing units by sampling "persons living in group quarters, such as dormitories, rooming houses, and religious group dwellings" (BJS, 1987: 105).

2.2.2 Types of Crime Covered

The NCS collects information on both personal and household crimes. In the personal category are rape, robbery, assault (aggravated and simple), and larcenies that occur away from the home. The household category consists of burglary, vehicle theft, and larceny of property from in or around the home.

While there have been periodic discussions about expanding the types of crime covered by the NCS, it appears that the only type of crime that is likely to be added in the near future is vandalism.

The NCS does not try to collect information about homicides of household members because the low rate of homicide would generate very few reports in the survey. Reasons for excluding some other types of crimes are less apparent. For example, the NCS personal crime category of assault includes threats of bodily harm, but only if they are made in a face-to-face encounter; telephone threats are specifically excluded.

3. Measuring Crime With Victim Surveys

The obvious reason for using victimization surveys to collect information about crime is to get a more complete picture of crime. It has been more than half a century since Sellin pointed out that "the value of a crime rate for index purposes decreases as the distance from the crime itself, in terms of procedure, increases" (1931: 346).

Thus, crimes recorded by the police are incomplete because many crimes do not come to the attention of the police, and furthermore, the police do not make an official record for every crime about which they are aware. Arrest data are even less complete because many crimes go unsolved. Further attrition affects data at the charging and disposition stages of the criminal justice process.

If the shrinkage in the numbers of crimes at each successive measurement point were caused by cases dropping out randomly, there would be few problems. The crimes in arrest statistics, for example, would be a representative sample of all crimes. The arrest data would not tell us about the total *number* of crimes occurring, but the data could be used with confidence to analyze the *characteristics* of crime.

However, the shrinkage in numbers is not a random process. There are factors that are systematically related to the likelihood that a crime will come to the attention of the police, that the police will record it, that an arrest will be made, and so forth. These factors can make the crimes recorded at one stage look quite different than the crimes recorded at previous stages in terms of variables, such as injury and weapon use, that are of interest to researchers and policymakers (for example, see Block and Block, 1980).

Following Sellin's dictum, researchers have tried to get information about crimes from sources as close to the acts as possible—namely, offenders and their victims. Studies of self-reported offending have been around longer than have surveys of victims, and have primarily involved juveniles as subjects (see Hindelang, Hirschi, and Weis, 1981).

The major impetus for surveys of the general population designed to locate and interview crime victims can be attributed to the President's Commission on Law Enforcement and the Administration of Justice in the mid-1960s. The Commission touted the victim survey as a method for studying the "dark figure" of crimes not reported to the police (Biderman and Reiss, 1967). Actually, the Commission did much more than tout; it sponsored several research projects that laid the early groundwork for the NCS (see Hindelang, 1976: Ch. 2).

While it is certainly true that victim surveys uncover crimes that are not known to the police, this does not mean that such surveys produce measures of the "true" amount or nature of crime. Like any other measurement technique, the victim survey has limitations. These limitations can be categorized as those that stem from (1) sampling, (2) the nature of the phenomenon being measured, and (3) the context in which data are collected.

3.1 Sampling Issues

As noted earlier, the Census Bureau samples housing units identified in the most recent decennial census and continually adds newly constructed units to the sample. To make interviewing efficient, the sample is drawn through a multi-stage clustering technique based on geographic areas.

3.1.1 REPRESENTATIVENESS

The techniques used for the NCS are similar to those used in other Census Bureau surveys and have proven to produce reasonably representative samples of U.S. households. However, all household-based surveys are plagued by undercoverage of certain subgroups of the population (National Academy of Sciences, 1972).

It has long been recognized that young, black males are under-represented in household-based surveys, and the probable undercounting of illegal aliens became an issue during and immediately after the 1980 census. People with particular lifestyles—drifters, street hustlers, the homeless—are missed. In addition, the NCS specifically excludes people in prisons, jails, and juvenile correctional facilities from its sampling frame. These subgroups almost certainly have victimization rates that are higher than the general population.

At the other extreme, the very wealthy are probably underrepresented because of their ability to insulate themselves from interviewers (for example, see Reiss, 1967: 146).

There have been attempts to collect data from some of the more elusive subgroups of the population (e.g., Boggs and Galliher, 1975). However, the representativeness of the subjects contacted through alternative means is uncertain.

Thus, surveys like the NCS, using relatively rigorous methods to select samples of housing units, probably end up with samples that are representative of what might be called the *mainstream* of the population. Fringe groups—from the homeless at one end to the super-rich at the other—tend to be underrepresented.

3.1.2 BASE RATES

The second sampling issue that affects the ability of victim surveys to measure crime is the relatively low base rates characterizing some crimes, particularly serious crimes. For example, despite the enormous number of interviews conducted during the course of a year, the average NCS data year during the first half of the 1980s contained information on less than 125 rapes, less than 900 robberies, and less than 1,300 aggravated assaults.

Because of the relatively low numbers, national estimates of the rates for serious crimes that are produced by the NCS will be subject to a fair amount of sampling error.

The Census Bureau provides guidance on how to compute standard errors and confidence intervals for some of the NCS findings. In an appendix to the annual report of the 1985 NCS data (BJS, 1987: 110), the procedures are illustrated for the robbery rate of persons, with a standard error of 1.2. The 95 percent confidence interval (plus and minus two standard errors) for the rate ranges from 8.0 to 12.8 per 1,000 persons in the age group.

The low base rates for serious crimes also have an indirect effect on the ability of victim surveys to produce measures of crime. Because of the low base rates, the surveys must use very large samples, and it is commonly accepted that increases in sample size increase the risks of non-sampling errors, such as errors in coding.

3.2 Nature of the Phenomenon Being Measured

Sampling issues are not the primary difficulties in using victim surveys as measures of crime. The very nature of crime itself interacts with the technique of victim surveying to produce some interesting problems.

It is doubtful that even a small group of experts could reach agreement in classifying every possible event as either "crime" or "no crime." It is even doubtful that they would agree, in every instance, on what constitutes an "event." "Crime" covers a very diverse range of behaviors and events, some of which are quite ambiguous. Many crimes are also well concealed; in some cases, only the offender is aware that a crime has occurred.

Questions about knowledge, perceptions, and definitions make it impossible to fully accept victim survey results (or the results of any other known measurement technique) as measures of the "true" amount or nature of crime.

3.2.1 Respondent Knowledge

Some of the people interviewed in a victim survey may not be aware of certain crimes directed at them. This has implications for what types of crime are included in a survey initially and for how exhaustively the included types of crime are measured.

Victim surveys are most useful for crimes that affect individual victims directly and that are readily apparent to their victims—e.g., robbery, burglary. Many crimes do not meet these criteria and, therefore, are not included in victim surveys such as the NCS.

Price-fixing and other restraint of trade actions by large corporation can inflate the prices paid for products by millions of consumers. Each consumer can be considered a victim of the illegal acts, but trying to measure victimization from such acts by surveying individual consumers and asking them if they have been the victims of corporate price-fixing during the prior six months is futile. Consumers never actually see the illegal behavior, and the effects are not only far removed (in time and space) from the illegal behavior but are also spread across a very large number of victims, each of whom may suffer a very small individual loss.

Even small-time frauds committed against individuals are difficult to measure with victim surveys because, almost by definition, if the fraud is successful, it is not detected. For example, an automobile repair shop might charge for name-brand replacement parts but install cheaper, or even used, parts. Unless an obvious problem develops or the customer has other reason for suspicion, the fraud will probably go undetected.

Other crimes are committed against organizations, the government, or the general public. Although these crimes can eventually lead to costs for individuals, the linkages between the crimes and the costs are very indirect. For example, vandalism of public schools and parks creates costs for local governments which are incorporated into local tax rates.

Because of the technique's limitations for measuring certain types of crimes, the NCS is restricted to the narrow range of crimes described earlier.

Even within the range of crimes covered by the NCS, respondent knowledge is not complete. A victim might believe that he/she lost a piece of property that was, in fact, stolen. An offender might try to burglarize a house, be frightened off by a barking dog, and leave no traces of the crime. Or, the traces of an unsuccessful burglary may be misinterpreted: e.g., a broken window is interpreted as vandalism (which is not covered by the current NCS) rather than an attempted entry.

Finally, respondent knowledge constrains the range of information that can be collected about crimes that are uncovered in victim surveys. The victim's perspective on the criminal event is tapped by the survey method. There are some aspects of the event about which victim knowledge will often be quite limited.

A good example of the limitations of the victim's knowledge is offender characteristics. In most crimes the victim does not even see the offender. When the victim and offender do come into contact, the victim's knowledge is limited to visible characteristics of the offender, unless the victim knows the offender from some other context. The NCS limits questions about offenders to victim's perceptions of the number of offenders, sex, age, race, and relationship to the victim (if any).

3.2.2 Ambiguity About Definitions

In most of the crimes covered by the NCS, the occurrence of a crime and the designation of the crime's victim are relatively clear. However, some events are ambiguous on both counts. This is particularly true for minor assaults, such as verbal threats and barroom scuffles. Since the victim survey asks one of the participants in the event to describe it, the results reflect the respondents' perceptions about the events in which they were involved.

The matter is complicated by the strong possibility that interpretations of events—particularly ones that might be minor crimes —vary across subgroups of the population. This is illustrated with the following numbers, which are assault rates (per 1,000 persons twelve and older) for whites and blacks from the 1982 NCS data.

	Aggravated	Simple	Total
White	8.7	17.6	26.3
Black	14.7	13.7	28.4

The data show that the very similar total assault rates for whites and blacks mask racial differences in the two types of assault. The data can be taken at face value; blacks have a higher risk of being victims of aggravated assault, and whites are slightly more likely to be victims of events that involve minor scuffles or threats (without physical attack or the presence of a weapon). However, the data are also consistent with the interpretation that whites are more *sensitive* to minor altercations; when such altercations occur, they are more likely than blacks to define themselves as having been victimized.

There is another whole group of crimes for which the meaning of the term, victimization, is ambiguous; the so-called "victimless" crimes, such as those relating to prostitution, drugs, and pornography. Illegal events in which people are involved in consensual exchanges are not well suited for measurement by the traditional victim survey technique. There is a great deal of ambiguity about who are the victims in these events, and collecting information about the events would require asking respondents about their own illegal behaviors.

Combining questions about victimization and offending in the same survey is certainly possible and, in fact, has been done on several occasions with juvenile respondents (see Laub, 1987). However, the issue of including questions about offending in an on-going, national survey of the general population conducted by a government agency is very touchy. Thus, the NCS does not try to measure the "victimless" crimes.

3.2.3 Discrete vs. Continuing Crimes

Victim surveys have proven most effective in measuring discrete crimes. A crime that has a definite beginning and end, marking a relatively short time frame, can be labelled (as a robbery, burglary, etc.). It can be placed in time (June of 1984, between 6 p.m. and midnight), and its associated features can be identified (amount of injury and loss, number of offenders, place of occurrence, whether or not it was reported to the police, etc.).

However, some crimes are not discrete events. They have a continuing, evolving nature. A few illustrations will be helpful:

> A neighborhood dispute characterized by periodic clashes, each involving a different triggering event, a somewhat different set of individuals, and different behaviors (shouting, threats, fighting).

A series of domestic assaults that may become increasingly serious but that occur sporadically and over a long period of time.

Recurring "shakedowns" of the same victim by the same group of fellow students, with each instance differing in terms of time of occurrence, loss, injury, etc.

Special questionnaires could be designed to cover continuous, evolving victimizations within the context of a victim survey. However, the questionnaires would be much more complex than ones used for discrete events, and the approach to administering them (screening procedures, probes, etc.) would probably have to differ.

The NCS does not include special instruments for non-discrete crimes. Rather, certain crimes are defined as "series victimizations:" "three or more criminal events that are similar if not identical in nature and incurred by individuals who are unable to identify separately the details of each act or recount accurately the total number of such acts" (BJS, 1987: 107). For series victimizations, interviewers are supposed to question respondents about the characteristics of the most recent instance in the series. The series victimizations are not included in the regular tabulations of NCS data.

3.3 The Interview Process

Victim surveys usually involve verbal interaction with respondents via telephone or in person, although some mail surveys have been conducted. Respondents are asked to recall and describe incidents that have befallen them during some previous time period.

While one might suppose that victimizations are significant events that respondents would recall easily and accurately, research indicates that memory problems are significant for victim surveys (see Skogan 1981: 15-22). Some incidents are forgotten; others are recalled as having occurred at some point in time other than when they actually did occur.

The NCS design includes features that are meant to minimize these problems. Respondents are asked about victimizations in the preceding six months (rather than twelve months or even longer) to minimize forgetting. The panel design, in which housing units are re-visited at six-month intervals, is meant to increase the accuracy with which victimizations are placed in time. Nevertheless, it is virtually certain that some relevant victimizations are not reported to interviewers because they are forgotten, and that others are recalled inaccurately as to when they occurred.

Prior research also indicates that, from among the types of incidents included in a victim survey, some types are more fully reported to interviewers than are others. Crimes of violence committed by persons known to the victims appear to be particularly underreported (e.g., Turner, 1972). However, this is probably not an example of forgetting. It is more likely that the sensitive nature of these events, combined with the setting of the interview (the home), inhibits full reporting. Undercoverage of these kinds of events limits the utility of traditional victim surveys, like the NCS, for measuring crimes such as domestic violence, child abuse and other household conflicts.

Another issue in the interview process is the likelihood that respondents differ in the extent to which they are comfortable with and adept at being interviewed. The NCS, for example, includes relatively long, complex interview instruments. It seems reasonable to assume that the verbal abilities of the respondent will be related to the "productivity" of the interview, i.e. whether they report some form of victimization.

Differential respondent productivity has been cited as an explanation for the anomalous NCS finding of a positive association between assault rates and levels of education, an association that does not occur between assault and family income level (Sparks, 1981: 32-34; Skogan, 1981: 22). The figures below, from 1982 NCS data, show assault rates per 1,000 persons 25 and older, by level of education.

	Aggravated	*Simple*	*Total*
No high school	4.0	4.1	8.1
1-3 yrs. of high school	8.0	9.8	17.8
4 yrs. of high school	6.1	10.1	16.2
Some college	6.1	15.6	21.7

As with the data on race and assault presented earlier, one could simply take the above figures at face value. However, the fact that the association is driven by the pattern for simple assaults suggests other possibilities. Perhaps people with higher levels of education are more sensitive to minor conflicts, as was discussed earlier. Or perhaps, they are just more productive in interviews—more willing to sit and talk with interviewers, more adept at remembering and at describing verbally.

4. The Limits of the NCS

This section discusses some of the major substantive limitations of the NCS. The discussion is not a critique of the NCS; rather it is an attempt to warn potential users about difficult or inappropriate applications of the data. In fact, some of the NCS's limitations stem from features that make it useful for other purposes. For example, interviewing a nationally representative sample permits the estimation of national victimization rates. At the same time, this feature limits the extent to which the data can be disaggregated geographically.

4.1 Information Not Collected

As discussed earlier, the NCS covers a relatively narrow range of crime types. But even for the crimes within its scope, the NCS does not collect some kinds of potentially very useful information. In some instances, this is because of limitations of the victim survey technique (e.g., victims limited knowledge about offender characteristics). In other instances, the NCS does not attempt to collect data on factors about which victims may be very good sources of information. Three examples are series victimizations, and the contexts and process features of victimizations.

4.1.1 SERIES VICTIMIZATIONS

In the prior discussion of continuing victimizations (as opposed to discrete events), it was noted that the NCS uses the designation "series victimization" when the respondent cannot recall the details of each event in a continuing, related string of victimizations. For series victimizations, the interviewer records the number of events in the series and details about the most recent event in the series. Because of ambiguity about how well the collected details reflect all of the events in the series, routine tabulations of the NCS exclude series victimizations.

If each series victimization is counted as one crime, about 3 percent of the personal and household victimizations in the NCS fall into the series category. Among household victimizations, the distributions of specific types of crimes do not differ much between series and non-series victimizations (although larcenies have a slightly higher representation among the series victimizations).

However, series and non-series personal victimizations differ considerably in the NCS. The series victimizations are twice as likely to be violent crimes rather than crimes of theft (63 percent vs. 30 percent for non-series), but they are also more likely to be attempted rather than completed crimes (47 percent vs. 23 percent). Simple assaults are especially prevalent among the series crimes. Simple assaults comprise 42 percent of the personal series victimizations, but only 16 percent of the non-series victimizations (BJS, 1987: 108).

A more detailed analysis of the NCS personal series victimizations (Dodge and Lentzner, 1978) found that the largest single category involves assaults against people in certain occupational groups, such as police and bartenders. Another sizable category consists of conflicts among family members, friends, and neighbors. The only other identifiable category with a significant number of cases was one involving violence against youngsters in which the incidents were primarily school-related and committed by offenders in the same age groups as the victims.

4.1.2 THE CONTEXTS OF VICTIMIZATIONS

Contextual information about events is very limited in the NCS. Questionnaire items dealing with time of occurrence, place of occurrence, and the presence of others provide the key bits of information. Although these items have been improved by questionnaire revisions in 1979 and 1986, they still allow only a gross understanding of the contexts in which victimizations occur.

The 1979 revision of the questionnaire (with which the most recently available data were collected) uses four six-hour blocks of time to categorize time of occurrence. It asks whether any other people (twelve years old or older) were present during the victimization and whether or not they were also victimized. The place of occurrence item has sixteen specific response categories, but many of these are too broad to provide a good sense of context (e.g., "inside office, factory, or warehouse," or "on public transportation or in station," which includes "bus, train, plane, airport, depot, etc.," or in a "park, field, playground other than school").

An extensive list of potentially useful contextual variables could be devised easily; amount of lighting, whether other people were within hearing distance, vehicle traffic, whether businesses were open nearby, what the victim was doing and carrying, how the victim was dressed, the physical characteristics of the immediate vicinity, and so forth. This type of rich detail is not available from the NCS.

4.1.3 PROCESS FEATURES OF VICTIMIZATIONS

All victimizations involve sequences of behaviors and results. The NCS asks a variety of questions about these behaviors and results, but does so without linking them together in a total process. This presents particular problems for personal crimes in which the victim and offender come into direct contact.

For example, the NCS can tell us whether or not the offender had a weapon, the offender physically attacked the victim, the victim used some form of resistance, and the victim was injured. But we cannot determine at what point during the victimization the offender displayed the weapon, if the victim's resistance was a stimulus to or a response to the offender's attack, and (in the case of a robbery) if the offender inflicted injury as a means of obtaining the victim's property or if the injury was inflicted after the property had been taken (see Block and Skogan, 1984).

To answer certain questions about crime prevention and to develop understandings of why some victimizations turn out differently than others, process information is invaluable. For each victimization, one would like to know what the victim was doing at the time, how the offender approached the victim, what sequence their interaction followed, how the encounter broke off, and what the victim did when it was over.

4.1.4 Structured Questionnaires and Unique Events

Criticisms about how series victimizations are handled in the NCS and about the lack of information on the contexts and processes of victimizations are not new by any means (e.g., Hindelang, 1976: 241-242; Penick and Owens, 1976: 88-93 and 158-159). The BJS and the Census Bureau have developed questionnaire revisions that are meant to provide richer data about the victimizations uncovered in the NCS. The new questionnaire implemented in 1986, for example, asks about the *results* of victims' attempts to resist offenders.

However, the NCS would have to undergo major changes in order to fully capture the complex details of context and process for single events and the dynamic, evolving features of continuing crimes. These phenomena are not well suited to being studied via highly structured questionnaires. Open-ended, flexible research instruments are more appropriate, and there are a number of reasons why the NCS is unlikely to utilize such an approach.

First, the NCS is meant to produce on-going indicators of the rate and nature of victimization in the U.S. and therefore, continuity in the questionnaire is important. Second, the necessity of using a large number of interviewers makes a highly structured questionnaire attractive because the problem of varying interpretations among interviewers is minimized. Third, the NCS interviews are already long, and detailed questioning about contexts, processes, and the dynamics of series crimes could add considerably to interview length, risking declines in the willingness of respondents to cooperate. Fourth, there is pressure to disseminate NCS results in a timely fashion, and highly structured questionnaires are easier to edit and code than are questionnaires with open-ended items.

In sum, detailed consideration of contexts, processes, and continuing events requires a focus on the uniqueness of individual victimizations. A large survey program like the NCS must limit its examination of the unique features of events in order to meet its goals of producing timely, on-going national indicators.

4.2 Measurement of Assaultive Crimes

The NCS does not do equally well in measuring all of the crimes that come within its scope. It appears to do quite well with robberies and thefts but not with purely assaultive crimes. This problem has been mentioned several times, both directly and indirectly, in earlier sections of this chapter. For example, assault data were used earlier to illustrate the issues of variations in respondent interpretations and productivity.

The problem is particularly acute for assaultive crimes (rapes and assaults) in which the victim knows the offender (Turner, 1972). In the 1985 NCS data, for example, women have an assault victimization rate of 17 per 1,000 compared to 32 per 1,000 for men, and 42 percent of the assaults against women were committed by strangers (BJS, 1987: 14 and 34-35). However, police data, either from crime reports or patrol dispatches, suggest that the rates for men and women are far less disparate and that a smaller proportion of the assaults against women are committed by strangers (see Nelson, 1984; Skogan, 1981: 30).

Whether the NCS's difficulties with non-stranger assaults arise because of respondents' interpretations, the setting of the interviews (the home), the sensitivity of the topic, or some other reason (or combination of reasons), the fact is that this portion of the NCS data has to be used very cautiously. In fact, it may be wise to limit analyses of assaultive victimizations to ones committed by strangers because we have no idea of how representative the non-stranger assaults are.

4.3 Utilizing the Panel Features of the NCS

The NCS does use a panel design, but it is a panel of housing units (addresses). If the occupants of a housing unit move, no attempt is made to follow them; if new occupants move in, they are interviewed. This may not be a problem for national estimates of victimization rates. On average, out-movers should be similar to the respondents who replace them in the housing units they vacate. It is a problem, however, for any attempt to analyze the victimization experiences of individuals over time.

The crux of the problem is that panel attrition does not appear to be independent of victimization. People who leave the panel before their full set of interviews are completed have higher victimization rates than people who stay at the same address (see Lehnen and Reiss, 1978; Skogan, 1981).

There is even a more practical problem in conducting longitudinal analyses of the NCS. A longitudinal data set (of individuals or households) is very difficult to construct from the public use data tapes. It involves manipulating a series of very large annual data sets and matching a group of identifying variables across these data sets.

4.4 Geographical Disaggregation

The NCS data are not very useful to researchers who wish to analyze variations in victimizations across specified sub-national areas. That is, the

NCS cannot be disaggregated to provide useful data about the individual states, counties, or a substantial number of cities. The two major reasons for this are confidentiality and sample size.

Census Bureau rules prohibit the release of individual records for geographic areas of less than 250,000 population. This is meant to prevent even the *possibility* that someone could identify an individual person or household from the data. While the restriction is quite stringent, it is understandable in light of the Bureau's desire to protect its reputation for safeguarding the confidentiality of the data it collects. This reputation is viewed as critical to the Bureau's ability to conduct the decennial censuses and to its success in maintaining low refusal rates for all of the surveys it fields.

Obviously, many people live in geographic areas with populations of more than 250,000. Many Standard Metropolitan Statistical Areas (SMSA) and all of the states meet this criterion. However, there are some general geographic identifiers on the NCS public use data tapes, such as the size of the place in which the respondent lives and the description of the place (SMSA inside central city, SMSA outside central city, outside of an SMSA). These variables, when used in conjunction with, for example, the identity of an SMSA of 750,000, could enable one to identify individual households or respondents. Thus, place size and place description would have to be removed from all public use data tapes before the Census Bureau would consider adding more specific place identifiers.

Even if confidentiality concerns could be addressed, sample size limits the potential for disaggregating the NCS data geographically. The NCS sample is large, but victimization—especially serious victimization—is relatively rare. The actual numbers of victimizations detected by the NCS in any given year are surprisingly small, as was noted in an example early in this chapter.

Raw numbers of victimizations can be increased by summing across data for several years, but even then, the numbers are not enormous. For example, summing across four years (1980-83) for black respondents produces 2,716 total personal victimizations, i.e., rape, robbery, aggravated and simple assault, and larceny with contact between the victim and offender. If these data are disaggregated for even 25 specific places, there is an average of only slightly over 100 victimizations per place, and this is before the data are subdivided by type of crime, age, or any other variable of interest.

Currently, the NCS data can be broken down by some geographic characteristics. The place size and place description variables have already been mentioned. Most of the NCS data sets up until now also include a set of "neighborhood characteristics," consisting of 55 aggregate variables pertaining to the (unidentified) area in which a sampled housing unit is located (e.g., percent of population in specific age groups, percent of housing owner occupied, median income).

However, the "neighborhood characteristics" do not necessarily pertain to real neighborhoods. The areas are:

> ... usually contiguous, computer-aggregated enumeration districts (ED's) or blocks with a population minimum of 4,000. ... Neither socioeconomic nor demographic data were used in forming neighborhoods. Similarly, maps were not used in constructing neighborhoods. Therefore, while neighborhoods rarely cross county lines, they may straddle a meaningful social boundary such as an urban freeway (Shenk and McInerney, 1981: 74).

Furthermore, the "neighborhood characteristics" are based on data from the 1970 census, and there are no plans to update them. For each year past 1970, the variables become less accurate, because the characteristics of areas change. Also, data records for the newly constructed housing units that are continually being brought into the NCS sample do not contain the "neighborhood characteristics" variables. Since these housing units represent a growing proportion of the sample as time goes on, the proportion of cases with missing information on the "neighborhood characteristics" increases with time.

The Census Bureau also produces an annual set of limited NCS data tabulations for the ten largest states, and some thought has been given to producing similar, routine tabulations for other areas with sufficiently large sample sizes (e.g., certain SMSAs).

There is one caution that applies to all of the geographic variables in the NCS—place size, place description, "neighborhood characteristics", largest states. The variables represent information about where the sampled housing unit is located, which may not be the same place where a victimization occurred. Not even all burglaries occur at the sampled housing unit; some may have happened at a respondent's previous address. The NCS questionnaire does ask whether or not a victimization occurred in the same city, town, village, state, and county as the current residence. It is important to take this information into account for analyses of where victimizations take place.

4.5 Timeliness

There is a substantial lag time between data collection and the availability of public use data tapes. Part of the lag is simply structural. Since the NCS asks respondents about victimizations that occurred in the six months preceding the month of the interview, the data pertaining to a given year are not all collected until June of the following year.

After being collected, the data must be edited and coded. Then the Census Bureau performs a series of computer runs to check for quality and to compute weights for national estimates. The Census Bureau and the BJS can then conduct the analyses that will go into the annual report (and other reports), and a data tape can be delivered to the Criminal Justice Archives at the University of Michigan. The staff of the Archives produces data tapes and documentation for distribution to the user community. By the time these processes run their course, researchers will receive data pertaining to two, or even three years earlier (e.g., 1985 data in 1987 or 1988).

Further complications arise when there are substantial changes in the NCS, such as sampling, weighting, or questionnaire design. For example, a revised questionnaire was implemented in 1979, but for the first few years thereafter, the data were recast in pre-1979 form before being released. Data tapes incorporating the questionnaire revisions did not become available from the Criminal Justice Archives until 1987.

5. Changes in the NCS: 1973-1986

Although the NCS places a premium on continuity of the data over time, some changes have been implemented. Additionally, more basic changes are being planned for the future as is discussed in the following chapter by Professor Lynch. Below, seven significant changes in the 1973-86 period are noted and discussed briefly.

5.1 Discontinuance of the City Surveys

As mentioned earlier, the original NCS program had a component in which separate surveys were conducted in selected cities (see Garofalo and Hindelang, 1977). The last of the city surveys were conducted in 1976. Since the city surveys were basically independent of the national panel survey, discontinuing the city surveys did not affect the continuity of the national data.

5.2 Discontinuance of the Commercial Surveys

A commercial survey component was part of the original national panel design, but, as noted earlier, this component was dropped in 1977. Although part of the national panel design, the commercial component utilized a separate sampling frame and a separate questionnaire, and therefore, its discontinuance had no affect on the continuity of the data from the national panel of housing units.

5.3 Telephone Interviews

As a cost containment measure, the NCS began to make more frequent use of telephone interviews in 1980. Under the change, the first interview at a sampled housing unit is done in person, but every other interview can be done by telephone. Since the change, about half of all interviews are conducted by telephone, compared to about 20 percent before the change (Paez and Dodge, 1982).

Before the change was implemented, the Census Bureau conducted a field test to compare in-person with telephone interviews. Telephone interviews tended to generate fewer victimization reports from respondents, especially for minor larcenies. However, for most comparisons, the differences between in-person and telephone interviews were not statistically significant (see Woltman and Bushery, 1984; Turner, 1984).

5.4 Sample Size

Over time, the NCS sample grows naturally in size, because the U.S. population increases and newly constructed housing units are added to the sample continually. To keep a relatively constant sample size, reductions of about 5 percent are made in the sample periodically. However, in 1984, a 20 percent reduction in sample size was made because of cost considerations. Because of the way this reduction had to be implemented, the remaining, unweighted sample was less representative of the U.S. population, so special weighting of the reduced sample was necessary. This problem will disappear at the end of 1987 when a new sampling design has been phased in completely.

5.5 New Sampling Design

In January 1985, the Census Bureau began to conduct interviews at housing units selected under a new sampling design. The new design still uses the basic multi-stage, stratified, cluster sampling technique, but the strata were formed on the basis of data from both the 1980 Census and 1980 Uniform Crime Reports. The utilization of UCR information as an independent indicator of crime rates is meant to make the sample more efficient.

As housing units from the new design are being phased in, housing units from the old design are being phased out. This process will be completed at the end of 1987. The Census Bureau expects that the process may have slight effects on rates of victimization in the NCS, particularly for 1986 (see Alexander, 1987).

5.6 Questionnaire Revisions

Two significant revisions in the NCS questionnaire have occurred in recent years. The first, implemented in 1979, primarily added new response categories to existing items. However, it did add a few new questions, such as victims reasons *for* reporting their victimizations to the police, in addition to the existing question about why victimizations were not reported to the police.

A new questionnaire, implemented in 1986, contains more far-reaching changes. For example, as noted earlier, some new questions have been added to elicit information about the process of interaction in face-to-face crimes. Unlike earlier questionnaire versions, respondents are asked if they know anything about offenders that they didn't see during the crime (e.g., as in most burglaries). A whole series of questions about criminal justice system response, after initial reporting to the police, has been added.

5.7 Supplemental Questionnaires

The Census Bureau and the BJS often use the regular NCS sample to conduct methodological tests. Two supplements dealing with substantive issues have also been used; one dealing with public perceptions of the severity of crime (Wolfgang, et al., 1985) and one addressing victim risk factors (Whitaker, 1986; Lynch, 1986).

The BJS views the use of such supplements as an efficient way to generate fresh information from the NCS while maintaining the continuity of the basic data. In recent years, BJS has been encouraging the development of new supplements.

6. Summary

The primary purpose of this chapter has been to make potential users of the NCS sensitive to the limitations of the data set. Because of its large sample size and great amount of information about individual victims and victimizations, the NCS is very useful to researchers. Periodic questionnaire revisions and supplements have enhanced its utility over the years, and forthcoming changes will enhance it further.

However, the effective use of any data set requires a strong sense of its strengths and weaknesses. This is particularly important with the NCS because it is such a large, complex data set. Inappropriate use of the NCS can be very costly in time and resources.

5

The Current and Future National Crime Survey

James P. Lynch

In 1978 the Bureau of Justice Statistics (BJS) of the U.S. Department of Justice issued a solicitation for the creation of a consortium of organizations that would evaluate and improve the National Crime Survey (NCS). This call for a redesign of the victimization survey was prompted by widespread criticism from the academic community and criminal justice practitioners. The National Academy of Science (NAS) was asked to evaluate the NCS, and issued a report in 1976 identifying areas in which the survey could be improved (Penick and Owens, 1976). The Justice Department considered suspending data collection in order to correct its deficiencies, but congressional hearings urged continued data collection while research was undertaken to identify solutions for the problems specified by NAS. The solicitation followed and a contract was awarded to the Bureau of Social Science Research, Inc. (BSSR) to form the Crime Survey Research Consortium (CSRC). From 1979 to 1985 the CSRC developed, tested and negotiated the implementation of major improvements in the NCS. Implementation is substantially completed. The redesigned survey is expected to correct many of the deficiencies of the current NCS without adversely affecting those things that the survey does well. This paper is designed to acquaint researchers interested in victimization data with the benefits that they can expect from the NCS Redesign effort. These benefits include not only improvements to the on-going NCS, but also useful data sets that were created as a by-product of the Redesign.

Before discussing the Redesign and its products, I will briefly describe the development of National Crime Survey. Secondly, the organization and strategy of the Redesign will be outlined to explain why some products will be available before others. The products of the CSRC's work will be presented in three different sections, according to the timing of their availability. The first section includes data sets that were created as by-products of instrument development, which was the principal work of the Redesign. Many of these data sets were developed to test the feasibility of a particular interview instrument or procedure, but they can be used to address other methodological and substantive questions. The second section includes changes in the on-going NCS which were introduced in July 1986, and the final section includes other major changes in the survey that will be implemented in the early 90's. This is not intended to be a detailed description of the data sets, but simply an introduction that will suggest how these data are a clear improvement over what was heretofore available and how they can contribute to substantive and methodological studies of crime causation and measurement.

This description of the future NCS must also be considered an approximation since the ultimate form of the long term changes in the survey must be decided by BJS and the Census Bureau. Logistical problems with implementation of recommended changes within the context of the Census may preclude some changes or alter them even radically. Budget constraints may prevent the implementation of recommendations that seemed feasible at the conclusion of the Redesign. This description then should be considered a good, but not exact outline of the future NCS.[1]

1. The Development of the National Crime Survey

The National Crime Survey was developed in the early seventies in recognition of the fact that our major indicator of the level and change in crime—the Uniform Crime Reports—included only those events reported to and recorded by the police. Obtaining an estimate of the 'dark figure' of unreported crime was considered essential for a complete crime reporting system that could be used to monitor the fight against crime (Biderman and Reiss, 1968). Sample surveys of victims of crime had been attempted in the late sixties and the method seemed workable (Biderman, et al., 1967). Consequently, the Department of Justice contracted with the Bureau of the Census (BOC) to survey large samples of the non-institutionalized population of the United States in order to estimate the level of criminal victimization, year-to-year change in the level, and the distribution of victimization in the population.

Initially the NCS program had three distinct components—the National Crime panel, the City Surveys, and the Commercial Surveys. The City Surveys were designed to provide detailed estimates of victimization among citizens of the largest metropolitan areas. Large numbers of interviews were conducted in the thirteen largest cities in order to provide reliable estimates of victimization for each of these areas. The Commercial Survey was designed to complement the Crime Panel and the City Surveys by collecting information on the victimization experiences of businesses which were excluded from the other two surveys. The Crime Panel was developed to provide reliable estimates of victimization for the nation as a whole. For budgetary reasons, as well as questions about the utility and quality of the resulting data, the Commercial Surveys and the City Surveys were discontinued and the Crime Panel became the National Crime Survey.

The NCS employs a multi-stage probability sample of housing units in the fifty contiguous states. Contacts with the occupants of these housing units yield a representative national sample of persons twelve years of age or older. This is the target population of the NCS. This sample is divided into six rotation groups with each group being interviewed every six months for three years (a total of seven interviews per household). Within each rotation group six panels are designated with a different panel interviewed each month during the six month period. This particular scheduling of interviews is referred to as a rotating panel design. It was chosen to increase the efficiency of interviewing by spreading the workload evenly through the year, to reduce seasonality effects on the data, and to increase the accuracy with which reported incidents are dated.

Interviews are conducted with all members of sample households who are fourteen years of age or older. The victimization experience of children twelve and thirteen was obtained, until recently, by asking an adult in the household. Similarly, interviews with persons who cannot speak the language[2] or are not mentally capable of responding are conducted by proxy. All members of the household are asked to report on their personal victimization, e.g., assaults, robberies, rapes, thefts from the person, but only a designated household respondent is asked to report on crimes against the household as a group, e.g., burglary, theft of household property and auto theft.

The NCS interview has two parts. The first is called the screening interview which is designed to elicit mentions of victimization experience occurring in the six months prior to the interview. This is administered to all respondents, although the interview administered to household respondents is obviously different from that given other members of the household. The second section of the interview is called the incident form. These questions are asked of all respondents who report a victimization during the previous six months. The incident form asks victims to report the particulars of the crime including: 1) the type of offense, 2) a description of the offender, 3) the location and time of the incident and 4) the outcome of the incident, i.e., successful completion, injury, loss, and days lost from work.

The information gathered in the interview is used to classify crimes as being within the scope of the survey and to group crimes according to major crime classes. These counts of victimizations and incidents are used to estimate the number and rate of victimization annually and the change in the level of victimization across years. Estimates are based upon counts weighted by the inverse of the probability that a particular respondent or household will be selected into the sample. Additional adjustments are applied to obtain incident weights which are used to estimate the number of crime incidents as opposed to the number of victimizations. These weighted counts provide estimates of the number of victimizations experienced by the target population—the non-institutionalized population of the U.S., 12 years of age and older.

2. The Redesign of the NCS

Since its inception, the NCS program was the subject of criticism regarding the accuracy, utility and cost of collecting these data. These criticisms lead to the suspension of the City Surveys and the Commercial Surveys. The Crime Panel was exposed to similar criticisms, but the consensus of researchers and practitioners within and outside the government was that the survey was worth saving. However, it was agreed that specific steps had to be taken to improve the accuracy and utility of the survey while reducing its unit cost. To this end, the Crime Survey Research Consortium (CSRC) was formed.

In its solicitation BJS stipulated that the NCS Redesign should be undertaken by a consortium of research organizations because no single organization possessed the requisite skills in sufficient quantity to complete the task. In response BSSR organized the CSRC. The Consortium included a mix of leading experts in the field of sampling, statistics, survey research and criminology. These experts could jointly address the problems of the survey, thereby ensuring in the deliberations equal representation of substantive, methodological and administrative concerns. Initially, the Consortium included: 1) BJS, 2) BOC, 3) BSSR, 4) the Survey Research Center of the University of Michigan (SRC), 5) the National Opinion Research Center of the University of Chicago (NORC), 6) Yale University and 7) Carnegie-Mellon University (CMU). Later, as the demands of the research required, NORC and CMU left the Consortium and the Research Triangle Institute (RTI) and Westat, Inc. were added. In addition, the Redesign was guided by an advisory panel of noted government and academic experts in fields relevant to crime statistics and victimization surveys.

The CSRC approached its task in an incremental fashion. First, major criticisms of the current NCS were identified, and possible solutions were matched with these problems where appropriate. Second, the various proposed solutions were evaluated in terms of their ability to redress the problem and the feasibility of the approach. For example, radically increasing the size of the NCS sample would address the criticism that the survey did not provide sufficiently reliable and detailed estimates for states and localities. However, increasing the sample size enough to yield such estimates would be prohibitively expensive and therefore infeasible. Those proposals which passed this initial review were the subject of more detailed research and development work designed to test both the feasibility and effectiveness of a particular remedy. Again specific solutions were rejected when this research indicated that they were likely to be ineffective or infeasible. In the fourth stage, the proposed remedies that survived this additional research and development work were combined in total survey designs which were recommended to BJS. The fifth and final phase of the Redesign appraised the probability of implementing specific designs. It involved lengthy and detailed deliberations by BJS, BOC and CSRC members to determine which of the designs were most desirable and most practical given the current or probable future technological and budgetary environment of the survey.

2.1 Three Stage Implementation

Given the length of the Redesign, the uncertainty of the budgetary climate and the pressing need to improve the survey, the Consortium proposed a three stage implementation of acceptable proposals for improvement. This would ensure that useful reforms could be introduced without awaiting the completion of the Redesign. Improvements to the current NCS that were recommended to and accepted by BJS would be introduced into the survey immediately. It was agreed that these recommendations would not affect series continuity nor would they be costly to implement. More substantial recommendations for change could be introduced in the near term, that is, before the end of the Redesign. These near improvements could affect rates if these effects could be estimated or adjusted for post facto. Finally, the most radical suggestions for reform would be introduced in the long term, that is, after the end of the Redesign at a time when budgetary conditions permitted. A likely estimate for the implementation of long term recommendations is 1992, but it is impossible to say when changes will occur with certainty.[3] The implementation of current system improvements was abandoned as impractical later in the Redesign but the plans for near and long term implementation were retained.

This brief description of the strategy for pursuing the Redesign is presented to explain the manner in which I will describe the future form and capabilities of the NCS. Some of the data currently available from the NCS program are by-products of the research and development work done by the CSRC. While these data are not part of the survey per se, they can usefully and immediately contribute to our understanding of crime and crime survey methodology. They are described in the first of the following sections. Additionally, some ways in which these data can uniquely contribute to substantive and methodological research are reviewed. The second section details the specific changes in the survey that were introduced in the near term. Again, suggestions are made as to how these changes may be useful to researchers. The final section outlines the changes in the survey that could be implemented in the long term. The implications for future research are discussed.

3. Useful By-products of the Redesign

The development of new instrumentation was a major emphasis of the Redesign and a great deal of the program's resources were devoted to this task. Efforts to test this new instrumentation in the field provided data that was not available heretofore. In addition, the consortium attempted to answer many questions crucial to the development of new instrumentation by innovative manipulation of existing data. Under the first category of by-product, the Washington Metropolitan Area Survey (WMAS) may be of interest to researchers as well as the Victim Risk Supplement (VRS). Under the later category, the development of a longitudinal file of NCS data covering the period 1976 through 1979 also permits the exploration of issues previously unexplorable with victimization data. Each of these data sets is described briefly below.

3.1 The Victim Risk Supplement (VRS)

The consortium developed the VRS in order to identify the more productive explanatory variables for inclusion in the survey, either in the basic questionnaire or in supplements to the survey (Martin, 1982). The supplement was designed to test the feasibility of specific operationalizations of key explanatory variables. Although the work of the Redesign Project was not explicitly the building of criminological theory, the VRS constitutes a rich data base that can be applied to this purpose (Lynch, 1987; Whitaker, 1986).

The supplement data, which is available through the Inter-University Consortium for Political and Social Research (ICPSR), includes the basic NCS information as well as an expanded set of explanatory variables to account for variation in victimization risk. Many of the variables currently included in the survey pertain to fixed characteristics of the victims and offenders (as reported by the victims)—traits such as age, race, sex, etc. The VRS expands the scope and number of risk factors measured, and in particular measures risk factors that are more manipulable by policies and strategies intended to reduce vulnerability to crime.

Some specific aspects of the supplementary data are worthy of note because they offer the possibility of distinguishing particular types of crime that may reduce the power of our explanatory models. By identifying and isolating these crimes, we may be better able to explain their occurrence.

Specifically, vehicle related crime such as theft of motor vehicle parts or theft from a motor vehicle comprise a large proportion of the NCS theft category (Lynch and Biderman, 1984). Combining vehicle related crimes with fundamentally different crimes such as thefts from the person or household can reduce the power of our models explaining the risk of theft. The VRS permits the identification of some vehicle related crime and can therefore permit the identification of conceptually cleaner crime classes that may be more amenable to quantitative modeling. Similarly, the VRS permits the location of incidents according to the activity in which the victim was engaged in at the time. So, for example, if the victim was at work when he was robbed, we can exclude from our explanatory models attributes of his non-work life that will be irrelevant to his victimization and concentrate on more proximate and potentially powerful causes (Lynch, 1987). Heretofore, this location of victimization by life domain was not possible with the NCS.

In addition to expanding the information on explanatory variables available in the survey, the VRS offers a much larger sample size than is usually available in ad hoc surveys that include comparable explanatory variables. The NCS sample of 72,000 households yields approximately 60,000 interviews for a six month period. This sample is divided into six rotation groups with each group being interviewed every six months for three years (a total of seven interviews per household). Within each rotation group six panels are designated with a different panel interviewed each month during the six month period. The VRS was administered to all of the panels interviewed in February 1984 for a total of 14,000 households or approximately 20,000 persons. This sample is several times larger than that used in most special studies of victimization (Greenberg, Rohe and Williams, 1981; Taub, Taylor and Dunham, 1981) and should therefore exhibit more variation on crucial explanatory variables and yield enough victimization for multivariate analysis (Lynch, 1987). Moreover, the sample is probably more representative of the U.S. population than that of previous studies. Each rotation group and panel is drawn to be representative of the non-institutionalized population twelve years of age or older. Changes in the panel composition over time will reduce the representativeness of the VRS sample, but it should be more representative of the national population than are those employed in special studies which tend to focus on larger cities.

3.2 The Washington Metropolitan Area Survey

The Washington Metropolitan Area Survey (WMAS) was commissioned by BJS at the request of a U.S. Senator who was concerned with the victimization of congressional staffers particularly, and more generally with safety in the metropolitan area. The survey was conducted by the Research Triangle Institute (RTI). The budgetary constraints on the survey and the information requirements of congress required an innovative approach. Specifically, RTI needed an extremely productive screening interview in order to obtain sufficient victimizations for reliable estimation. Since the CSRC has been experimenting with new screening techniques, the Consortium was asked to develop instrumentation for use in the WMAS. Such cooperation served the ends of the Capitol Hill sponsor who wanted reliable estimates and the Redesign program which needed vehicles to test experimental instrumentation.

The WMAS possesses several features that are distinct assets for research on substantive and methodological research. First, the survey substantially expands the amount of information collected from victims beyond that obtained in the current NCS. Although the scope of explanatory variables is not as extensive as that of the VRS, there is considerably more information available than there is in the NCS. As in the VRS, the WMAS permits the isolation of vehicle related crimes and the allocation of victimizations to particular activities or life domains. The scope of crimes was expanded to include vandalism. Preliminary analysis of these data suggest that, in terms of dollar loss, vandalism is, on the average, as serious as most crimes of theft; when auto theft is removed from the theft category vandalism involves greater dollar loss (Lynch, 1984). The WMAS is one of the better data sets currently available for the study of this under appreciated crime.

Second, the WMAS is particularly well suited to the study of the distribution of victimization in metropolitan areas. The survey was administered to a sample of approximately 5,000 persons in the D.C. metropolitan area, which includes the District and the surrounding counties in Maryland and Virginia. The interviews yielded approximately 1,600 victimizations. A data set of this size should support most conceivable analyses. Since the specific jurisdictions are identified, it is possible to use data on those jurisdictions from sources other than the survey. For example, in a cursory analysis of victimization risk on mass transit in the metropolitan area we combined victimization occurring on the Washington Metro system with ridership data for the area to obtain a crude estimate of risk. Other combinations of survey data and external information are possible. The WMAS also distinguishes victimizations by jurisdiction of occurrence so that we can distinguish victimizations that occur in the jurisdiction of residence from those that occur in other jurisdictions. Not being able to make this simple distinction has seriously hampered our understanding of the dynamics of victimization in metropolitan areas. Again, preliminary analyses of these data suggest that the stereotype of the dangerous central city surrounded by the safe suburbs may need to be modified. Although a substantial proportion of victimizations of suburbanites occurred in the central city, this pattern varied by the nature of the suburb. Moreover, a surprisingly large proportion of the victimizations befalling city residents occurred while they were in the suburbs. This surprising finding is open to a number of explanations. Certainly, one possible interpretation is the change in metropolitan shopping patterns. City residents may now travel to the suburbs to shop rather than the suburban residents traveling to the city to make their purchases. Whatever the causal process, the WMAS is fertile ground in which to search for the distributions of victimization.

The experimental nature of the WMAS instrumentation offers some disadvantages among its many advantages. Many of the questions and procedures were new and we do not have a good idea of the errors and artifacts that they may produce. Also some procedures were adapted to meet the particular constraints of the WMAS. These adaptations can also introduce errors or otherwise limit the utility of the WMAS data. Three such peculiarities are especially noteworthy. First, the survey employs a rolling recounting period such that some respondents were asked to report victimizations occurring in the calendar year prior to the interview while others were asked to report for the prior 18 months. Only those victimizations reported as occurring in a particular calendar year are included in the main data set. Other victimizations that were reported in the recounting period, but not in the calendar year used as the reference period, are included in the section of the data set called out-of-scope incidents. The incident form used to describe these incidents includes much less information than that for in-scope incidents. This particular procedure was used because RTI could not collect all of the interviews within one or two weeks as the BOC does. We do not know whether this procedure introduced bias into the data. Since both the in-scope and out-of-scope data are available, it may be possible to estimate this bias, but as yet this has not been done.

The innovative screening procedures used in the survey may also be a source of error or bias in the data. The CSRC developed a screening strategy that used a large number of short cues to prompt mentions of victimization rather than the long, complete sentences that are used in the current NCS. So, for example, the NCS would ask, "During the last six months, that is, since January 1, 1984, have you been hit, kicked or punched?" The WMAS screener would open with a similar question and then follow with a series of short cues that referred to possible attributes of the event that may encourage greater recall, e.g., at work, by a family member, hit with an object. Although the short cues did encourage significantly higher reporting, we do not know if this increase was evenly distributed across respondents and events. Consequently, the data may be biased in unknown ways.

Finally, we know that the particular procedures used to identify thefts from motor vehicles is flawed. While there is no reason to believe that the reporting of thefts is in error, we do know that those involving thefts from vehicles are often not correctly identified as such. Thefts from motor vehicles are underestimated in the WMAS (Lynch and Biderman, 1984).

These problems with the data set may not greatly diminish its usefulness, but analysts should be aware of these peculiarities so that they can estimate their probable effects on specific analyses. The idiosyncracies of the WMAS are probably less than those afflicting other one-time data collections, particularly the City Surveys conducted in the early part of the NCS program.

3.3 The Longitudinal File of NCS Data

There is a general interest in longitudinal data in the social sciences because it gives a very different perspective on social phenomena than more prevalent cross-sectional data. The rotating panel design of the NCS offers a longitudinal view of housing units over a three year period. Most analysts, however, are equally or even more interested in longitudinal information on persons or groups of persons. The crucial question for the NCS was whether the following of housing units over time provided useful longitudinal information on persons and households. The NCS Redesign addressed this issue because a longitudinal file of NCS data was an efficient means of providing empirical data on issues affecting proposed instrumentation and procedures. For example, debates over the effectiveness of current procedures could not be resolved because the effects of procedures were often confounded with selection effects. A longitudinal file of NCS data can be used in quasi-experimental designs in which procedural effects can be assessed for the same individual over time, thereby separating procedural and selection effects (Biderman, Cantor and Reiss, 1982; Reiss, 1982).

The Consortium first addressed the question of whether the various segments, housing unit, household and person identifiers used by the BOC could be used to link households and persons across interviews. Earlier efforts to construct a longitudinal file from NCS data had found that these identifiers were often in error and could not be used as matching keys. The BOC maintained that, while controls on these items were faulty in the early years of the survey, they had been improved to the point that they could be used to link persons across interviews. The CSRC tested the accuracy of the identifiers on data for the period 1975 through 1979 and found that linking interviews with the identifiers on the NCS resulted in an accurate match approximately 95% of the time. The Consortium used the BOC identifiers to build a longitudinal file of NCS data for the period 1975 through 1979. Questionable matches were identified and validated by the Census Bureau. This file includes approximately two million incident, person, household and housing unit records. The file contains all of the information included in the current NCS.

This longitudinal file offers several advantages over the standard NCS data. First, as we mentioned above, the linking of data over time permits the use of quasi-experimental research designs that can be used to separate treatment or substantive effects from selection effects. Second, the file can be used to construct procedural or methodological variables, such as an individual's interview history, that are not readily available in the standard NCS data sets (LaVange and Folsom, 1984). These procedural variables could explain some of the observed variation in victimization risk so that including these variables could clarify anomalous findings and increase the explanatory power of our models. One example of such a variable is the bounding status of a respondent. Earlier research has shown that respondents who were interviewed previously consistently report fewer victimizations than persons who cannot bound the reference period with a prior interview. With the current NCS data, we know the bounded status of the household, that is, whether anyone in the household had been interviewed at the previous time in sample, but we do not know the bounding status of all individuals in that household. The longitudinal file permits the determination of prior bounding status for individuals. Finally, the longitudinal file reduces some of the problems caused by the rare event nature of victimization by allowing the accumulation of experience over time. In any given year only 10% of the respondents report any victimizations. This skew in the distribution leaves relatively few cases for analysis. Moreover, many of the factors that affect the risk of victimization in a given period of time can be random. By accumulating experience over time we are able to more precisely define that group of persons who remain victimization-free for extended periods of time as well as those who are repeatedly victimized over the three year period. This more reliable differentiation of victims and non-victims can lessen the effect of random "noise" on our attempts to model victimization risk. Accumulation need not be restricted to persons, but can be applied to higher units of aggregation such as households, housing units or segments (Cantor, 1982).

This longitudinal file does have some problems and limitations. First, it is not a true longitudinal file of persons or households. People are included in the NCS as they move through the sample housing units that are followed over a three year period. Those who leave sample housing units are not followed. Consequently, the effects of mobility are hopelessly confounded with the period over which a respondent is interviewed. Analyses relating time to the risk of victimization will underrepresent that risk, because the highly mobile and highly victimized populations will be underrepresented. Similarly, accumulating experience over time will underestimate risk for certain groups because they leave the sample. We do not know how much the NCS' longitudinal file of housing units departs from the results that would be obtained from a true longitudinal file of persons or households. A test comparing the two designs was developed and proposed, but funding was simply not available.

Second, in the course of our analyses of the longitudinal file, we have discovered matching errors in the file. Although this error is well within acceptable ranges for the entire file, it is concentrated among movers. Consequently, analyses that concentrate on highly mobile portions of the sample may be adversely affected.

The third disadvantage of the longitudinal file is that it is massive and complex and, therefore, expensive and difficult to use.

4. Near Term Changes in the NCS

In keeping with the plan for a two phase implementation, the CSRC proposed a series of improvements in the survey that could be implemented in the near term, that is, on or before July 1986 (Lynch, 1981). These changes in the survey were restricted to those that 1) would increase the utility of the survey to various user audiences, 2) would not substantially affect rates in unknown and unknowable ways, and 3) would be implementable at reasonable cost. The Census Bureau reviewed and commented upon these recommendations and BJS decided which of the proposals would be implemented (Taylor, 1984). The specific changes in instrumentation and procedures required by these recommendations have been made, and these new instruments have been tested by the BOC. They were introduced into the on-going survey in July 1986.

Four general types of changes in the survey were recommended for introduction in the near term (1) expansion in the scope of crimes, (2) improving the accuracy of data currently collected, (3) expanding the range of explanatory variables, and (4) expanding the range of information on outcomes of victimization events. The specific recommendations made within each of these general areas are presented below with a brief discussion of their importance for analysis purposes.

4.1 Changes in the Scope of Crimes in the NCS

It was recommended that the scope of crimes included in the survey be expanded to include vandalism. Although BJS endorsed this recommendation, neither the CSRC nor the Census Bureau could devise a method for including vandalism without adversely affecting rates for other types of crimes or without severely undercounting vandalism. Consequently, the inclusion of vandalism in the NCS was postponed until the long term.

4.2 Improving the Accuracy of NCS Data

In an effort to improve the accuracy of NCS data on juvenile victims the Consortium proposed that twelve and thirteen year olds be interviewed in person rather than by proxy, as they are currently. A quasi-experimental study conducted by the CSRC using the longitudinal file presented persuasive evidence that proxy reporting resulted in substantial under estimates for this youngest age group (Reiss, 1982). The current procedure was adopted by BOC because they feared that parents would object to the interviewing of young children, and that the difficulty of contacting younger adolescents would threaten their response rates. The Census agreed to attempt to interview twelve and thirteen year olds in person, but reserved the right to obtain the information by proxy if the parents objected to the in-person interview. Although this change may not affect most users of NCS data, it will improve considerably the quality of data on juvenile victimization.

Similarly, the Consortium attempted to improve the completeness of our information on offenders in the survey by asking all knowledgeable victims about offenders rather than simply those victims who were present (according to the Census criteria) at the time of the incident. Procedures tested using the WMAS suggested that as much as 20% more information could be obtained about offenders by asking victims who were not present at the time of the incident. Many victims receive information about the offender from neighbors and other witnesses who are not members of the victim's household and are, therefore, not in the NCS. Others obtain information from the police. Still others simply identify the offender by a process of elimination. Some of this information is quite reliable while other information is not. By including all available information on offenders, the analyst can selectively exclude that deemed too unreliable to use. This new information could change our understanding of who are the victims and offenders in various types of crime incidents. With this expanded information, the proportion of stranger-to-stranger crimes may be reduced substantially. We may also be able to find out more, albeit somewhat selectively, about non-contact crimes. At this point the survey is completely silent on this issue by virtue of using the presence criteria for asking about offenders.

4.3 Expanding Explanatory Information in the NCS

The opportunity to add potential explanatory variables to the survey in the near term was extremely limited because of the cost and respondent burden involved. Questions can be added to the incident form without substantially adding to cost or burden, because so few respondents are administered most of the questions on the incident form. There are relatively few victims in any given period and the skip pattern of the incident form further reduces the questions asked any single respondent. Explanatory variables must be asked of both victims and nonvictims so they involve more cost and more respondent burden. Within these limitations, however, the Consortium recommended the addition of several items to the basic survey instrument. More importantly, BJS has begun a program of periodic supplements to the survey which can vastly increase the number of explanatory variables while keeping cost and respondent burden within reasonable bounds.

The Consortium recommended the following changes to the basic NCS instrument in the near term:

1. record of respondents mobility in the last five years: Currently the respondent is asked if he has resided in the same housing unit for the last five years. If the respondent responds negatively, it is unclear whether he is a highly mobile individual or a one-time mover. The addition of this question will permit the distinction.

2. greater specification of major activity e.g., work, school: The Current Population Survey (CPS)-like battery of questions used to define major activity in the current NCS leave substantial gaps for the purpose of building theories of victimization risk. Participation in school in lieu of or in addition to work is more important for the exploration of victimization than it is for the estimation of the unemployment rate. Changes were made in the employment questions to obtain a more complete recounting of activities out of the home. Questions were also added to the incident form to link major activity at the time of the incident as opposed to major activity at the time of the interview or the previous week.

3. additional descriptive information on housing structure that may be pertinent to security of the dwelling, e.g., type of access.

4. change in marital status: Social mobility can contribute to victimization as much as changes in residence.

While these changes are quite modest in comparison with the desired information and that which may ultimately be added to the survey, this additional data on possible explanatory variables can give analysts something to work with while they await the more substantial additions planned for the long term Redesign.

Periodic supplements to the on-going NCS offer the greatest hope for expanding the explanatory information available immediately in the NCS. Supplements that include information can be changed, thereby keeping space with, and adding to our theories of, crime causation. Even in a modest supplement the survey offers a sample size much greater than most special purpose surveys at a much lower unit cost. Information collected in supplements can be linked to the high quality data on victimization available in the NCS.

The idea of supplementing on-going surveys is not new. Major health and economic surveys routinely employ supplements to provide information at reasonable cost without disrupting the continuity of level and change estimates. The Redesign demonstrated that this idea could and should be implemented within the NCS. The VRS described earlier served as a prototype for supplements to the NCS that could be reasonably well-integrated into the survey. This experience demonstrated that supplements could be a routine feature of the survey and not a special event. BJS moved quickly to institutionalize this feature of the survey by issuing a joint solicitation with the National Institute of Justice (NIJ) for funding subsequent supplements. More solicitations are planned in the near term and a more ambitious program of rotating supplements is being considered for the long term.

Supplementation as a strategy for increasing explanatory information in the NCS has it limitations. As long as supplements are linked to on-going surveys, the requisites of annual level and change estimates will influence the content of supplements. Questions or procedures that are useful for research purposes, but adversely affect estimates will not be allowed in supplements. Moreover, since the NCS is conducted by the Census, the content of supplements could be limited by policies and procedures unique to the Census Bureau, e.g., confidentiality restrictions. These problems not withstanding, the use of periodic supplements to the NCS has increased and will continue to increase the amount of explanatory information available in the near term.

4.4 Expanding Descriptive Information in the NCS

The amount of descriptive information on crime events included in the current NCS is extensive and underutilized, but in a few specific areas small increases in the information collected could offer substantial dividends for our understanding of crime and criminal justice. To this end, the CSRC recommended adding to the scope of descriptive information in several areas, including: 1) more logical and extensive location codes, 2) more information collected on stolen objects, 3) greater description of victim-offender interaction, 4) more data on the type of police service received, 5) additional information on offender motivation and 6) contact with the criminal justice system beyond the police.

4.5 Changes in Location Codes

The location codes in the NCS evolved in response to the categories mentioned by respondents. While this is a perfectly good method for developing codes, it does not always yield the kinds of distinctions useful for analysis. For example, the current codes cannot be used to identify crime in a victim's residential neighborhood. Crimes occurring on the street adjacent to the dwelling can be identified, but not those that happen down the block. Similarly, public and private places are inconsistently distinguished from more exposed locations. Systematically distinguishing such attributes of location will contribute to investigations of victimization risk.

Changes were also recommended in the handling of the jurisdiction in which the incident occurred. Currently, the survey collects information on the specific jurisdiction in which an incident was reported to have occurred, but this information is not included in the public use tapes. The CSRC recommended that, at a minimum, the distinction be made between incidents occurring in the jurisdiction of residence as opposed to some other jurisdiction. This distinction is pertinent for any analysis which includes size or type of place variables. It is also helpful in comparisons between the NCS and those data systems based on jurisdiction of occurrence such as the UCR (for subnational analyses). Ideally, we would want to be able to identify incidents by both jurisdiction of occurrence and jurisdiction of residence. The information is in the survey, but an expensive crosswalk procedure is required to match jurisdictions, and the jurisdiction of occurrence variable would have some 3,000 codes. Until such problems can be dealt with, the distinction between coincident jurisdictions of residence and occurrence, and non-coincident will be an improvement.

4.6 Expansion of Property Codes

The great bulk of offenses included in the survey are property offenses in which some object is taken. The only way to make sense of this large and heterogeneous category of crime is to subdivide it into more internally homogeneous types. One way to do this is to differentiate according to the type of property taken. Unfortunately, the property codes included in the NCS do not provide a sufficiently detailed description of stolen objects to be useful, in this regard. Consequently, the Consortium recommended that these property codes be expanded. The more detailed codes used in the WMAS and the various Canadian surveys were offered as a model.

4.7 Expansion of Information on Victim-Offender Relationship

The degree of relationship between the victim and the offender is one of the most analyzed variables in the survey. It is used to distinguish stereotypic street crime from crimes among intimates over which social agencies have less control. Similarly, relationship is a crucial determinant in the decision to call the police (Skogan, 1976). While the two end points of the relationship scale are reasonably clear, i.e., stranger and relative, the middle range is ambiguous. The exact meaning of friend and acquaintance is ambiguous and this ambiguity contributes to unsatisfactory analysis and confusing findings. For example, the relationship between reporting to the police and intimacy of victim-offender relationships is curvilinear rather than linearly negative. The police are less likely to be called for incidents involving strangers and intimates than they are for incidents involving relationships in between. This may be attributable to the fact that victims have no information on strangers and feel that calling the police would be useless. In the case of intimates, they may be unwilling to call because it is a private matter or they fear retribution because they are in such close contact. Acquaintances, however, are known sufficiently to be able to find, yet they are not so central to the victim's life that the victim is reluctant to call. This hypothesis and others can only be tested when we have more information about the middle range of victim-offender relationships. To this end the Consortium recommended expanding the questioning on the degree of relationship between victim and offender. Specifically, the casual acquaintance and well-known categories of relationships were expanded to include various types of non-relative relationships, such as boyfriend or girlfriend, or ex-boyfriend or ex-girlfriend, roommate or boarder, school mate, neighbor, co-worker or customer, and the like. For persons known by sight, additional questions were asked about the amount of information that the victim had about where these persons lived, worked, etc. These additions should help us untangle the somewhat confused web of findings surrounding degree of relationship and crime.

4.8 Expanding Information on Police Service

The current survey asks whether the victim reported the event to the police, and if not, why not. The Consortium recommended that this questioning be expanded to include more information on the type of service provided by the police. This information is important for two reasons. First, there are no nationally representative data on the nature of police service.[4] Major changes have been taking place in the way in which police departments respond to citizen complaints, but we have no way of assessing these changes. For example, most police departments emphasize full service, that is, a patrol car is dispatched to every call for assistance. There are signs, however, that full service is fast disappearing and that different types of calls receive different types of service (Lynch and Biderman, 1983). Some receive a patrol car while others receive a reporting form in the mail. These changes are important for the criminal justice system. They should be monitored, and the NCS is a good, if not perfect, way of doing so. Second, the divergence of the UCR and NCS trends over time have been a source of concern to the crime statistics community (Biderman, Lynch and Peterson, 1983). In some ways this divergence threatens the credibility of crime statistics. A large part of our confusion about this divergence is the result of the lack of systematic information about what the police do with a citizen's report after it is made. The NCS could help illuminate this dark area by collecting some minimal information on the police response. For example, if the police are called, but they do not respond at all, then we may be safe in assuming that no report is filed and that we can exclude this event for purpose of NCS and UCR comparisons. More stringent criteria can be applied, such as restricting the comparisons to those NCS incidents in which the victim knows that a report has been filed. The contribution of police response to the divergence of the trends can be investigated more adequately in specific jurisdictions, but these studies will not be generalizable beyond that jurisdiction. NCS data on police response may not be as good as that available from special studies, but it does have the advantage of being nationally representative.

Victims are asked if they reported the incident to the police, why or why not, whether the police responded in any way, how they responded, i.e., by phone, mail, or in-person, and if in-person, what exactly they did when they arrived or afterward, e.g., made an arrest, completed a report. The victims who had contact with the police were also asked if they had contact with any other authorities regarding the incident.

4.9 *Increasing the Availability of Local Area Data*

One of the major, longstanding criticisms of the NCS is that it could not provide estimates of victimization for a wide range of sub-national area without substantially increasing its sample size or threatening the quality of the national estimates. The demand for sub-national data was made by two groups—planners and other officials in specific localities who wanted level and change estimates for their areas and academics who wanted data on a wide range of areas for research purposes. The former wanted the Census Bureau to publish annual estimates for their area. The latter simply wanted the data in any form that could be used in analyses. The size and type of the sample employed in the NCS would not permit the production and publication of reliable estimates for any but the very largest metropolitan areas. BJS and the Consortium questioned the utility of these estimates, and the Census Bureau was reluctant to publish them because they were concerned about their quality. BJS has asked the Census Bureau to investigate the possibility of producing model-based estimates for local areas rather than estimates based only on interviews conducted in those areas.

The CSRC, BJS and the Census Bureau were able to reach an agreement on making data available for the purposes of analysis. Census disclosure strictures prohibit the release of individual level data for areas with less than 100,000 population. Moreover, they will not release aggregated information for jurisdictions when these aggregated data can be linked with micro or individual level data for the same aggregate because it may permit the identification of individual respondents. After some negotiation, the BOC agreed to construct a public use tape that would make aggregate estimates of victimization rates available at the county level for most counties in the NCS sample. This data set would provide estimates of victimization as well as offense specific estimates of victimizations for a particular county. Some county level sociodemographic characteristics would be included and the county would be identified by name so that analysts could add county level data from external sources such as the *City-County Data Book*. Some lower limits on the size of included counties was imposed and some random noise was introduced to preserve confidentiality. Although these data cannot escape the problems that thin numbers bring, they should contribute to our understanding of the relationship between victimization and ecological factors at the county level and higher.

The near term changes in the survey may seem quite modest to some. A few words changed here, a few codes changed there, and an all but invisible procedural change somewhere else do not appear dramatic, but those who have used these data realize that it is the little things that stand as the great impediments to the proper and fruitful use of these data. Bold strokes that add vast amounts of information to the survey are undone by the manner in which the specific questions are cast. These seemingly small changes can pay great dividends in the hands of competent and experienced researchers. Moreover, these modifications were restricted in their scope because of the need to have them implemented and available immediately. These changes were put into the field in July 1986. More ambitious changes would have required much more development work and a longer phase-in unless BJS could tolerate radical discontinuities in the NCS trends.

5. The Long-Term Redesign of the NCS

The changes scheduled for implementation in the long term were not constrained by regard for series continuity. The principal objective of these changes was to improve the accuracy and utility of NCS data while reducing the unit cost of the survey. The recommendations were constrained only by the need to stay within reasonable cost limits for the on-going survey. Even considerations of implementation costs were precluded from the early considerations of the most desirable long-term design. Every aspect of the survey was open for reconsideration, including the continued administration of the survey by the Census Bureau.

The Consortium considered a wide range of changes in the basic design features of the survey including:

1. Sample Design

    —an area frame rather than a list frame

    —a true longitudinal design of persons and households

    —a triennial cross-section design

    —a dual frame telephone design

2. Mode

    —maximum telephone interviewing

    —centralized telephone administration

3. Reference Period

    —three-month

    —four-month

    —six-month

    —twelve-month

    —alternating three- and six-month periods

4. Instrumentation

    —uniform screening procedures

    —new screening interview and incident form

    —core and supplement format

5. Estimation

    —error adjustments for major sources of measurement error

    —adjustment and use of the bounding interview

Ultimately, the CSRC recommended that the NCS design should have the following major design features. First, it should be a true longitudinal design of persons and households or include a longitudinal component. Second, it should employ the new short cue screener and uniform screening procedures tested in the Redesign. Third, it should take the form of a core instrument to which one-time and periodic supplements could be added. Fourth, a dual frame, mixed mode design should be employed if Census cold-contact telephone interviewing tests prove successful. Fifth, centralized computer assisted telephone interviewing should be employed if the on-going tests of CATI within the Census demonstrate its desirability.

While all of these changes have repercussions for the quality and utility of the NCS data as well as the cost of the survey, two design features have particular importance for analysts—core and supplement format and the longitudinal design. The advantages of longitudinal data were discussed earlier. Since the future NCS will be a true longitudinal design of persons and households, these advantages will be that much greater. Moreover, the problems of attrition which affect the current longitudinal design of household will be much less severe in a longitudinal design of persons. The advantages of a core and supplement format in the NCS have also been discussed in the previous section. In the long-term, the proposed program of supplements is more ambitious. Rather than periodic supplements to the existing instrumentation, the long term Redesign urges an extensive program of routine, periodic and one-time supplements with a substantially altered core instrument. The core instrument of the NCS would be administered to all eligible respondents at all interviews. It would serve the purpose of 1) eliciting mentions of victimizations, 2) providing the basic information required to classify events and 3) providing the data necessary for weighting. The core questionnaire would also include some questions for rare populations for whom we would want to collect information at every opportunity, e.g., rape victims. All other questioning could be conducted in specific periods or with subsamples of respondents. This format would make available the funds and the respondent burden necessary to construct and field supplements that would include much more varied information than can be accommodated in the current fixed format design. Periodic and one-time supplements could focus on specific types of crime, such as crime at work, and much more detailed questioning could be administered to employed persons to isolate those factors that affect the risk of victimization at work. Similarly, supplements could address incidents with specific outcomes such as calling the police and much more detailed questioning about police service and other services of the criminal justice system could be included. The CSRC has recommended several candidates for periodic supplements to be funded by BJS (Lynch, 1984). The core and supplement plan also seeks to expand the participation of the academic and practitioner communities in the routine formulation of supplements. BJS would continue to solicit ideas from the research community and fund those ideas for supplements as it has in its recent joint solicitations with the

National Institute of Justice (NIJ). The agency could also entertain supplements proposed by researchers with independent funding. Whatever the source of the supplement idea, the use of the NCS as a vehicle for supplements greatly increases the flexibility of the survey and its potential as a research tool.

Two cautionary notes are in order. The broad outlines of the long-term survey design have been recommended to BJS, but the final decision on these recommendations must await feasibility testing within the Census Bureau environment which are currently underway. Implementation of this design depends upon the availability of funds, so that the implementation of some or all of the recommendations and the timing of that implementation is not clear at this time (see Taylor, forthcoming).

6. Summary

The NCS Redesign was an ambitious and courageous undertaking for which BJS should be given appropriate credit. The project was begun with high hopes. In some cases those hopes were unrealistic and they were soon abandoned. In other cases, these hopes were well-founded and the objectives achieved. At the end of these five years, however, it became clear that the improvement of a major survey was an on-going process. Hopefully, the extraordinary effort put forth in the Redesign will leave in place those institutional structures that will facilitate the constant improvement of the NCS. A core and supplement format should routinize the change process that was so difficult the first time around. Making provision for continuous contributions and stimulus from outside of the Federal government will sustain the interest in improvement. The specific changes in procedures and instruments described here are important in themselves, but it is equally important to routinize the process of Redesign. Researchers are encouraged to use what the Redesign has wrought and to become part of the process for continuing improvement by participating in the NCS program with their ideas and their interest.

6

State Prisons and Inmates: The Census and Survey[1]

Phyllis Jo Baunach

Less well-known than the UCR or the NCS are the surveys of inmates in state and local correctional facilities and the censuses of state and local correctional facilities. Unlike either of its other two more widely-used sister data series, the surveys and censuses make no attempt to measure crime trends or crime rates. Rather, these rich data sources provide national information on the demographic, social, and criminal characteristics of the confined adult populations and the facilities that house them.[2]

Perhaps because they were developed more recently and are collected less frequently than either the UCR or the NCS, the censuses and surveys, to date, have not been used or reviewed extensively in the literature. Yet the wealth of data on inmate and facility characteristics is worthy of note. For this reason, the present chapter provides an historic overview, a descriptive analysis, and a brief discussion of the utility and limitations of two of these series —the Survey of Inmates of Adult State Correctional Facilities[3] and the Census of State Adult Correctional Facilities.[4]

The Survey and Census, are part of the National Prisoner Statistics (NPS) Program. First begun in 1926 at the U.S. Census Bureau, the purpose of the NPS Program is to "collect and interpret data on state and federal correctional institutions and their inmates" (Cantwell, 1974: 111). The program was transferred to the U.S. Bureau of Prisons in 1950 and to the National Criminal Justice Information and Statistics Service (NCJISS) of the Law Enforcement Assistance Administration (LEAA) in 1971. The program is now part of the Bureau of Justice Statistics (BJS). The Census Bureau has served as the data collection agent for NPS since its transfer to LEAA.

Over the past few years, the NPS has developed two major foci, one dealing primarily with annual counts,[5] and the other covering the Surveys and Censuses. The Survey and Census provide a snapshot of inmates and facilities, respectively, at one point in time. They are done roughly every five to seven years.

1. Why Study the Inmates and Institutions?: Census and Survey Objectives

Within recent years there has been a dramatic increase in the numbers of men and women incarcerated in prisons and jails across the country. From 1980 to 1981 there was a 12 percent increase (roughly 40,000 inmates) in the prison population, which was the largest increase in the nation's history (Gardner, 1982: 6; Minor-Harper, 1982: 1). Similarly, from 1981 to 1982 there was a 12 percent increase in the prison population size, bringing the total number of persons incarcerated in prison to well over 412,000 (Minor-Harper, 1983: 1; Gettinger, 1983: 6). At the end of 1983, the prison population figure was 437,248, a 6 percent increase over 1982, and at year end 1987, a record 581,609 inmates were held in state and federal prisons (Greenfeld, 1987: 1). The 1987 figure represents a 7 percent increase over a year earlier and a 76 percent increase since 1980.

These staggering increases in the size of the prison population have exacerbated already crowded prisons throughout the country, and have stimulated resounding cries for additional reforms in sentencing policies, ceilings on prison population sizes, greater use of alternatives to incarceration and, among a more conservative faction, more prison construction.

In an era when the primary focus of correctional philosophy is on punishment (von Hirsch, 1976) or incapacitation (Sherman and Hawkins, 1981), rather than on rehabilitation, one may well ask why there should be an interest in collecting information about inmate characteristics. Three points are relevant to this concern. First, despite the decline of rehabilitation as the focal point of correctional philosophy and effort, there is still a need to provide services for incarcerated offenders, and there is still a recognition of the rehabilitative ideal among corrections practitioners (Morris, 1974). This point was articulated by the American Correctional Association in its recent correctional policy statement. Among the goals and objectives of corrections in this country are: ... to offer the widest range of correctional options ... to meet the needs of both society and the individual" and "... to provide humane program and service opportunities for accused and adjudicated offenders that will enhance their community integration and economic self-sufficiency..." (Nesbitt, 1983: 86).

Second, particularly because of the massive increase in the numbers of incarcerated offenders, there is a need to determine the nature of the population for whom correctional practices are devised. The development of services in the institution must begin with an understanding of the population for whom these services are being provided (Conrad, 1967: 288). Without some understanding of client characteristics, it would be impossible to provide meaningful services.

The significance of this point has been echoed by those who argue that programs for incarcerated offenders may be effective in changing post-prison behavior, but that it is imperative to ascertain under what conditions which programs work for whom (Palmer, 1976: 42). Determining the "for whom" underscores the importance of carefully identifying the population served.

Finally, in planning for reforms in the processing, handling, and housing of offenders, some have argued for a need to "selectively identify" (Montilla and Harlow, 1979: 28) the problems to be addressed. An accurate identification of problems begins with a clear understanding of both the inmates and the environment within which they live.

Within this framework, the primary purpose of the Survey is to describe the characteristics of the inmates housed in adult state correctional facilities nationwide. Similarly, the main purpose of the Census is to describe the facility characteristics. These Surveys and Censuses remain the only source of comprehensive information about the inmates and facilities in this country. More specifically, the common objectives of the surveys and censuses are:

- To obtain a detailed profile of the facilities housing inmates and of the inmates housed in State-operated confinement and community-based corrections facilities. These data may be used to assess trends in such areas as demographic or socioeconomic characteristics, nature of offenses among incarcerated populations, capacity and confinement conditions, programs provided and staffing patterns.

- To obtain information on major issues in corrections related to facilities and inmates. Issues pertaining to inmates include, for example, sentences imposed on incarcerated offenders, patterns of repetitive criminal behavior, gender differences in crimes and criminal background, and the relationship between drug and/or alcohol use and involvement in crime among incarcerated persons. Issues pertaining to facilities include, for instance, characteristics of capacity and confinement space, occupancy rates, trends in population growth, expenditures, staffing patterns, and program availability.

- To obtain information on special issues of concern regarding facilities and inmates. For instance, the 1979 Survey and Census included extensive information on veterans, and on specific aspects of health care afforded inmates in facilities; the 1984 Census included special inmate counts of Mariel Cubans, illegal aliens and persons under the age of 18, and the number of inmate deaths due to AIDS. The 1986 Survey included information on the victim-offender relationship.

- To provide public-use data tapes for use by interested practitioners, planners, academicians and researchers through the Criminal Justice Archive and Information Network (CJAIN) at the University of Michigan.

With a focus on the collection and dissemination of information about inmates and facilities, the Surveys and Censuses gather data about current conditions and inmate characteristics that may be used by administrators, practitioners and planners in making informed policy decisions, and by researchers in their examination of specific corrections issues. In this sense, the Census provides a national picture of the prison environment, a backdrop against which decision-makers may gauge the conditions of their own jurisdiction relative to the rest of the country. This information may be used at the federal, state, or local level to assess existing conditions within the state correctional facilities and the need for change. Similarly, the Survey provides a national profile of incarcerated persons, and a starting point for developing programmatic changes in processing, and handling criminal offenders.

2. Historic Overview

2.1 Survey of Inmates of Adult State Correctional Facilities

To date, three Surveys and three Censuses have been conducted. The first Survey was conducted in January 1974 with individual interviews using a representative sample of roughly 10,000 inmates. The information obtained in the Survey included demographic and socioeconomic background, military experience, prior criminal record, current offenses, history of incarcerations, adjudication experience, prison routine and drug and alcohol use. The information was presented in two reports, *Survey of Inmates of State Correctional Facilities, 1974: Advance Report* (1976), and *Profile of State Prison Inmates: Sociodemographic Findings from the 1974 Survey of Inmates of State Correctional Facilities* (1979). The first report presents a broad overview of the major topics covered in the 1974 Survey; the second report delineates socioeconomic and demographic characteristics in relation to one another and in relation to various criminal characteristics. The most frequently used variables include race, offense, and number of past sentences an inmate had served. In addition, comparisons were made between the inmate population and the U.S. population on selected characteristics.

The second Survey was conducted in November, 1979 using a representative sample of about 12,000 inmates from adult state correctional facilities. In addition to the topics raised on the 1974 Survey, the 1979 Survey covered grievance mechanisms, use of legal materials since incarceration, parole hearings, work assignment and health care during confinement. Preliminary information was presented in *Prisons and Prisoners* (1982). Three topical bulletins and two special reports were prepared by BJS staff, including *Veterans in Prison* (1981), *Prisoners and Alcohol* (1983), *Prisoners and Drugs* (1983), *Career Patterns and Alcohol* (1983) and *The Prevalence of Imprisonment* (1985).

The most recent survey, conducted in February and March, 1986, included roughly 15,000 inmates and added the topic of the victim-offender relationship. The first report, *Profile of State Prison Inmates 1986* was released in January 1988.

2.2 The Census of State Correctional Facilities

The first Census was conducted among approximately 600 facilities in January 1974, and included type and security status of institutions; population size; age of physical plant; staff complement; payroll and operating expenses; and programs and services provided for inmates. This information was presented in the Advance Report published in July 1975 (Advance Report, 1975).

The second Census was done in November 1979, among 568 secure confinement facilities and 223 State-operated community-based correctional facilities. The variables collected covered security classification of facilities; facility functions; rated capacity; inmate count on the reference date; number of inmates by security classification, race and sex; veteran status of inmates; confinement space; nature of the programs provided for inmates; employment characteristics (i.e., nature of position by payroll status; race of staff by payroll status); level of health care evaluation provided for inmates; nature of medical facilities; number of inmates on medication; and number of inmate deaths during calendar year 1978. To date, there have been no publications specifically devoted to these data. A brief overview of the number of inmates by type of facility in which they were housed was included in the bulletin *Prisons and Prisoners* (1982).

The third Census conducted in June 1984, collected data from 903 facilities, including 694 confinement facilities and 209 community-based facilities. To date, BJS staff have written two reports based on these data. One report, the *1984 Census of State Adult Correctional Facilities* (1987) is a collection of tables highlighting key findings; the other is a special report, *Population Density in State Prisons* (1986). For both Censuses, public use data tapes were prepared and sent to the Criminal Justice Archive and Information Network (CJAIN) at the University of Michigan in Ann Arbor.

Until the most recent cycle, Censuses were conducted in tandem with Surveys. The rationale for conducting these two efforts simultaneously was twofold: 1) to provide a snapshot of inmates and the facilities that house them at about the same point in time; and 2) to allow for weighting the Survey data by the universe represented by the universe of inmates in the Census. In the past, since the Surveys and Censuses were done at about the same time, selection of the sample of facilities to be used in the Survey was based on an updated universe of facilities from the previous full Census conducted five years earlier. However, to enhance the accuracy of the Survey sample, it would be more appropriate to select the sample of facilities from the most recently completed full Census. For the most recent cycle, 1984-1986, this procedure was used. The Census was conducted in advance of the Survey, and the sample of facilities for the Survey was selected from the completed Census.

Initially the Census was to be done about a year in advance of the Survey. However, given extensive revisions and refinement of the Survey questionnaire, the Census was conducted in 1984, and the Survey, in 1986.[6]

3. Methodology: How are the Censuses and Surveys Conducted?

The Census and Survey differ considerably in their methodologies. The Census, as the name implies, includes every State prison and State-operated community-based corrections facility in the country. The Survey, on the other hand, includes a nationally selected random sample of inmates from several facilities across the country. The Survey entails a two-stage sample: (1) a representative sample of facilities selected from the universe of facilities and (2) a random sample of inmates drawn from those sample facilities. Since the Census includes all facilities in the defined universe, there is no need to weight data to obtain a national picture of facilities. Survey data, however, derived from a sample, are weighted to the national total of inmates included in the universe of facilities. Given the differences in approach, the key elements of the Census methodology include defining the universe, and data collection. Key elements of the Survey include devising the sample, pre-testing and data collection.

3.1 Census Methodology

3.1.1 DEFINING THE UNIVERSE

The definitions of the universe used in 1974 differed from the definition used in the 1979 and 1984 censuses. The 1974 universe included facilities that were:

- Operational on January 31, 1974;
- Administratively capable of providing a unique inmate count, staffing pattern, payroll figure and budgetary information; and
- Defined as a state correctional facility for adults or youthful offenders; or, a non-state operated facility where the clear majority of residents were state inmates.

Within this definition, both private and local facilities housing mainly inmates under state jurisdiction were included. Most of the non-state facilities were classified as community centers, as they were privately operated but funded through the state on a per diem basis. Except as noted above, Federal, county, municipal and local facilities were not included (Advance Report, July 1975: 15).

For the 1979 and 1984 Censuses, the universe of facilities included the following:

- Prisons; prison farms;
- Classification/diagnostic/reception/medical facilities;
- Hospitals exclusively for state prisoners;
- Drug/alcohol treatment facilities exclusively for state prisoners;
- Road camps; forestry camps;
- Special function facilities: youthful offender facilities except the sixteen facilities operated by the California Youth Authority that house both juveniles and adults, and are included in the Census of Public Juvenile Detention, Correctional and Shelter Facilities; vocational training facilities; honor camps; state-operated jails in Alaska, Connecticut, Delaware, Hawaii, Rhode Island and Vermont;
- Community-based pre-release facilities: halfway houses; pre-release/parole facilities; work release facilities and study release facilities.

Facilities excluded from the universe were:

- Privately operated facilities that house state prisoners even if they are supported with state funds on a contractual or per diem basis;
- Facilities financed and operated by the military, the Federal government, and local governments even if they house state prisoners;
- Facilities located in U.S. territories;
- Treatment facilities for drug addicts and/or alcoholics not exclusively for state prisoners.

In addition, the facility had to be staffed with employees hired directly by the state; and the facility must have been functionally distinct in a separate physical location under the executive control of its own warden, superintendent, etc. (Census of State Adult Correctional Facilities, 1984: Codebook, 1986). The reason of this last criterion was to ensure a separate administration for each facility. For instance, a women's prison physically located within the same walls as the men's prison, but which had its own warden was classified as a separate facility rather than as a part of the men's facility. The distinction, then, allows for considering the women's facility independently in analyses.

The 1974 Census differed from the 1979 and 1984 Censuses in the definition of the universe in at least four respects. First, the universe used in the 1974 Census was not specific in listing the types of facilities to be included. Second, the later two Censuses clearly distinguished between community-based and more secure confinement facilities (prisons), whereas the first Census did not. Community-based facilities were defined as those in which at least half of the population was allowed to leave the facility grounds regularly, unaccompanied by an official, for the purpose of seeking and holding employment, and/or making daily use of community resources such as schools or treatment programs. Secure confinement facilities were those facilities in which at least half of the inmates could not routinely leave the facility grounds. Third, the 1974 Census included private and local facilities in which most of the inmates were under the jurisdiction of the state; the later two Censuses specifically excluded facilities that were not run by staff hired directly by the state. Fourth, the earliest Census specifically consolidated institutions that were unable to provide an inmate count, staffing pattern, payroll or budgetary information; the later two Censuses made no mention of such a consolidation in their definitions of the universe.

Distinctions in the definition of the universe among Censuses were brought about by at least two factors. The first factor was the orientation of the branch of the U.S. Census Bureau that collected data for each Census. The earliest Census was conducted by the Demographic Surveys Division of the U.S. Census Bureau, and the later two Censuses, by the Governments Division. These two separate branches of the Census Bureau have different approaches to defining the universe. The former branch, which focuses on people as the unit of analysis, emphasized the inmates, whereas the latter branch, which focuses on governments, emphasized the governments that operate the facilities. As a result of these diverse perspectives, the 1974 Census universe included private or local facilities wherein most inmates were under State jurisdiction, and the later two Censuses limited the universe to facilities that were State-funded and State-operated.[7] If a local facility housed inmates who were under State jurisdiction but was funded by the State on a contractual or a per diem basis, that facility was not included in the universe for the 1979 or 1984 Censuses.

The second factor that accounts for differences in the definitions from the 1974 and later Censuses stems from the information derived from the 1974 Census. This was the case, for instance, with the distinction between community-based and more secure confinement facilities. Community facilities differ from confinement facilities in many respects, such as employment (i.e., in community facilities staff are not called guards; executive administrators are directors, not wardens); confinement units (i.e., residents live in rooms, not cells); medical facilities (i.e., medical staff and equipment are not usually located within the community facility itself); recreational areas (i.e., recreation is more frequently found in the community, not in the facility); furloughs or weekend passes (i.e., usually a part of the program itself in community facilities); and prison industry (i.e., not part of a community program). Given these distinctions between confinement and community-based facilities, a separate questionnaire was designed for community facilities in the 1979 and 1984 Censuses.

For each Census, prior to data collection, the universe of facilities was updated from the previous Census in a two-stage process. First, the list was initially updated using information provided by Abt Associates from their 1978 Survey of State Correctional Facilities, and from other sources. In 1984, the universe was first updated using the annual American Correctional Association facility directory. In the second stage, in both years the revised listing was then sent to the Department of Corrections in each jurisdiction for review (Census of State Adult Correctional Facilities, 1984: Codebook 1986: ii).

In 1984, the universe consisted of 915 facilities, including 693 confinement facilities and 222 community-based facilities. When data collection was completed, the final response included 903 facilities, 694 confinement facilities and 209 community-based facilities. Four facilities were added, and sixteen were eliminated from the Census (Census of State Adult Correctional Facilities, 1984: Codebook, 1986: ii).

3.1.2 DATA COLLECTION

For each Census, data were obtained through a mail canvas. In 1974 and 1984, questionnaires were sent directly to the facilities. In 1979, 129 questionnaires were sent to individual facilities in 11 states, and 672 questionnaires were sent to a central location in 40 states. The questionnaires sent to central sources were either completed at the State Department of Corrections or distributed to the individual facilities after receipt (28 states). In 1984, questionnaires were sent directly to the facilities. Expenditure data, however, were collected directly from State Departments of Corrections. For each Census, second and third questionnaires were sent to administrators who had not yet responded to the Census several weeks after the initial questionnaires were sent out. Telephone follow-ups were made to obtain missing data or to clarify inconsistent entries. Census Bureau staff keyed and edited data and prepared the public use data tape and documentation.

3.2 Survey Methodology

The issues of concern in the Survey methodology are sample selection, pre-testing instruments and data collection.

3.2.1 SAMPLE SELECTION

The Survey sample selection procedures provide a representative sample of inmates in state correctional facilities across the country. Institutions include both confinement and state-operated community-based facilities. Sample selection for the Survey entails a two-stage process. The first stage involves selection of a representative sample of facilities from among the universe of correctional facilities included in the Census. In all three Surveys, conducted in 1974, 1979 and 1986, stage one involved stratification of facilities by the four Census Bureau regions, and the selection of facilities according to population size.[8] The second stage involves selection of a random sample of inmates from within each facility sampled in stage one. Interviewers at each facility select the inmates based upon predetermined sampling instructions devised by Census Bureau staff in accordance with BJS specifications.

3.2.2 PRE-TEST

For the 1986 Survey, a pre-test of the questionnaire and interviewer training materials was conducted in 1985. Roughly 200 male and female inmates from three states, Michigan, Florida and Delaware, were included. The purposes of the pre-test were twofold: to determine the appropriateness, readability and flow of items included on the questionnaire; and to determine the utility and clarity of the home study training materials prepared for interviewers.

Interviewers were selected through the Census Bureau's Field Division to collect the pre-test data. BJS staff accompanied interviewers as observers. Interviewers were debriefed after the pre-test to obtain their input on the items and procedures. In addition, the pre-test included a records check to get a rough idea of the extent to which information obtained from inmates, particularly relating to current offenses and prior criminal record, reflected information reported in the records. Information from the pre-test was used to revise the questionnaire and training materials.

3.2.3 DATA COLLECTION

Immediately prior to the data collection effort a formal training session for Census Bureau region supervisors was held to ensure their understanding of Survey objectives, and enlist their support in conducting the study.

This session included an overview of the nature and purposes of the Survey, an explanation of the criminal justice process, and a brief description of the timetable for completion of the data collection effort.

In addition, formal training for the interviewers was held in each regional office across the country. This training consisted of two phases. In the first phase, interviewers participated in home study of materials related to the criminal justice process and the questionnaire. Information regarding the criminal justice system was incorporated into the training materials to acquaint interviewers, who generally have little background in this area, with criminal justice issues they might encounter in talking with inmates.

Training included such areas as an explanation of the differences between probation and parole, the definition of a current offense for purposes of the study, and an explanation of the movement through the criminal justice system from arrest through release from parole.

During the second phase, interviewers participated in group training sessions in the regional office. Included in these sessions were taped simulations of interviews with inmates to give interviewers practice in accurately recording information from possibly difficult situations.

The actual data collection effort was conducted in February and March, 1986. A total of 15,000 inmates were interviewed. U.S. Census Bureau staff coded and keyed the data, and in conjunction with BJS staff, edited the data. The Census Bureau prepared documentation and a data tape for the CJAIN.

4. Topics Included in the Census/Survey

4.1 Facility and Inmate Characteristics

To achieve the objectives of devising a profile of state-operated correctional facilities for adults, the Census collects information on both facility and inmate characteristics. The nature of the data collected in each of the Censuses has varied to some extent. In the 1984 Census, facility characteristics included:

- Community access: whether 50 percent or more of the inmates are regularly allowed to leave the facility grounds unaccompanied usually to attend work or study release.

- Physical security level of the facility: maximum, medium, minimum, and the characteristics that relate to this security level.[9]

- Facility function: all the functions the facility serves, including reception and diagnostic center, medical unit, general adult population confinement, work release, or prerelease.

- Capacity: rated, or design.[10]

- Age of facility: the year in which the facility was constructed, the original purpose of the facility if it was not originally constructed as a correctional facility, and the year in which it was converted into a correctional facility.

- Health and safety conditions: the nature of medical facilities available, whether inmates are on medication, the number and causes of inmate deaths during the annual period covered by the census, whether the facilty is under court order or consent decree for conditions of confinement and the reasons for the court order or consent decree, the number of assaults and incidents of inmates during the annual period covered by the Census.[11]

- Expenditures: operating and capital expenditures during the annual period covered by the Census.[12]

- Employment: the number, race and ethnic origin of full or part-time, payroll or nonpayroll staff employed by the institution on the reference date of the Census, and the sex and work assignments of staff on the reference date.

Inmate characteristics included:

- Inmate population size: the number of inmates in the facility on the reference date by sex, race and ethnicity, and custody level, and the average daily population by sex of inmates housed in the facility during the annual period covered by the Census.

- Program involvement: the number and sex of inmates enrolled in academic, counseling, and work release programs on the reference date.[13]

- Work assignments: the number and sex of inmates enrolled in industries, maintenance jobs, and vocational training on the reference date, and the average hourly wage paid to each inmate.[14]

- Special inmate counts: the number of Mariel Cubans, illegal aliens, and persons younger than age 18 housed in the facility on the reference date, or admitted to the facility during the year covered by the Census.

4.2 Criminal Characteristics

The Survey serves many purposes. It provides an overview of inmates at one point in time, enables comparisons of inmate characteristics over time, and allows for analysis of specific timely issues. Given these broad purposes, the 1986 Survey provided general information on a wide range of issues pertaining to adult offenders incarcerated in state-operated correctional facilities. Topics included both criminal and noncriminal characteristics.

Much of the Survey focuses on criminal characteristics, which include prior criminal involvement from youth through adulthood and the offenses for which the inmate is currently incarcerated. More specifically, criminal characteristics cover current offenses, victim-offender relationships, pre-trial experiences and adjudication process, and prior criminal record. Each of these factors will be discussed briefly.

4.2.1 CURRENT OFFENSES

In the 1986 Survey, the current offense was the crime or crimes for which the offender was most recently sentenced to prison just prior to the most recent admission to prison. In determining which offenses were the current ones, two factors were considered: 1) whether the inmate was on some type of release just prior to the current incarceration; and 2) if the inmate had been on release, whether the inmate was imprisoned for violating the terms of the release, or whether the inmate had been sentenced to prison for one or more new offenses. The types of release included probation from court or from prison, parole, conditional release, or escape. Given these factors, the Survey allows the user to track an inmate's current offenses in one of the eleven groups. These groups are illustrated in Table 1.

Table 1

Determining the current offense of inmates in the 1986 Survey of inmates of state adult correctional facilities

Type of release:	*New sentence**	
	Yes	No
None—new court commitment	X	
Probation from court	X	X
Probation from prison	X	X
Parole	X	X
Conditional Release	X	X
Escape	X	X

*If the inmate was sentenced for a new offense just prior to the current incarceration, this offense was the current offense. Otherwise, the offense for which the inmate had been on release was the current offense.

For an offender who had been sent to prison directly from court, and who had not been on any type of release at the time of sentencing for this offense, the current offense was the offense for which the inmate was sent to prison. This person was considered a new court commitment. For an offender who had been on some type of release at the time of sentencing but who had not been sentenced for a new offense, the current offense was the offense for which the person had been placed on release. As an example, consider an inmate who was on probation from court for burglary, who violated the terms of the probation, and who was sent to prison; the current offense was burglary.

For an offender who had been on some type of release and who had been sentenced for a new offense just prior to the current incarceration, the current offense was the new offense for which the person was sentenced. In the example presented above, if the inmate had not only violated the terms of the probation but had also been sentenced for robbery, the current offense would be robbery. The burglary, then would be the most recent prior offense. For each respondent, five current offenses were listed. Counts were considered as separate current offenses.

Other current offense variables included the sentence length imposed for the current crimes, and the estimated date and type of release the offender expected. For offenders who had more than one current offense, the offense with the longest sentence imposed was called the controlling offense. This offense was used in other sections of the questionnaire to focus attention on various activities that may have occurred in conjunction with this offense. For instance, information on drug and alcohol usage just prior to involvement in the current offense was geared to the controlling offense.

4.2.2 VICTIM-OFFENDER RELATIONSHIP

The purpose of this section was to obtain a profile of some basic characteristics of victims of violent offenses from the offender's perspective, just as the National Crime Survey (NCS) attempts to profile the characteristics of offenders from the victim's perspective.[15] Data on the victim-offender relationship were collected for offenders incarcerated for violent offenses only.[16] The rationale for this limitation was that it would be difficult to identify the victim for a property offense such as burglary. For this kind of offense, the offender might not have seen anyone at the place of the crime. Moreover, an insurance company might be considered the victim, as the company would have been forced to pay for the lost property. However, since a violent offense entails a face-to-face encounter between an offender and a victim, the offender would have a greater likelihood of confronting one or more victims directly.

4.2.3 Pre-Trial Experience

Pre-trial experience refers to an offender's criminal activities and involvement with the criminal justice system prior to and during the trial for the current offenses. Data were collected on the nature of pre-trial crimes, the type of pre-trial release, and jail time.

Since many jurisdictions release offenders prior to trial, there is the possibility that the offender will commit additional crimes before the trial is over. Thus, data on whether or not an offender had been involved in crimes while on release awaiting trial, and the nature of these crimes were obtained. However, since the Survey is limited to those who were incarcerated at the time of the interview, generalizations about the nature of pre-trial crime for all offenders are not possible.

The type of pre-trial release refers to whether the offender had been released on one's own recognizance, conditional release, bail, or any other type of pre-trial release. Within recent years, the use of bail has come under attack since those who are unable to raise the required amount of money, or other collateral, may be denied release. Thus, requiring excessive bail serves as a form of pre-trial detention for those unable to pay. The threat of pre-trial confinement may be used to coerce defendants into accepting guilty pleas or risk spending time prior to trial in jail (von Hirsch, 1976: 114). Advocates of pre-trial release contend that the use of bail poses an undue burden on indigent offenders, and should be reserved only for offenders who have committed heinous crimes.

Although the parameters of the Survey do not allow an in-depth study of the nature and extent of bail, the Survey provides an opportunity to examine the extent to which persons imprisoned for various types of offenses had been required to post bail, the amounts required, how much of the bail was returned, if any, whether they had been released on bail prior to trial, and if not, what factors precluded their release.

Data on the amount of time the offender served in jail prior to and during trial were obtained to assist in determining the total length of sentence imposed for the current offense.

4.2.4 Adjudication and Prior Criminal Record

Although the Survey is not designed to obtain information on the intricacies of the adjudication process for all offenders, data were collected on some of the key factors as they relate to the incarcerated population. These factors include whether legal counsel was appointed by the court or hired by the offender, whether the offender had pled guilty or was found guilty for the crimes charged, and whether the crimes charged differed from those for which the offender was incarcerated at the time of the interview.

Prior criminal record includes the inmate's offense history from the first arrest as a juvenile through the time of release for the most recent prior crime. Although for some research prior criminal record often encompasses arrests, convictions, and incarcerations, the Survey focused on incarceration history, partly because of limitations in the amount of information that can be asked in an interview, and partly because incarceration history would likely be recalled given the nature of the experience. Additional information on the number of prior probations both as a juvenile and as an adult, the age at first probation, and the offenses for the first probation were also collected.

4.3 Noncriminal Characteristics

Noncriminal characteristics refer to those factors other than an offender's criminal involvement that may be useful in describing the offender population, and in understanding the nature and extent of criminal involvement. These factors may be used in developing a profile of the entire prison population or subgroups of the population (i.e., those incarcerated for a single offense such as robbery or murder, or those incarcerated for a class of offenses, such as violent crimes, and career criminals). These factors include demographic characteristics, socioeconomic characteristics, military service, history of drug and alcohol use, and prison activities.

4.3.1 DEMOGRAPHIC AND SOCIOECONOMIC CHARACTERISTICS

Demographic characteristics include age, sex, race, ethnicity, date of birth, and marital status. Socioeconomic characteristics include education, employment immediately prior to incarceration, and family background.

Family background includes two separate elements: Information about the family from which the inmate came (i.e., parents and siblings), and information about the family with which the inmate was closely associated at the time of the interview (i.e., spouse, children.) With respect to the first element, the family from which the inmate came, there were three variables of interest: who the offender lived with most of the time while growing up, whether any other family members had been involved in the criminal justice process, and the inmate's relationship to those family members.

In terms of the second element, the family with which the inmate associates most closely at the time of the interview, there were seven variables of interest: whether the inmate had any children under age 18 at the time of the interview, the number and ages of such children, where these children had been placed during the inmate's incarceration, whether the inmate was living with them just prior to the current incarceration, whether the inmate retained legal custody of these children, and whether the inmate planned to live with these children after release.

Most of the previous research on inmates and children has focused on inmate-mothers (Baunach, 1985; Stanton, 1980; McGowan and Blumenthal, 1978; DuBose, 1974; Bonfanti, et al., 1974; Zalba, 1964), perhaps because child-rearing traditionally has been associated primarily with the role of women in our society. However, there are many fathers in prison as well. The data from the Survey provide a national overview of the extent to which inmates of both sexes are parents. These data will be useful in determining the need for resource allocation to develop parenting programs or programs to retain ties with children, and in estimating the numbers of children whose lives have been affected by their parent's incarceration.

4.3.2 MILITARY SERVICE

In 1979, roughly one-fourth of the inmates in state prisons were veterans. Of the approximately 65,500 veterans in prison, most had served in the Vietnam era (39,500); many had served in the pre-Vietnam era (19,500), and the least number had served after the Vietnam era (6,000) (Cantwell and Masamura, 1981: 1). Given the relatively large proportion of veterans in the 1979 inmate survey, the 1986 Survey collected information to update these data.

Variables of interest included whether the inmate had ever served in the service and in what branch, when the offender entered and was discharged, the type of discharge that was issued, whether the inmate had served in Southeast Asia, whether the offender had become dependent upon drugs while in the military service, and if so, on what type of drugs this dependency had developed.

4.3.3 ALCOHOL AND DRUG USE

At the present time, the nature of the relationship between alcohol consumption and criminal behavior is ambiguous (Collins, 1981). Yet there is a common sense assumption that intoxication may disinhibit an individual such that hostile propensities emerge, and that aggressive or criminal behavior may be ascribed to alcohol use.[17] In the 1979 Survey, the assessment of drinking habits among incarcerated inmates was determined based on three measures: the frequency of drinking during the year just before the current incarceration and just prior to the current offense, the amount of alcohol consumed at these times, and the inmate's perception of his level of intoxication after he had stopped drinking.[18]

The first two measures are closely akin to those developed by the National Institute on Alcohol Abuse and Alcoholism (NIAAA) to assess the quantity and frequency with which individuals consume alcohol. The index, called the Quantity-Frequency, Adjusted (QFA), combines measures of the frequency of consumption of a particular beverage over a given time period (usually thirty days), the typical quantity consumed on that day, and the number of days during a given time frame, usually a year, wherein a person has consumed large quantities of a beverage (i.e., twelve or more cans of beer at one time). The latter is usually referred to as binge drinking. The QFA provides a valid, reliable means of determining total volume of consumption that takes into account both average drinking and binge drinking over a specified time period (Armor and Pollich, 1982).[19]

The third measure used in the 1979 Survey attempted to assess heavy drinking by asking the inmates how drunk they felt after they had finished drinking.[20] Because of the importance of the role that alcohol consumption plays in criminal behavior, the 1986 Survey included questions to address the usual drinking habits of inmates over the year prior to incarceration, during the month surrounding the offense, and just prior to the crime itself. Variables of interest included the quantity of alcohol consumed during these periods, the frequency of alcohol consumption, the social context within which drinking occurred (i.e., alone or with others), and the age at first alcohol consumption. In addition, the Survey included questions regarding involvement in alcohol treatment programs prior to incarceration.

As with alcohol consumption, the known linkages between crime and drug use are tenuous at best, (Gettinger, 1979; Greene, 1981; Ball, et al., 1983; Anglin and Speckart, 1984; Johnson, et al., 1985; Watters, et al., 1985; and Gropper, 1985)[21] and there is little empirical research describing the history and characteristics of incarcerated drug users. The 1979 Survey included information on lifetime use of drugs, use of drugs during the month preceding the crime, and use of various types of drugs just prior to the offense.[22] The 1986 Survey included similar items.

4.3.4 PRISON ACTIVITIES

Prison activities include the programs and work assignments during incarceration. Variables of interest in the 1986 Survey included whether inmates had been involved in educational or vocational training programs since prison admission, the grade they had completed prior to incarceration, and whether they had a work assignment inside or outside the institution, the number of hours assigned to this work, and the nature of the remuneration received for their efforts. In addition, items regarding the number of inmates in a sleeping unit, and the number of hours inmates were allowed out of their sleeping quarters each week were included.

5. Limitations of the Data Sets

5.1 The Survey

Perhaps the most significant drawback to the Survey data is the limitation in the generalizability of the findings. Because the universe for the Survey includes only inmates incarcerated in state-operated prisons and community-based facilities, the data obtained from this Survey cannot be used to make generalizations about all offenders, or about any specific aspect of the criminal justice process. For instance, information about bail and about pre-trial crime may be generalized only to the adult inmate population in prisons.

A second limitation is the lack of sufficient data to address issues that relate to the causes of crime. Although socioeconomic characteristics as they relate to crime could be the basis for separate in-depth studies, the fact that the Survey covers only incarcerated individuals precludes analysis of these factors as they relate to the causes of crime. To obtain accurate and complete information to examine causal relationships requires much more data than the Survey can feasibly collect. For instance, to examine the relationships between economic status and involvement in crime would require an understanding of factors associated with the opportunity costs of crime (Sullivan, 1973). Since Survey resources do not permit a thorough examination of the records, interviews with staff, counselors, peers, and family members, this kind of analysis is impossible using Survey data.

A third limitation is the reliability of self-report data. Since the data collection relies on the recall of past events in inmates' lives, the extent of forgetting will influence the validity of the data. Related to this limitation is undetected interviewer error. Interviewers may, for instance, complete questionnaires incorrectly and not realize their mistakes. Despite rigorous editing procedures, some errors may slip by.[23] The extent of interviewer errors in the Survey has never been assessed.

5.2 The Census

The major difficulty with the Census data is the mode of data collection. Since data are collected through a mail survey, administrators in each facility complete the questionnaire independent of one another and of the Census staff. Thus, each administrator may interpret items differently and responses may inconsistently refer to different things, despite the fact that the questionnaire includes detailed definitions for many items. The principal check on the consistency of interpretation of the questionnaire items across facilities is done during the pretest. However, limited resources, restrict the pretest to only a handful of facilities.

A second limitation of the Census stems from the differential definitions of the universe used in the 1974 and subsequent Censuses. As noted previously, the 1974 Census used a jurisdictional approach, whereas the 1979 and 1984 Censuses employed a custody approach (see footnote #7). Given these differences, the nature of the population included in the Censuses varied between the 1974 Census and the other Censuses. Thus, comparisons of specific population-related data, such as inmate counts, is troublesome because of differences in who is being counted.

Related to this limitation is the differential inclusion of youthful offender facilities in the Census universe. The 1974 Census counted inmates in youthful offender facilities. However, these inmates were also included in the Children in Custody series, a biennial census of juvenile correctional, shelter, and detention facilities. Thus, in 1974 these inmates were counted twice. In the 1979 and 1984 Censuses, youthful offender facilities were excluded from the definition of the universe to eliminate double counting. Data analyses must therefore, take into account this differential inclusion of youthful offender facilities in determining such things as accurate counts for the 1974 as opposed to the other Censuses.

6. Utility of the Data Sets

6.1 The Survey

The data from previous Surveys have been used in a number of articles and reports. BJS has used these data to prepare reports on career patterns of criminal behavior, veterans in prison, and the drug and alcohol use of inmates. Others have used these data to profile drug histories and criminality (Barton, 1980; Piercy, 1984; Miller, 1984; Miller and Welte, 1987).

Given the wealth of information provided in the 1986 Survey, other reports could include:

- A profile of the demographic and criminal characteristics of inmates serving time for specific offenses, such as murder, robbery, or burglary.

- A retrospective recidivism study using prior criminal record data. This kind of study could estimate such factors as the nature and extent of the prior records for those incarcerated for violent as opposed to nonviolent crimes, and would shed some light on the development of varying criminal patterns among incarcerated offenders.

- An analysis of the changes in specific demographic and criminal characteristics of the inmate population since 1974, when the first Survey was first undertaken.

- An analysis of the similarities and differences in the characteristics of male and female inmates incarcerated for similar offenses, controlling for such factors as prior criminal record.

- A comparison of the victim's perceptions of the offender using data from the National Crime Survey with the offender's perceptions of the victim at roughly the same point in time.

- An assessment of the extent to which drug and/or alcohol use preceded criminal involvement for imprisoned inmates. Although it would not be possible to definitively answer the question of whether drug involvement or criminal involvement came first for all offenders, the Survey data provide an opportunity to consider the linkages between drugs and crime more closely for incarcerated persons.

6.2 The Census

As noted previously, Census data have been used in some descriptive BJS reports already. However, many additional analyses could be done. Since the Census includes all facilities nationwide, analyses may be done for a specific region (i.e., Northeast, Midwest, South and West), as well as for the nation as a whole. Particularly since the 1984 Census covered topics not included in previous Censuses, additional analyses could fruitfully yield many other reports.

For example, a trend analysis of population sizes and facility characteristics from 1974 to 1984 might be done. With a decade of data, analyses that are mindful of the variations in the definition of the universe among the Censuses, could provide useful profiles of population characteristics in State-operated community as compared with secure confinement correctional facilities over time.

A detailed examination of changes in capacity and confinement conditions from 1979 to 1984 must also be done. Using the initial BJS report on this topic as a starting point, a more thorough exploration of the changes could be undertaken.

A comparative study of the nature of programs in male, female, and coeducational State-operated community and secure correctional facilities could be undertaken. Since the 1984 Census includes the sex of inmates involved in various types of programs for each facility one question that may be addressed is whether both women and men in prison are afforded similar vocational programs, or whether women in prison still have access primarily to programs that emphasize the traditional "female role," such as cosmetology or secretarial skills.

Reported differences in the physical security level between State-operated community correctional facilities and secure confinement facilities might be examined. Questionnaires for both community-based and secure confinement facilities asked respondents to classify themselves as "maximum," "medium," or "minimum" security. Respondents were then asked about characteristics that may be related to these security level designations. One research question is to what extent facilities termed "community" corrections differ from secure confinement facilities in the presence and number of towers, the type of perimeter, the extent of patrols, the type of inmate housing, and the nature of surveillance and detection devices. One would expect community-oriented facilities to be more "open" than more secure confinement facilities.

Another issue that might be addressed is the characteristics of facilities that classify themselves as maximum, medium, or minimum security level. The question of interest in this kind of study would be the extent to which facilities that classify themselves as "maximum" security differ from their "medium" and "minimum" security counterparts on specific characteristics. That is, do those facilities that classify themselves as "maximum" security have more secure perimeters, more towers, more patrols, and more surveillance and detection devices than "medium" or minimum" security facilities, as one might expect?

A study of the relationship between the number and type of various kinds of incidents (i.e., riots, strikes) that occured during the period covered by the Census, and other facility characteristics, such as population size or density might be examined. One question of interest is whether more heavily populated facilities tend to have more incidents of certain types than less populated facilities.

The data also lend themselves to a detailed analysis of the characteristics of State-operated community corrections facilities. This study would be especially useful, since prisons are becoming increasingly crowded and the need for alternative housing sources continues to grow.

7. Summary

Data from the Census and Survey provide an underutilized source of information about the characteristics of incarcerated offenders and the facilities that house them. Despite some limitations in the data collection mechanism, the Census profiles every State-operated adult corrections facility nationwide and allows for detailed comparative analyses of State-operated community corrections facilities and secure confinement facilities on both a regional and national level that have yet to be undertaken. Similarly, despite its limitations, the Survey is the only comprehensive national periodic data collection effort of its kind, and provides a way to track the changing characteristics of inmates in this country.

As prison populations continue to swell, there will be a perennial need to understand the characteristics of both the correctional facilities and the inmates in them. The information from the Census could be instrumental in detecting deficiencies and in designing programs and facilities to house the burgeoning prison population. By the same token, the information from the Survey could be useful in understanding the demographic, social, and criminal characteristics of these inmates and in planning for the needs of the incarcerated population.

Part II

Measurement and Analysis

7

Using Archival Data for the Secondary Analysis of Criminal Justice Issues

Michael W. Traugott

The development of archives for computer-readable criminal justice data reflects the joint interests of individual criminal justice researchers and agencies of the federal government in pursuing empirically-based studies of crime and the criminal justice system while taking advantage of the availability of substantial data resources which have already been collected. Particularly where large, continuing federal data collections efforts are concerned, such as the National Crime Surveys (NCS) conducted by the Bureau of Justice Statistics (BJS) or the Uniform Crime Reports (UCR) prepared by the Federal Bureau of Investigation (FBI), the analysis which supports initial printed reports is usually quite limited statistically and conforms to a standardized presentation of information. By making these data available to other researchers, the return on the investment in data collection costs can be increased substantially at the same time that knowledge in criminal justice is expanded.

But the use of archival data is not without its pitfalls and potential problems. By definition, secondary analysis is conducted by individuals who were not part of the original research team. Without appropriate documentation, their initial absence may put them at a disadvantage with regard to matters of conceptualization and operationalization in the original research design; the ability to reproduce derived measures may also be severely limited. These problems obviously have consequences for the operationalization of new concepts as well. The successful use of archival data will therefore, be constrained by the degree to which documentation can provide important, if vicarious, links between secondary analysts and the principal investigator(s).

Nevertheless the potential clearly exists for the relatively rapid and cost-effective expansion of our understanding of crime and the criminal justice system through the use of archival data resources. This chapter reviews the general principles of secondary analysis and their application to criminal justice research; the problems of secondary analysis and the ways in which they can be addressed by social science data archives; and notes specific examples of the potential applications of three large-scale criminal justice data bases.

1. The Principles of Secondary Analysis

Secondary analysis is sometimes referred to as "extended" analysis because it involves the use of data to conduct research beyond the theoretical or analytical goals and interests of the original principal investigator(s). An original research project is one whose development includes a data collection activity designed to generate information to produce estimates of a given level of precision, to test specific hypotheses, or to replicate the findings from one research context in another. Even as these goals are accomplished, the resulting data may lend themselves to other analyses which were never anticipated by the original researchers. A secondary analysis effort may arise because a researcher has a different set of theoretical interests or reconceptualizes the problem. Or it may result from the accumulation of data in an archive. Multiple datasets, each originally collected for a different purpose, may take on new analytical utility based upon their possible combinations or a series of complementary analyses which none of the principal investigators could have contemplated.

The potential value of secondary analysis can be seen in both the scientific and administrative goals which may be achieved. Each of these goals in turn encompasses a set of principles which can be met through the use of archival resources in secondary analysis. From the scientific perspective, these principles include replication, the development and inculcation of data sharing as a norm, and the ability to analyze data of such high quality and complexity that it is unlikely that most individual researchers (if any) would have been able to collect them on their own. From an administrative perspective, the principles include recapturing some of the substantial initial investment in data collection which is involved in many large data bases, making resources available to multiple analysts at very low costs, and the potential to stimulate research in selected areas by making appropriate resources available for secondary analysis.

1.1 A Scientific Perspective

Perhaps the greatest scientific value of secondary analysis lies in the potential for one set of researchers to replicate the findings of another. Our confidence in the validity of a relationship increases as it can successively be reproduced in a variety of settings. As a fundamental condition, the original analysis should be reproducible, although this is sometimes a more complicated task than it appears to be at first glance, especially when the calculation of complicated derived measures is involved (Schneider, et al., 1986). In a limited number of cases, attempts at replication may indicate a fundamental flaw in the original analysis, particularly with regard to the possible spurious nature of a relationship after appropriate controls are applied (see Hirsch, 1980, commenting on Gerbner and Gross, 1976, and Gerbner, et al., 1978, for example).

Replications can only be pursued, however, when the original data are made available for secondary analysis. Ideally data should be made available in a timely manner. When the principal investigator is in fact a government agency which sponsored the data collection and preliminary analysis, data availability generally has not been a problem. The interest and support of the BJS and the National Institute of Justice (NIJ) for data archiving is one indication of their appreciation of this value.

Obtaining data from individual principal investigators is frequently more problematic. However, the norm of data sharing is more widely held in the social sciences for a number of reasons (Fienberg, Martin and Straf, 1985). Many more researchers have, themselves, become secondary analysts in the last several years; their use of archival data inevitably increases a sense of the value of sharing data. Federal agencies have encouraged their grantees to archive their data and have developed formal mechanisms to ensure that data are archived.[1] And many journals have adopted editorial policies which require that data on which published manuscripts are based be made available for secondary analysis as well.[2]

For many users of archival data, the available resources represent data of high quality and reflect a level of complexity commensurate with their research interests. These data would not have been available if archive users had to write a proposal themselves to secure funds for data collection. Through the archives researchers have access to data from projects for which they could not have been the principal investigator, because resources are too limited to support multiple data collections on a grand scale, or because the data collection activity was so complex that it involved an administrative operation of its own at one or more agencies. The NCS represent one of the clearest examples of such a data collection effort. This complex and expensive national project involves collaboration between the staffs of BJS and the Bureau of the Census. While no individual researcher could hope to organize and implement such a massive project alone, hundreds of researchers have access to these data for analysis.

1.2 An Administrative Perspective

The most important administrative value of secondary analysis is that it provides a mechanism for recapturing what is frequently a substantial investment in original data collection costs. This principle is especially important when one takes into account the limited analyses of many data collection efforts designed to accomplish limited goals. Data collection efforts such as the NCS, which were designed to generate relatively simple but necessarily precise estimates of the incidence of victimization, for example, will support many other types of analysis.

Sometimes there is a charge for purchasing a copy of a data set from the principal investigator or the agency responsible for the data collection. Data archives sometimes function as a form of "buyers cooperative" in that they pay the initial costs of data acquisition and amortize these costs across multiple secondary analysts. This process results in more data becoming available at lower cost to more researchers. In the case of the National Criminal Justice Data Archive, for example, the archival acquisition costs are covered by grant funds or waived by BJS, reducing the effective user costs to nothing. On the dissemination side, a variety of mechanisms and associated charging algorithms can be employed to cover the costs of duplicating data and documentation, and the costs to data analysts can be reduced substantially as well.[3]

When appropriate data resources are available to support a secondary analysis project, they can be made available on a much more timely basis than would be the case if the researcher were to start from scratch to design a project and collect the data. While not all research projects can be conducted with archival data and the problems of operationalization and conceptualization may sometimes be severe, those whose needs can be met with this type of resource can usually begin data analysis within a month after selecting their datasets. This time lag results in a substantial cost reduction in terms of the researcher's time and may be particularly important for policy-related research.

As archival resources accumulate, they can provide a core of data upon which substantive areas can build (Miller, 1976). Such data lead to a convergence in measurement and conceptualization which may permit increasing attention to analytical issues. At the same time, such developments may lead to the stimulation of research in other areas as more data resources become available or as agencies support programs of secondary analysis.[4] In either case, the administrative convenience associated with secondary analysis can have a direct impact on the direction which research takes in specific fields.

2. The Problems of Secondary Analysis

There are several factors which complicate the use of archival data. These factors include issues of conceptualization and measurement which derive from not being part of the original research team, and issues related to possible technical problems associated with working in a different computing environment than the data supplier. This first set of problems must be dealt with through appropriate documentation, or codebooks, for the data sets. The second set of issues depends upon the technical versatility and flexibility of the organization which disseminates the data.

2.1 Documentation

By definition, secondary analysts did not participate in the original research design, data collection activity, or statistical manipulation of the resulting information. They did not contribute to decisions about hypotheses to be tested or matters of conceptualization or operationalization. In one sense, then, these issues have to be taken as "givens" in extended analysis of the data set. But potential problems can be minimized if appropriate documentation can be prepared and disseminated with the data to describe the initial decision-making process as well as its results. High quality documentation is a critical precondition for successful secondary analysis.

The codebook must contain a careful presentation of documentation. In addition to appropriate descriptions of each variable, the codebook must adequately describe the study design and essential elements of the original data collection and processing procedures. The description of the study design includes the conceptual or theoretical genesis of the study, basic decisions about which concepts were to be employed and the intended units of analysis. In many cases, this description covers the sampling frame and the sampling design. When field procedures were involved, the codebook should further provide a description of interviewing or data transcription techniques, data preparation, and editing procedures.

Beyond the manipulation of the basic elements of the data collection, most analyses will involve the computation or calculation of derived measures. These may include recodes of individual variables or combinations of variables into indexes or scales. In the criminal justice area, many seemingly simple concepts are subject to quite different operationalizations. A concept such as "risk" or "exposure to crime" can be constructed in a number of alternative ways which take into account life styles, personal characteristics and place of residence. Unless a detailed description is available of which variables were used in what combination, there is little, if any, utility to a measure described simply as a "Risk Index."

2.2 Technical Considerations

The range of potential technical obstacles to data sharing arises from two sources (Clubb, et al., 1985). The first source is the use of increasingly complex research designs and associated data structures to reflect more accurately the real-world environment in which social problems and policies are studied. The second source is the ability of the disseminator of the data to provide information which can be employed in a variety of technical environments which differ from those in which the data were originally processed. Because of differences in both software and hardware options which are currently available, analytical flexibility must be preserved by disseminating data in a wide variety of technical formats.

On the matter of data structures, we have moved quite a distance from a technological stage when simple rectangular data files were used to store information in a common format. Each variable was located in the same place in each unit of analysis. In the NCS, for example, information is collected in a panel study about individuals who are twelve years of age or older in a representative national sample of households. The data collection includes information about the characteristics of the household in which they live, about themselves and about any incidents of certain types of victimization which may have occurred in the previous six months. Households will obviously vary in their composition and the number of persons about which information will be collected. Incidents of victimization will occur with varying frequency as well. As a result, there is an implicit hierarchical structure to the data collection which can be reflected in the techniques for storing the data, if appropriate software is available. In such a format each household record (of one fixed format accommodating data content) is followed by as many person records as appropriate for the household (in a second fixed format), each of which is in turn followed by as many incident records as appropriate (in a third fixed format). In smaller data files, the difference in storage requirements for this hierarchical structure—rather than a fully "padded" fixed format structure—might be marginal. But the NCS involves the collection of interviews with approximately 20,000 households per month, so the savings in storage and associated data manipulation costs are significant.

Even more importantly, however, the NCS structure lends itself to alternative analyses based upon different conceptualizations of populations of inference or of events. Some researchers will want to analyze the data by households (touched by crime) while others will want to look at individuals. And some will want to compute rates of victimization for various crimes while others will only want to look at victims. In order to accommodate these different interests, then, analytical software must also be capable of extracting appropriate subsets of the basic data files in the required alternative units of analysis. This sensitivity to software issues will preserve the maximum amount of flexibility for data analysts while balancing the costs of data storage and the required retrievals.

At the same time, provisions must be made to distribute the data to individual researchers who are working in technical environments which involve a wide variety of software and hardware alternatives. Analysis cannot be limited to those who function in a technical environment which corresponds exactly to that in which the data were originally processed and analyzed. Thus, the organizations or operations that are responsible for data dissemination must have the flexibility to distribute the data in a number of alternative forms. This flexibility includes sending out full copies of data files as they are prepared by the principal investigator or the sponsoring agency, or creating customized subsets or extracts of the data to satisfy the secondary analyst's needs. Satisfying these needs may involve retrieving selected variables, cases or both, according to specifications. Most data files are distributed on magnetic tape and shipped through the mails; but some analysts may require information on floppy diskettes as the storage medium. And still others may be best served by accessing the data remotely in order to take advantage of the technical facilities—both hardware and software—of the organization disseminating the data.

For all of these reasons, social science data archives have come to play an increasingly important role in providing services to secondary analysts of criminal justice data. These archives operate on the basis of preparing "readily usable" data which are appropriately documented and can be supplied in a number of technically usable formats. In some cases they even provide for remote access to the data, so that software and hardware which are not available at a local site can be employed in the management and analysis of the data files. It is also common for archives to provide a number of aids for locating appropriate data sets—or even variables within data sets—for secondary analysis.[5] The advent and development of secondary analysis in the criminal justice field, especially when very large data bases are involved, has been substantially promoted through the use of social science data archives.

3. Examples of Archival Holdings of Large-scale Criminal Justice Datasets

Several of the essays in this volume describe the research designs which currently underlie the major large-scale criminal justice data sets and the developmental work which is underway to improve their analytic potential. And there is substantial content devoted to the publications' series which are generated by the research staffs at the BJS and the FBI which contain the initial analysis of the data collections. Other chapters review the current research interests of many secondary analysts using these same data files. The purpose of this section is to describe the technical characteristics of three major criminal justice data collections and the special files which have been prepared from them by the National Criminal Justice Data Archive for use in extended analysis. These three data collection efforts include the National Jail Census, the UCR, and the NCS.

3.1 The National Jail Census

The National Jail Census is one of the central data collection activities of the National Prisoner Statistics Program at the BJS. It and the National Prison Census comprise the major quinquennial efforts to obtain information about correctional confinement facilities in the United States. With the current interest in prison overcrowding, increasing attention in the data collection activity has been devoted to obtaining information which can be used to describe space allocations for inmates in each facility.

The latest available public use data file contains information from the 1983 National Jail Census, which covered 3,338 facilities. Because there is one record per institution, the data are available in a fixed format record containing 452 variables for each facility. This is a relatively small data matrix by most standards, and therefore no special extracts or subsets of the data set have been routinely prepared in anticipation of special analytical needs.

The basic information about each facility is divided into ten sets of variables. These include data which identify the facility (19 variables) and describe the detention authority (20 variables), its capacity (7 variables), building and/or renovation plans (16 variables), inmate population (91 variables), program (7 variables), confinement space (201 variables), personnel (42 variables), expenditures (11 variables) and health and safety matters (38 variables).

The documentation for this data file contains all of the essential elements which a secondary analyst needs to understand the genesis of the data. In addition to a description of the study design, documentation includes copies of the data collection instruments and editing procedures, a description of the imputation techniques which were used to deal with missing data, and for each variable, either a set of frequencies or summary statistics which provide the secondary analyst with information about its basic distributional properties.

3.2 The Uniform Crime Reports Collection

This data collection actually consists of three types of data which are supplied by local police agencies to the FBI. The FBI in turn processes and edits these data for publication in its series Crime in the United States. The FBI releases public use versions of its basic data files, but they are difficult to work with technically and cannot be used in a straightforward fashion to reproduce the published crime counts (Schneider and Wiersema, 1985). This difficulty is partially a function of estimation procedures used by the FBI to impute unreported crimes as well as editing and correction procedures which are applied to the published reports but not necessarily to the base data files.

There are approximately 16,000 reporting agencies which voluntarily file three reports with the FBI on a monthly basis. These cover information on offenses known (or reported crimes), property stolen, and law enforcement officers killed or assaulted. Because the filings are extensive but incomplete both by agency and calendar month, the data are processed by the FBI and distributed in a hierarchical form. There is limited information about the agency itself and then up to twelve monthly reports for each on offenses known, property stolen and police employees killed or assaulted. Conceptually each annual file contains more than half a million records (16,000 agencies submitted three reporting forms for each of twelve months). The archive has been processing two years of UCR data during each of its recent annual grant periods, adding the most recent year available from the FBI and the one preceding the current collection in each cycle. Data are currently being disseminated for the period from 1976 to 1986, with the data for 1975 and 1987 forthcoming. The amount of information available for each agency in any given year is quite substantial as well. There are approximately 2,900 variables in three groupings for the data on known offenses, about 1,130 variables for the reports of stolen property and about 2,250 variables related to law enforcement officers killed or assaulted.

For these basic elements of the UCR collection, the archive has prepared a set of standardized data files which involve the equivalent of a rectangularization and subsetting of the FBI files. Based upon its early experience in disseminating various versions of the UCR data and in consultation with a project advisory committee, these versions of the data were created with an eye toward the most common and standard analytical uses which have been made of the data. A fixed format version of the data on offenses known has been created with the agency as the unit of analysis, for example, with the data for each month arrayed in chronological order and annual totals calculated from the monthly reports. These totals sometimes do not correspond to the published data, for the editing and imputation reasons cited above.

The documentation for the UCR collection now incorporates a guide to use of the data as well as the standard elements of a codebook. In addition to the description of the data collection procedures and the characteristics of each variable, text has been added to the codebook which describes the imputation procedures used by the FBI in the preparation of Crime in the United States. The purpose is to anticipate questions about the slight discrepancies which will appear periodically in the computer-readable versions of the data files compared to the published reports, as well as to provide some insight into the use of the data by the FBI in its publications.

3.3 The National Crime Surveys

This data collection series represents the focal point of BJS analytic efforts for the last fifteen years. The basic national surveys have been conducted since 1972 on a monthly basis, but the data are distributed by BJS through the National Criminal Justice Data Archive in collection quarters comprising the four contiguous three-month periods of a calendar year. These data are to be distinguished from a "full file" for a twelve-month period, which actually consists of six collection quarters. This organization takes into account the six-month reference period which each respondent is asked to use in recalling incidents of criminal victimization which they have experienced.

The structure of the basic file is hierarchical as described above, with information on the characteristics of the household (consisting of 103 variables) followed by as many person records as appropriate (each consisting of 43 variables), followed by a number of incident records as appropriate (each consisting of 201 variables). In a typical collection quarter there will be interviews with approximately 35,000 households, comprised of approximately 65,000 persons age twelve or older, with about 8,000 reported incidents of victimization in this period. This form of the data is appropriate for analyzing households touched by crime, persons and incidents when data analysis and management software is available which deals with hierarchically structured data.

But this structure itself, however, is not conducive to other important conceptual approaches to the data. For example, there is no straightforward way in which rates of victimization can be computed from these data files based upon numerators consisting of counts of victims and denominators consisting of relevant population counts. As a result, the National Criminal Justice Data Archive routinely creates an incident level extract file for each calendar year. Here the unit of analysis is a reported incident organized in a fixed format record with the appropriate characteristics of the victim and the household in which the respondent resides. There are approximately 32,000 such records in an annual file, each composed of 347 variables describing the incident, person and household characteristics.

Even this file is not appropriate for the study of victims, as it contains multiple incidents associated with a limited number of individuals. As a result the archive routinely prepares a second special subset called the person-level file. This file consists of a fixed format data record comprised of 935 variables containing information about the person, the household in which they reside, and up to four incidents of victimization.[6] Prepared on a quarterly basis, the units of analysis consists of data for every victim and a sample of one-in-ten of the nonvictims. This file is appropriate for the analysis of either victims or incidents of personal victimization, taking serial victimization control into account.

Because of the close collaboration of the archive, the staff at BJS, and the people at the Bureau of the Census who supervise the data collection work, the documentation for the NCS is very complete. BJS has also conducted an on-going program of methodological studies of the NCS, and the results of this effort have contributed to our knowledge of the analytical strengths and limitations of the data.

As a result of this methodological emphasis, the basic survey instrument for the NCS has undergone some changes, and data are now being released going back to 1979 in the so-called "new format." These changes, all of which are documented in the codebooks distributed by the archive with the data, include revisions in the computation of certain derived measures, such as the type of crime involved in each incident, well as changes in the structure and content of the questionnaire. Ancillary data collections on which the methodological research has been based will be publicly available. To date this means information from the victim risk supplement study conducted in February, 1984, but this component of the collection will eventually include the major studies of the use of telephone survey techniques and the redesign of the sample and the questionnaire. These data sets will provide important information about the meaning of the respondents' survey replies, in conceptual as well as methodological terms, and will be useful in assessing a variety of potential measurement errors associated with current data collection efforts.

4. Summary

This chapter has described the value of secondary analysis for research on crime and criminal justice issues, as well as important contributions which social science data archives can make in disseminating such data and facilitating their use. Three specific examples of large-scale criminal justice data bases were cited to show how archival activity enhances the basic data products prepared and distributed by major federal agencies involved in original data collection activities. Such large-scale criminal justice data bases would not be possible without the cooperation and assistance of the federal agencies; their interest in these efforts reflects their desire to increase the use of these data that are expensive and time consuming to collect.

Archival data provide an efficient, cost effective and timely way for criminal justice researchers to pursue important theoretical and policy-related questions about crime and criminal justice issues. More researchers are working with better data than would be available if they had to organize and administer their own data collection projects. And they are devoting more of their effort to analysis than to the necessarily time-consuming administrative tasks associated with managing large-scale data collection projects. While due care must be taken in reviewing the principal investigator's decisions about conceptualization and operationalization, secondary analysis has increased research opportunities and, hence, has resulted in an extension of our understanding of the criminal justice process.

8

The Use of Microcomputers with Large Data Bases

Edgar Barry Moser

The great advances made in microcomputer technology have put tremendous, affordable computing power in the hands of almost everyone. In fact, most data analysts have access to one or more microcomputers. It is very common to find systems with 640K (kilobytes or thousands of bytes) of main memory, 20 megabytes of on-line hard disk storage and capable of executing millions of instructions per second. Their interactive operating systems and software, and instantaneous feedback for most operations makes them suitable for word processing, spreadsheet computations, sophisticated graphics modeling, games, and data base management. It is reasonable to assume that much of the data and statistical analyses performed on mainframes today will be relegated to microcomputers, while new data intensive and Monte Carlo methods (See Efron, 1979) will become popular on mainframes as their capabilities increase. Thus the microcomputer user will need access to standard data bases that were once only in the domain of mainframes. Specifically, much of the large-scale efforts to measure crime based on the large criminal and demographic data bases will be moved to the realm of the microcomputer.

This chapter will examine the capabilities of microcomputers for handling large data bases, as well as many of the issues in dealing with large data bases on a microcomputer system. Reference will be made to the popular literature for articles dealing with data base evaluations and reviews and discussion of data base issues. Many reviews, articles and advertisements pertaining to microcomputer data base and analysis software can be found in *Byte, PC Magazine, PC World, Personal Computing, Computer Language, InfoWorld* and many others.[1] The number of data base software vendors is so large and upgrades to software occur so rapidly that even the latest reviews in these references are often outdated by publication time. The mention of a specific software or hardware product is for example only and not intended as an endorsement of the product. Readers interested in the more technical aspects of data bases should consult a reference such as Date (1981).

1. Microcomputer Systems and Capabilities

Before examining the specifics of data bases and data management on a microcomputer it is important to discuss the capabilities and limitations of using microcomputers for managing large amounts of data.

1.1 On-line storage capabilities

The first limiting factor is the amount of on-line storage available for storing a large data base. Many microcomputers are now equipped with at least 10M (megabytes or millions of bytes) of hard disk storage and so are able to store approximately 10 million characters of information. One alphanumeric character can be stored as one byte of information, a byte consisting of eight bits or binary digits. A document of 2,500 pages averaging 4,000 characters per page could be stored on this disk.

The amount of on-line storage is becoming less of a concern now since hard disks of 120M and larger are available and those of 20M, 30M, 70M and even 110M are standard on some models. The new compact disk (CD) technology permitting read-only access (ROM) can hold over 600M of data for microcomputer access. One advantage to the CD ROM is that it is a "removable" medium, that is, many of them may be used by a single CD reader. Some of the magnetic "hard disks" also have a removable storage medium permitting disks or cartridges to be swapped. Obviously this is a desirable characteristic for large data base users. Not all data bases and software would need to be kept on the same storage device but could be inserted when needed. Further, the standard, large capacity half-inch 9-track magnetic tapes of mini- and mainframe computers can be used directly by microcomputers with appropriate tape drives.

To relate microcomputer storage to the traditional mainframe on-line disk or DASD (Direct Access Storage Device) storage that is often used to store data bases, a single IBM 3350 disk pack, a type of hard disk, can store up to about 303M per pack, while a 3380 disk pack can store about twice this amount. Thus the CD ROM technology permits a microcomputer to access the same amount of data as that stored by a conventional mainframe storage device. The difference is that the CD is read-only and may not be altered whereas the disk packs may be rewritten with other data bases and information. To further illustrate the data storage capability of microcomputers, assume that a selected study containing 16,413 observations from the Uniform Crime Report (UCR) data base is to be stored on a microcomputer storage device. Each observation is composed of 2,015 characters of information. Since each observation requires 2,015 bytes or characters, a minimum of 31.6M of hard disk storage will be required and is well within the range of commonly used microcomputer storage devices.

1.2 Processing speeds

Another important factor pertaining to the on-line storage is the time required to read and write large quantities of data to these devices. For example, the time required by the IBM AT^2 microcomputer to read all of the characters stored on a 20M hard disk in 2K blocks without examining the characters was about five minutes. An application program would be required to examine the data for the requested information resulting in greater access times. Consider again data bases stored on the large capacity CD ROM. The current CD readers are about five to ten times slower than conventional hard disk drives. To speed access on the CD drives requires a hierarchical data base structure with data base keys stored in the computer memory and random access data retrieval. This requires microcomputers with large memories and processing speeds. Fortunately, most large data bases stored on microcomputers will not be of this magnitude so that conventional strategies may often be used. Additionally, statistical analysis may consist of analyzing contingency tables, for example, that can be constructed from the large cumbersome data base and then stored for all future analysis without need to reread the large data base. It is obvious, however, that the microcomputer database software must be very efficient when working with a large data base.

Hard copies, in the form of a computer printout, are often needed as backups of the data base as well as for reporting purposes. Most microcomputers are attached to printers delivering no more than 200 characters per second (cps) maximum throughput and some are much slower than this. Operating at 200 cps, a two-page report would require about one minute to print. Listings of large data bases could easily take hours. Fortunately, print spooling utilities can print files while simultaneously permitting the microcomputer to be used for other tasks, such as editing or analyzing the data base. Alternatively, spool buffers that attach between the computer and the printer can be used to store the large amounts of data to be printed, freeing the computer from waiting for the printer and allowing the computer to deliver the data to the printer at its maximum rate. Advances in hardware are ever increasing the speed and print capabilities of printers, especially of laser printers. Laser printers can print from six to ten pages per minute and have the ability to produce graphics as well as text output (McCown and Clark, 1987). These are now comparable in price to many of the dot matrix-type printers.

Processing speed and RAM storage are also important concerns when working with large data bases on microcomputers. The amount of random access memory, or RAM, accessible by the new microcomputers exceeds that of mainframe computers of only a few years ago with many of today's microcomputers accessing 16M or more of RAM memory. Microcomputer software has generally lagged far behind the advancements made with hardware. So although the computer may have a large amount of memory, the software may be limited in its ability to use it. It should not be long before operating systems will use all available memory, and like many mainframe computers, will be able to work with virtual memory or RAM memory simulated with a hard disk.

To elaborate on the developments in microprocessor technology, consider the evolution of the IBM microcomputer line. When the IBM PC was first released, the Intel 8088 microprocessor that it contained operated at 4.77MHz and it communicated with the RAM through an eight-bit data bus, that is, it could access only eight bits or one byte for each memory read or write operation. The IBM PC/AT uses an Intel 80286 microprocessor running at 8MHz and communicates with the RAM using a 16-bit data bus or two bytes at a time. The IBM Personal System/2 model 80 contains an Intel 80386 microprossor operating at 20MHz with a 32-bit data bus. Similar or greater advances have been made by other microcomputer producers. The Apple Macintosh SE uses a Motorola MC68000 16-bit microprocessor operating at approximately 8MHz while the Apple Macintosh II uses a 16MHz MC68020 32-bit microprocessor. This is a far cry from the popular Apple II microcomputer that started much of the personal computer revolution. IBM PC compatibles, clones, add-on boards and hardware modifications to existing machines, make available speeds in excess of 16MHz. Other microcomputers and several of the computers-on-a-board that attach to existing machines, have speeds comparable to that of a VAX 11/780 minicomputer (Marshall, Jones and Kluger, 1986) and communicate with the RAM, four bytes (32 bits) per access. In fact, many of the newer minicomputers are housed in units that look very much like microcomputers.

2. Data Base Terminology

A data base is usually stored in the form of a file or set of files. A file has a name associated with it and this name is kept in the disk catalog directory. A file is usually composed of records of the same type. A record is also referred to as an observation or case, and is composed of fields that identify the specific data. For example, a record might be the information about a specific person whereas the fields would be that individual's name, birth date, sex, and height. A collection of data about several individuals would be stored together as a file.

The data types that the data base software supports is also important. The most common type is character data. The other common type would be the numeric type. Numbers could be split into integers or whole numbers (numbers without fractional parts) and real or floating point numbers. Some data bases have separate types for each, while others treat all numbers as of the real type. Numeric data are usually stored using a binary number format which results in a constant number of bytes needed regardless of the value of the number. Integers are usually restricted to the word size of the microprocessor, the number of bits that can be processed in memory at once by the microprocessor, often two or four bytes. Floating point numbers are often stored as four or eight bytes depending upon the precision required, single or double. Numbers can also be stored as character data but must be converted to the specific machine format for numbers if arithmetic operations are to be performed using them. Other types include Boolean (Logical or true-false) and date and time. The date and time types can be important if time series analysis are to be performed on the data or if the data are to be sorted by dates. One would want August 1 to be one day later than July 31 of the same year. Alphabetic sorting may not guarantee this order, while date types will store the dates so that this proper order is maintained.

The other major terminology associated with microcomputer data bases concerns the structure and linking of related files. A flat file data base is composed of one file, usually of only one record type. A simple example would be the listings in a phone book. The UCR data base would be another example of a flat file. All of the information specific to a record is recorded as a single observation. One data base access can retrieve all of this information.

A relational data base on the other hand links two or more files by a common field or fields called an index. This permits hierarchical data bases as well as permitting the simultaneous use of more than one data base. A search could be performed on one of the data bases while the information displayed for the located record could come from the other data bases depending upon the indexed fields. The data from the National Crime Surveys (NCS) available from the Inter-University Consortium for Political and Social Research (ICPSR) are maintained in an hierarchical data base. Here, more than one data base access is required to retrieve all of the information associated with a specific person-record since all of the information for the record is not stored together. This can actually result in a very efficient data base as few records need to be processed at higher levels in the hierarchy to locate specific records lower in the hierarchy. Furthermore, less storage space is required because considerable duplication of information can be avoided. For example, the household information for several persons within a household need not be included for each person. Rather, the household information is stored only once along with a pointer to the several person-records of the household. If the data are moved to a microcomputer, it is likely that this structure will be important to maintain on the microcomputer. Indexing would be the method of maintaining this structure and for these data could link person records with their household records.

3. Data Base Software

Our attention now turns to a discussion of the requirements and needs that should be incorporated into microcomputer data base software.

3.1 Data Management and Storage

The primary consideration of the data base software is its ability to store and manage the data that is to be placed within it. Many of the data base programs have limitations on the sizes of records, the number of fields per record, the field sizes and the number of records per file. In addition, some will only permit use of one file at a time. Others require that the entire data base be loaded into RAM while in use. This greatly limits the amount of data that can be stored but these data bases tend to be very fast since no disk access is required for searching and sorting. For text or character data, a field size restriction of 80 characters might be unreasonable unless the use of multiple 80 character fields is acceptable. A data base with some size restrictions, however, might be more efficient, i.e., faster search and sort times, than an unrestricted data base because the additional overhead required for handling unlimited records is absent. In addition, some data bases support the attachment of notes or pages of text to specific records in the data base. These are usually stored in separate files and do not slow the searching and sorting of the data base. Data base software should not be overlooked solely because it has restrictions placed on its structure, as many of the restrictions would not limit most data base users and usually make the software more efficient.

If data are to be entered using the microcomputer, the ability to restrict input to specific values, a range of values, or to a specific format can help reduce entry errors. Some systems require that specified fields be validated through reentry of the data and non-matches require the user to begin the entry process anew. If a field has been assigned for phone numbers, then the data base could require entries in a phone number-like format for the field and not allow further entry until the requirement is met. The ability to specify field default values, for previous values to carry over, or the ability to use look up tables are desirable features. Many times the data are similar over several fields so data input can be speeded greatly by not having to reenter these fields for each record.

It can be very important for a data base to support a diversity of data types. This can additionally be used to partially validate data entry by restricting entries to only the specified data type. In some instances, only incomplete information will be available for a record. In these cases, provisions for missing data must be made. Some data bases handle this simply by leaving the fields blank while others may require a special missing value code.

Since an interactive microcomputer is used, the software should be user friendly. Some products support on-line help and tutorials, pull-down menus from which choices are selected, menu-driven actions and queries, windowing for viewing different parts of the data base simultaneously, intelligent interfaces for aiding the user, and the ability to recall previous commands in the event that syntax or logical errors are made in using the data base. The ability to create macros that can be invoked by a single command to perform multiple commands can make the data base easy to use. Some software can be written into a turnkey system whereby the specific data base application is automatically executed when the system is invoked. The actual user of the software may not even know what data base software is being used.

For large data bases, the ability to restructure the data base without intricate procedures or without reentering the data is desirable. Transformations of data may be required for analysis purposes. Can the data be transformed at a later time? Can new transformed variables be created? If additional data becomes available, can it be added by requesting more fields? For example, an analysis of the number of felony crimes for cities might be desired using the UCR data base. If the analysis is to be detailed, then a felony field might be added to the data base rather than computing this value for each analysis. The tradeoffs of storage space, input speed and speed of calculations would need to be analyzed before making the decision.

For hierarchical data bases the ability to index on more than one field is important. For many surveys, the data are collected using an hierarchical sampling scheme. The data could be stored using this structure by indexing the files on the hierarchies. Again, the NCS data base is stored in this manner.

Many data base systems come with their own programming language. This is especially advantageous if turnkey systems are to be developed, or if involved analysis and queries are to be performed on the data. In addition, several have interfaces to other high-level languages such as Pascal, C, Cobol, Prolog and Basic. Other ways of making the data base accessible to other software is the ability of the data base software to read and write ASCII text files and DIF files. An ASCII file consists of data stored in a human-readable form. Many data bases, word processors and statistical programs store data in their own special data formats that make data retrieval faster for the software.

However, these individual formats may differ so that one program may not be able to read a data file of another program. To avoid this problem, the DIF or Data Interchange Format standard was created so that a standard data file could be written by one program and retrieved by another. Most data base and data analysis software can read one of these formats. The ability to read or generate ASCII text files is also important for those users that may download or upload data from a host mainframe computer to the microcomputer. With the great number of systems linking mainframe computers around the world, ICPSR or other information managers may distribute information to microomputer users through these links or networks. For example, a user may request information through a link. The information agency would then process the request extracting only the information requested from a very large data base, and then send the data back to the microcomputer user through the link. This could all take place within a single day. Obviously, security procedures would need to be operational but the ability to transfer information in this manner is in place. There would be no waiting for tapes or other hard media for the distribution of information. One such network linking most major universities in the U.S. and many abroad is the BITNET network.

Good data base software should include powerful report generation capabilities. Some software permits the user to "paint," or position by the use of the cursor, the actual phrases and positions of the text and output on the CRT as it is to appear on the report. The report forms can be quickly modified and can be designed to work with preprinted forms. Other programs are, however, quite rigid in their report generation capacities by only permitting, for example, a column-style listing of the data with possible summaries. Many are intermediate, giving limited report generation capability through report commands but permitting flexible formats for those with programming skills. Some also permit easy generation of mailing labels.

3.2 User Interfaces

The most recent development in microcomputer data base software is the incorporation of natural language and expert systems into their user interfaces (Aarons, 1986; Baran, 1986). These artificial intelligence products have been around for quite a while, but they usually require fast processors to make them viable for interactive systems. The increased speed of microprocessors has made them reasonable additions to the software. Rather than require a rigid syntax for using and consulting the data base, the user can use his native language in issuing commands and in some instances can "teach" the program how to respond to specific questions. These programs are therefore easier to use by non-programmers. Additionally, some of these systems can train the user in how to use the software and how to find the information requested. Other programs are making use of artificial intelligence to speed the processing of the data base by selecting optimal paths for solving the requested problem, thus making for very efficient processing. For example, if you wanted to process the NCS data base in the order of the number of individuals in households, the complete data base could be read in and sorted, or, alternatively, only the household records would be sorted, and then the person-records read in, according to the new household order. The AI interface would be able to select the most efficient solution. There are also "intelligent" program generators that use artificial intelligence concepts to help the user write a data base program using simple and nontechnical language. The program itself generates or writes the actual code or programming statements used by the data base software.

3.3 Data Recovery

Another very important consideration in selecting software is how the software recovers, if it does at all, from power failures and program interruptions. Some data bases can easily recover from interruptions with minimal, if any, loss of data. If the data base is kept entirely or partially in RAM, then interruptions can be disastrous with complete loss of data. Even with disk-based systems, interruptions could result in leaving the data base in an unrecoverable state. Since data bases are typically stored using the software's special record structure, typical text editors or word processors cannot be used to repair the files. Special utilities and debuggers may be required to attempt repairs. In these cases, one must have a very detailed understanding of the file structures and of the machine's data storage details. In most cases, the only recourse is to restore a backup of the data base. This may result in considerable loss of information so it is important that backups be kept as current as possible. Additional protection may come from investing in an uninterruptible power supply (Rosch, 1986) that supplies power to the computer when the main source of power goes out, thus permitting the data base to be saved using normal procedures.

3.4 Statistical Analyses

Most microcomputer data base software do not include sophisticated data analysis features, although they usually offer routines to compute simple statistics. Some microcomputer statistical packages, however, will often provide tools as advanced as time-series forecasting and nonlinear regression. Most are restricted in their capabilities relative to the traditional mainframe statistical analysis products such as SPSS^x and SAS. Both of these mainframe statistical packages are available in PC versions, however, and contain most if not all of the same analysis capabilities as their mainframe counterparts along with some data base capabilities. PC SAS stores data in a flat file data base with random access capability, and the SAS/FSP, full-screen products, permit interactive editing, searching and sorting of the data base. For many data base applications this capability would be more than adequate. In addition, many of the statistical packages have routines to access and retrieve data stored with several of the more common microcomputer data base programs. For example, PC SAS supports dBASE files through the SAS DBF procedure, and DIF files, which most spreadsheet programs can produce, through the SAS DIF procedure. These are programs designed to read the special data formats that other software such as dBASE use in storing their data. On an IBM PC, these utilities would permit the exchange of dBASE III files with SAS data sets and with DIF supported products such as Lotus Symphony. Products similar to those mentioned above for the MS DOS compatible computer are available for other machines such as the Apple Macintosh. An obvious requirement of any microcomputer data analysis program is the ability to process large data bases. Several have a limit to the number of cases or observations that are permitted in the analysis and equally important, some have restrictions on their ability to read the data from ASCII text files or directly from the data base. Most quality software should support at least ASCII files with large record lengths.[3]

3.5 Security and Shared Files

Data base security and multi-user file sharing are two requirements that have received attention recently. Some data bases support coordinated simultaneous data base access. This has become important in corporate and university settings where several PC work stations are attached through a local area network (LAN). In order to preserve the data base integrity, the software must support multi-user access or all other users must be prohibited from using the data base until a specific use has been completed. Most of the available software contains little, if any, provisions for security. Security would include protecting the data from unauthorized users as well as protection from undesired alterations whether by physical damage, shared access to the data or erasure. These damages may be entirely accidental and not due to vandalism. In either event, the damage may result in the complete or partial loss of the data base.

A careless user can easily erase files on most microcomputers. Fortunately several utilities exist to recover deleted files if they can be executed immediately after the file deletion and before any other files are created. Otherwise, only partial recovery may be possible. Programs that are used to format diskettes will destroy data on the disk being formatted. If the hard disk is reformatted, then everything on the disk will be lost and no recovery is possible except from backups.

Several vendors have designed hardware and software to prohibit accidental deletion or alteration of data. Some products can restrict the hours of access to the machine, require passwords for authorized entry and can log all uses of the system. Others require setting a physical switch to the unprotect position before permitting alterations. These devices are not failsafe as they depend upon the software being loaded into the system or on the board being installed. Someone really wanting access to the data could circumvent these devices. To alleviate these problems, many companies require that the data be stored on media such as floppy disks, tapes or cartridges so that they can be locked in the company safe when not in use. In addition, data encryption programs can be used to store sensitive information in a form that is almost undecipherable.

At other times, deletion of a file containing sensitive data is desired. One must be careful, since as discussed above, utilities exist to aid in the recovery or partial recovery of files. Specifically, file deletion usually only involves removing the file name from the file directory and releasing the space back to the system so that new files can use the space. The actual file is not erased until new files use the old space. This is the basis on which the file recovery utilities work. To physically erase the file, the storage space of the erased file must be written over. Several utility programs are available to do this.

The third major topic under security involves the security of the data base when file sharing is permitted. Several of the microcomputer operating systems have incorporated file-sharing capabilities that can restrict and regulate access to specific files. Installing this software in a system, however, is not for the casual user and file sharing through a network may not result in protection if each user is running his own copy of the operating system. For networks, file protection must reside with the file server program.[4]

A security topic only recently made public is the "microspy" (Donlan, 1986). Special devices, not expensive, can tune in on the radio frequencies emanating from a PC, permitting the spy to view the data appearing on the PC terminal from as far as one-half mile away. The U.S. government has been aware of this capability for some time and has required special protection of their computers where national security is involved. This protection standard has the code name TEMPEST for transient electromagnetic pulse emanation standard. Thus a data base user working with very sensitive data might require TEMPEST protection to keep the microspy from the data.

4. The Mainframe Connection

When large data bases are involved, larger mainframe computers or minicomputers are also often used. In some cases, the larger machines are needed for the data analysis and report generation. In other cases, the data base may reside on a mainframe. It is often the case that the data may be moved from one processor to the other for specific applications. The data may be entered, verified and summarized using a microcomputer and then moved to a mainframe where the data are added to an existing data base. If the data are moved through a direct link between the microcomputer and the mainframe, the technique is called uploading or downloading, depending upon the direction of data flow. Alternatively, the required data may be a part of a data base available to the mainframe from which part of it is downloaded to a microcomputer for queries, report generation and analysis. Thus there is a need to be able to move data in both directions.

Data transfers between microcomputers and mainframes are dependent upon several factors. One of the most important is the compatibility between the host and the microcomputer acting as a terminal. For direct links to mainframes, special hardware and software are required. For example, to attach an IBM PC to an IBM 3084 mainframe requires special hardware, such as a 3270 attachment. Other attachments are possible, and to attach to other computers, different hardware may be required. On some systems, protocol converters permit asynchronous communication with the host while maintaining much of the power of the terminal-type being emulated. File transfers, however, may not be simple under these circumstances and special software may have to reside on both the host and the micro-computer. The big advantage to having a direct attachment, whether through a converter or not, is the fast transmission rates. Over leased phone lines, speeds of 9600 baud are common. Fiber optics lines can support far greater speeds.

The baud rate is the number of bits transmitted per second. There are usually seven or eight bits of data and two or three bits for parity checking and timing for each transmitted character. For most transmissions, the baud rate is the number of characters times 10 that can be transmitted in one second. Most microcomputer modems today operate at 1200 to 2400 baud or 120 to 240 characters per second. To transmit one megabyte of data at 1200 baud, nonstop, would require about two and one-half hours. New developments in modems may soon lead to ordinary transfers over standard phone lines at 9600 baud (Stone, 1986).

One of the first file transfer techniques for microcomputers was the data capture method, whereby anything received from the host is automatically logged to a file which is later edited to remove host-user commands and notes. No integrity checks other than parity checking are used by this method so that it is not very safe over "noisy" phone lines. The worst problem with this method is with the loss of data since the losses are difficult to detect.

To assure the integrity of the data, most file transfer programs have adopted a special file transfer protocol. This consists of parity checking and checksum calculations of the transmitted data. The data are transmitted as blocks or packets with special characters signifying the beginning and ending of the block and several other characters containing various sums of the binary representation of the characters. The receiving computer recomputes these sums based on the received data and compares them to the transmitted sums. If they do not match, then a transmission error has occurred and the block is requested to be retransmitted. Otherwise the block is saved and another block is requested. Obviously more time is required for these file transfers but the integrity of the data is insured. One popular file transfer protocol is Kermit (Hansen, 1985) and several public domain programs have implemented this protocol into their terminal software.[5]

Before data from a mainframe can be downloaded, it must be converted to a form suitable for transmission and for use once it gets to the microcomputer. Most mainframe data bases such as OSIRIS or SAS/BASE use their own special data file formats. The formats are usually unsuitable for downloading as is. Usually a program is executed on the host to extract the necessary records from the data base, and then a new file, compatible with the microcomputer, is created using these records. The form of the record structure is usually altered by this process. The most common procedure is to put the data into human-readable text form although some programs, such as PC SAS, have the capability to move their specially formatted data sets to or from a host mainframe without the need to convert the file structure to text format.

Other considerations in file transfer include the legal restrictions that may be put on a data base. Permission to use a mainframe data base may not include permission to download and analyze that data on a microcomputer. Because of the sensitive nature of some data bases, agreements to keep the confidentiality of the data may need to be signed or guarantees on the security of the data may need to be met.

5. Future Developments

In the very near future we should expect to see the development of still faster machines with graphical and intelligent interfaces. Multi-tasking should be standard in operating systems and artificial intelligence technology will make them easier and more personal to use. Compact disk (CD) technology can currently permit the storage of 600 megabytes on a single disk (Williams, 1987). Slater Hall Information Products of Washington, D.C. currently distributes economic and demographic data bases from the U.S. Census Bureau, Bureau of Labor Statistics and the Bureau of Economic Analysis for processing with microcomputers via compact disk. Each disk can contain up to 500 megabytes of information. It will not be unreasonable to assume that ICPSR and other information organizations will distribute their data bases to microcomputer users via compact disk or other optical-type media. The newer magneto-optical technology will extend this capability. The write-once read-mostly devices, WORMs, are an example in that they permit the computer user to store new data on the medium, unlike a CD that must be mastered and pressed like an audio CD. The old data on a WORM is not destroyed and new data must be written on previously unused parts of the medium. This may not be bad as it permits an audit trail of corrections and additions to the data base. It also adds security to the data base because changes are obvious. In addition, this medium can be kept secure, as with the CD, since the disk can be placed under lock and key. The CD and WORM cartridges are also much more durable than floppy or hard disks with life expectancies of 10 to 20 years. Erasable optical drives are currently being perfected that will work like standard magnetic media (Kryder, 1987; Williams, 1987). This technology will be exploited much more fully and may permit a standard method for the distribution of large data bases.[6]

Again, mainframe-to-mainframe links along with microcomputer-to-mainframe links will also permit quick and easy distribution of data. Transmission rates of information across phone lines will be increased both due to improvements in modem transmission rates and improved protocols as well as improvements in communication systems through fiber optic lines and satellite connections. Networking systems will become common in organizations supporting multiple microcomputers and these networks will make the minicomputer-mainframe computer connections transparent. The user may not even know on what computer, microcomputer or mainframe, his program is executing. Certainly developments in software will make microcomputers very easy and pleasant to use.

6. Example Using UCR Data

Many of the concepts discussed above can be demonstrated through an example.[7] This example illustrates the process of extracting data from the distribution medium, here magnetic tape stored on a mainframe computer, transferring the data to a microcomputer for analysis, and then undertaking a statistical analysis. Although this example uses software implemented on MS DOS machines, similar software exists for other microcomputers. Since many people use spreadsheet programs such as Lotus Symphony to view, summarize, print and graph the data, the example will show how the data base can be imported, processed and exported using a spreadsheet. As stated previously, several of the large data bases are hierarchical by design and the usual flat file formats of spreadsheets and statistical programs are not appropriate or are inefficient with them, therefore the use of a typical data base program will also be shown. Finally, an analysis using a traditional statistical package, PC SAS/BASE and SAS/STAT, will be undertaken. The main data base used in this example is a subset of the 1980 Uniform Crime Report data base.

6.1 Data Extraction

The data were delivered on a standard magnetic tape medium for use with a mainframe computer. The data were moved from tape to direct access storage, a disk pack, and were written in an OSIRIS format (i.e., written by OSIRIS software in their special data format). A mainframe SAS program using the CONVERT procedure converted the data from the OSIRIS format to a SAS data set format, because this was convenient for this user. Only a subset of the data set was needed for analysis on the microcomputer so another SAS program was used to select the variables of interest and the cases matching the specified criteria. Considerable mainframe familiarity was required to convert the original data base into one that could be downloaded to a microcomputer. For this example, 13 variables were selected for only those cities with a population of between 100,000 and 249,999 and no missing data. This resulted in a data base of 112 records.

This new data set was written to a text file for downloading. The IBM RECEIVE program was used to download this data set to an IBM PC/AT microcomputer through a 3270 type link. This program converts the EBCDIC characters of the IBM mainframe to ASCII so that they are usable on the microcomputer. The data was stored on the microcomputer in an ASCII text file. If the data had been available on a CD ROM, then the mainframe procedures could have been bypassed entirely and the selected records could have been removed directly from the CD.

6.2 The Microcomputer Data Base

The Ashton Tate dBASE III Plus software was used to manage this data base. For this small example, any data base program, spreadsheet, or even a word processor would have been sufficient for managing the data. For larger subsets, however, the ability of data base software to manage, quickly search, sort and summarize the data would be necessary. The field names, data types and lengths were entered in dBASE III to create the layout of the data base. The program provides an input window for describing the data base. The UCR records were then added to the new data base using the APPEND command. The following dBASE commands were executed to create the crime data base for the UCR data,
    CREATE UCRDBASE
    APPEND FROM UCR.TXT DELIMITED WITH BLANK

The UCR data were then contained within a dBASE III data base file and can now queried or analyzed using dBASE commands. The DISPLAY command can be used to list the entire data base to the console or to list selected records. Display of selected records is easier using dBASE III than for most spreadsheets or statistical packages and additionally could be used to create a data subset for analysis by these programs. The CREATE REPORT command could be used to organize a formatted report of the data with a column-style listing. Averages can be obtained using the AVERAGE command; however, to do more sophisticated types of analysis, such as correlations among the variables or analysis of variance among division or principal components of the variables, requires extensive dBASE programming, or more practical, the use of additional software.

6.3 The Spreadsheet

Spreadsheets are often convenient for data entry, editing, limited modeling and for providing summary statistics of the data as well as some transformations and graphs. The Lotus Symphony software is a typical spreadsheet. In order to use the data, first the Translate facility in Symphony must be used to change the data base format to a worksheet format, or an ASCII file must be created that can be imported into Symphony. The latter is used in this example since it is a more general technique; spreadsheets, word processors and statistical packages can usually read ASCII text files and may not, in general, be able to read a specific software's data format. From dBASE the ASCII text file can be created simply by:

COPY TO UCRASCII.TXT DELIMITED

To import both character and numeric data into Symphony, the character data must be delimited by double quotation marks. The DELIMITED option of dBASE will put quotation marks around character data and will separate fields with a comma. In this particular case, no character data are present so the SDF (standard data file) option could have been used in place of the DELIMITED option to create the ASCII text file. Additionally, the new text file could have been restricted to certain fields and records by other dBASE options if the entire data base was not needed for the analysis.

Once in Symphony, the File-Import-Structured options are selected from the Symphony menus and the file name UCRASCII.TXT is specified for retrieval. The data will be added to the worksheet, each column of numbers occupying a separate worksheet column. The data base can now be saved as a worksheet file if desired.

6.4 Statistical Analysis

A standard data file was also created from the dBASE data base by replacing the DELIMITED option with the SDF option. A PC SAS program can then be used to read the data and compute the necessary statistical analysis.

7. Summary

Microcomputer speeds and the new microcomputer storage devices permit the use of large data bases on microcomputers. Speed and storage capability have been in the past, the primary hardware limitations to the use of large data bases on microcomputers. Although limitations still exist, in the near future, microcomputers will perform practically all of the data base functions that mainframes currently do. Very efficient, flexible and multi-user data base software have been developed incorporating new artificial intelligence technologies permitting microcomputers to manage large data bases without the need for highly trained computer technicians. Many of the obstacles blocking the sharing of data bases among mainframes and microcomputers have been eliminated through the advent of new storage devices, modems and networks.

Because much of the data analysis software for microcomputers is interactive with graphical displays, more in-depth and exploratory analysis is likely to occur with microcomputers than with traditional mainframes. Many researchers have access to microcomputers although few have access to mainframe graphical work stations. Young, Kent and Kuhfeld (1987) and others have developed exploratory and dynamic graphics programs for use on microcomputers. This should result in further understandings of the relationships among the variables in the data bases, the major motivation for collecting and storing the data in the first place.

Currently the microcomputer is quite capable of handling many large data bases, although there are still many occasions when larger computers are more efficient and sometimes necessary for data management and analysis. However, recent advances in microcomputer hardware and software technology have made microcomputers currently worth considering for large data base management assignments and the norm for the future.

9

Nationwide Homicide Data Sets: An Evaluation of the Uniform Crime Reports and the National Center for Health Statistics Data

Marc Riedel

Because there is general agreement that most homicides find their way into a reporting system, it is easy to assume that there are few problems with homicide data sets (Sellin, 1962; O'Brien, 1985; Gove, Hughes and Geerkin, 1985). That there are other dimensions of the problem is implicit in what has come to be referred to as the "Sellin dictum:" "the value of a crime for index purposes decreases as the distance from the crime itself in terms of procedure increases" (Sellin, 1931: 346). While this dictum is usually meant to emphasize the greater value (for index purposes) of data gathered from police rather than from sentencing agencies, the dictum also suggests that what and how data are reported is affected by the reporting organization. As O'Brien (1985) indicates, reporting systems are "filters" which affect the kind of information that is ultimately used as data by researchers. Thus, while homicide may be a highly reported crime, an examination of the reporting systems indicates undocumented variations, errors in classification, and difficulties with missing cases and values.

Unlike other crimes, homicide is the only offense in which there are two nationwide reporting systems that gather detailed information on the entire population of events. The present chapter describes and assesses the homicide data provided by these two reporting systems. One of these reporting systems is the Federal Bureau of Investigation's (FBI) Uniform Crime Reporting Program (UCR Program) for which the most detailed source of information is the Supplementary Homicide Reports (SHR). The other reporting system is the National Center for Health Statistics (NCHS) through which information on homicides is collected as part of mortality data.

Two types of comparisons will be made: intrasystem and intersystem. Intrasystem comparisons focus on similar variables collected at different times by various organizational levels within the same reporting system. An example of an intrasystem comparison is the relative level of agreement between frequency distributions of victim-offender relationships for several cities as reported (1) by the SHR and as recorded (2) by local police departments. Intersystem comparisons, on the other hand, examine the extent of agreement between two different homicide reporting systems. At a national level, intersystem comparisons contrast information available from the SHR or the UCR with that available from the NCHS. State and local intersystem comparisons focus on the extent of agreement between police departments and the offices of medical examiners in reporting.

1. The Uniform Crime Reporting Program

According to the UCR definition, criminal homicide is composed of two categories: murder with nonnegligent manslaughter, and manslaughter by negligence. Murder and nonnegligent manslaughter are defined as "willful (nonnegligent) killing of one human being by another" (FBI, 1985: 6). As a general rule any death due to injuries received in a fight, argument, quarrel, assault or commission of a crime is counted as a murder or nonnegligent manslaughter. Suicides, accidental deaths, assault to murder, attempted murders, justifiable and excusable homicides are not included in the category of murder and nonnegligent manslaughter.

Manslaughter by negligence includes the killing of another person through negligence. Traffic fatalities are excluded. While manslaughter by negligence is part of the definition of criminal homicide, it is not included in the Crime Index. In the research reported here, the focus will be on murder and nonnegligent manslaughter.

One of the early critics of the UCR indicated that, with respect to definitions of crime, the United States "is in effect 50 separate sovereign countries rather than one" (Beattie, 1962: 39). The definitions provided by the UCR Program are meant to be sufficiently general so that information about the relevant act could be collected under the various state statutes. However, as Wolfgang (1963) has indicated, there is no assurance that these definitions will be applied correctly or consistently.

In addition, when multiple crimes are committed by the same person at the same time, only the most serious will be reported in the UCR. Because homicides are considered the most serious offense, the UCR reports the large majority of homicide occurrences (Cantor and Cohen, 1980).

1.1 Methods and Measures

The methods used by the UCR Program have been subject to extensive evaluation and criticism (Beattie, 1960, 1962; Sellin, 1962; Wolfgang, 1963; Robison, 1966; Lejins, 1966; Savitz, 1978; National Commission on the Causes and Prevention of Violence, 1969). While some of these criticisms are applicable to homicide data, many of the problems that beset homicide data are peculiar to it. To understand these problems, it is necessary to point out how the UCR Program collects information on homicides. Each of the three forms[1] used to gather homicide data is procedurally independent from the others. Since there is no identifier for the same event on more than one form there is no way to determine which cases are represented by more than one form. Comparisons, therefore, cannot be made by individual case, but must be made on aggregations of cases.

1.2 FBI Estimates

The extent of coverage for reporting homicide is a function of the number and population of jurisdictions. The extent of Return A coverage has increased over the years until, in 1984:

> law enforcement agencies active in the UCR Program represented approximately 227 million United States inhabitants, or 96 percent of the total population as established by the Bureau of the Census. The coverage amounted to 98 percent of the United States population living in MSAs, 94 percent of the population in "other cities," and 90 percent of the rural population (FBI, 1985: 3).

At least part of the UCR's estimation process assumes that homicide is not a seasonal crime. This assumption has been supported in a recent analysis of homicide in the United States (Block, 1984).

Incomplete coverage on Return A necessitates estimation. Historically, methods to estimate the total number of homicides have varied considerably. According to Cantor and Cohen (1980), various methods were used to arrive at estimates of total homicides prior to 1948. From 1948-1958 all such estimates were based on the aggregate percentage change for comparable reporting areas in adjacent years. Even though the pre-1958 figures were later revised numerically, the percentage changes used to obtain the original estimates were preserved.

From 1970 through 1975, the UCR Program annually revised past homicide figures. These six series were different because each year the UCR Program revised previous estimates on the basis of additional information from newly acquired reporting areas.

For their analysis, Cantor and Cohen (1980) examined two series. The first, from 1935-1976, consisted of estimates reported in each of the annual editions of the UCR. The second series, available from 1933-1972, was published by the Office of Management and Budget. The latter revised the UCR series to adjust the pre-1958 series so that they would be compatible with the post-1958 series. According to the authors, inspection of the eight series over the period from 1960 through 1970 indicated that none of these series differed in their estimates by more than one-tenth of a homicide per 100,000 population. Because of problems with revisions, Cantor and Cohen (1980) suggest that the UCR series not be used as source of data to study homicides prior to 1958. For homicides prior to that date, the Office of Management and Budget series appears to provide the best available FBI estimates.

Finding a reliable series of the total count of homicides for the nation does not necessarily mean that the same data source can be used for geographical subsets. The completeness of the Return A data varies for states, regions and cities in terms of quality and coverage. The completeness of a national data series when compared to other sources may hide large sources of error when smaller units are tabulated. Researchers are generally sensitive to this problem, however, the author knows of no research whose purpose is to generally assess underreporting of the Return A for different geographical subsets.

1.3 Supplementary Homicide Reports (SHR)

Return A forms and their estimates represent an aggregated total number of offenses from a law enforcement agency for a given month. In 1961, the SHR of the UCR Program began requesting detailed information on each murder and nonnegligent manslaughter case. For that year, information was collected on 3,008 murders (primarily from cities) out of a national estimated total of 8,600 murders (FBI, 1961). Although national coverage was attempted in 1962, until 1965 most of the information on murders and nonnegligent manslaughters came from large cities. For 1962 through 1975, the SHR was primarily a record of the age, race and sex of victims, weapon and the circumstances of the offense. Beginning in 1976, information about the offender and additional information about the homicide event were requested.

Until 1976, the various editions of the UCR Handbook provided general directions to law enforcement personnel for completing each form. Although computer processing was used, there was little effort to give clear unequivocal instructions which could be easily translated into computer codes. For example, the 1965 UCR Handbook gave the following written instructions for completing information on three variables: "Provide the data requested as to age, sex and race of the victim" (p. 51). When the SHR form was received by the UCR Program, codes were assigned and used to prepare tapes that are currently made available to researchers. From the perspective of a user who is accessing an SHR computer tape, what is needed is an understanding of major changes in categories of the coding guides as well as the handbook.

The instructions given in the UCR Handbooks (1965, 1974) do not vary in content during the 1962 through 1975 period. With respect to the coding guides, sex, as expected, was not changed from the inception of the form to the present. Similarly, age codes have undergone minor changes, and this is primarily at the younger ages. Codes for race of the victim and offender remained the same: White, Negro, Indian, Chinese, Japanese, Other, Unknown.

The major changes occurred in the codes given for weapon and circumstances. For the period 1962-1967, weapons were divided into firearms, stabbing and piercing instruments, other dangerous weapons, personal weapons, strangulation, and unknown; no more detailed breakdowns were given. Beginning in 1968, the weapons breakdown became more specific. Handguns, rifles and shotguns, for example, were distinguished from each other as well as from other types of guns.

From 1962-1975, the "circumstances" records were broken into three major categories. They were: (1) murder and nonnegligent manslaughter occurring within the family unit, (2) altercations outside the family but usually among acquaintances, and (3) felony or first degree-type murders where the death penalty may result. Beginning in 1968 each of the categories were further refined. For example, "altercations outside the family, but usually among acquaintances" were divided into lovers and triangles, drunken brawls, altercations over money, and other arguments.[2]

From 1973 through 1975 an additional refinement was added to the circumstances code. Where the SHR indicated a crime-related murder, a set of sub-circumstance codes relating to the type of crime were provided.

It is very difficult to develop a usable variable or variables from the circumstances data for the period 1962-1975. In his research, Curtis (1974) was able to develop a distinction between family murders, murders involving friends, neighbors and acquaintances, and non-primary relationships using the circumstances variable. For the friends, neighbors and acquaintances categories, he used the SHR categories of "romantic triangles," "lovers' quarrels" and "other arguments." For the non-primary relationships, characterized as "mostly strangers," he used the categories of "known felony type" and "suspected felony type." This effort probably represents the best approximation of a usable variable, given its nature during this period.

The major problem with the circumstances category was that it represented a combination of several variables. For example, crime related murders may also occur among family murders. What was needed, and provided beginning in 1976, was a distinction between victim-offender relationships and circumstances.

For the period 1976 through 1985 beginning with the data reported in 1976, the SHR underwent an extensive revision which substantially improved its utility as a nationwide source of homicide data. The handbook and the coding guides became more congruent with each other because some of the codes used in preparing the data were given to the law enforcement personnel completing the form. While Return A and the estimates remained a victim-based reporting form, the SHR became an event based system. In other words, when the murder or nonnegligent manslaughter involved multiple victims and offenders, information was collected on each of the offenders and victims who participated in the same event. Codes were provided in such a way that users were able to disaggregate the data and create a victim based system. Second, as has been mentioned earlier, information was collected on both the victim and offender.

Rather than confusing victim-offender relationships with other aspects of circumstances, a separate victim-offender relationship variable with a series of detailed codes was used. Circumstances were divided into codes for types of felonies, codes for circumstances that did not involve felonies, and one code for suspected felony type.

Two changes were made in the SHR in 1980: the race codes were changed and both race and ethnicity information was requested for both victim and offender. It is instructive to note the increase in highly specific and codable instructions currently used for these variables, in contrast to the handbook instructions used in 1965:

> Race designations for both victims and offenders are as follows: White—W, Black—B, American Indian or Alaskan Native—I, Asian or Pacific Islander—A, and Unknown—U. Only those race designations are to be used.
>
> Ethnicity designations are as follows: Hispanic Origin—H, not of Hispanic Origin—N, and Unknown—U. (FBI, 1980: 59).

1.4 Intrasystem Comparisons of SHR Data

Research on the SHR and NCHS can be conveniently divided into three groups: (1) agreement between the SHR and city police records, (2) studies of corrections for missing data and (3) studies of the problems of classification.

1.4.1 POLICE REPORTS AND THE SHR

Three studies examine the amount of agreement between SHR and city police information with respect to both case and variable completeness (Zahn and Riedel, 1983; Riedel and Zahn, 1985; Riedel, 1987). As part of a larger project, Riedel and Zahn (1985) collected detailed information from police records for one year (1978) on seven United States cities selected for geographic representativeness (Zahn and Riedel, 1983). The information on the number of cases and distributions on several variables for each of the cities was compared to similar distributions found in the SHRs of the same city and year. Table 1 reports the overall amount of agreement between the number of cases found in police departments and those reported by the SHR.

Table 1

Total number of murder cases as reported by police departments and SHR in seven cities*

City	City Freq.	SHR Freq.	Agreement Ratio**
Philadelphia	362	353	.97
Newark	102	109	1.07
St. Louis	207	210	1.01
Memphis	116	114	.98
Dallas	233	232	1.00
Oakland	98	96	.98
Ashton***	90	88	.98

*Revised table taken from Zahn and Riedel, 1983, page 109.
**The amount of agreement is measured by dividing the SHR frequency by the frequency recorded by city police
***Ashton is the pseudonym for a non-California city located in the western part of the United States.

The greatest agreement was found in Dallas in which the SHR reported one less murder than the city police. In five of the seven cities, there was a slight tendency for police departments to record more murders than the SHR. In St. Louis and Newark, the tendency was reversed, with the SHR reporting more murders than the police department. While it is not known what accounts for these discrepancies, the comparisons support the hypothesis that, at least for large cities, the SHR is reasonably complete with respect to the number of cases.

Zahn and Riedel (1983) also examined the amount of agreement between police department records and the SHR for sex, race and age of murder victims, weapon and victim-offender relationships. For male victims in the seven cities, the agreement ratio ranged from .95 in Oakland to 1.02 in Newark, indicating high agreement. For female victims, there was much less agreement—generally in the direction of overreporting by the SHR. The agreement ratios ranged from .96 in St. Louis to 1.29 in Newark; three of the cities had ratios larger than one. Because of classification difficulties, only data on black victims were used in comparing police records to SHR. The range of differences was from one case in Ashton to nine cases in St. Louis, where the SHR reported more black victims than were recorded in police records.

Although age classifications are somewhat arbitrary, age was grouped in ten-year intervals for making comparisons among the seven cities. In general, there was less agreement in reporting age than in reporting any other victim variable. In addition, there was no clear pattern that characterized the comparisons across cities. For example, in Oakland there was almost complete agreement in the youngest ages (1-19) and a fairly linear progression in discrepancy as age increased. On the other hand, Ashton had fairly high rates of agreement, with the greatest discrepancy in the 60-69 and 70-79 age groups.

For weapons, the level of agreement was more than 90 percent in five of the seven cities. Except for Newark, reporting between the two series was consistent across cities when the weapons were knives or guns. The discrepancies between the two series were greater when data for other types of weapons were compared across cities.

These comparisons support the lack of a systematic reporting pattern. For example, Newark city police frequently reported fewer murders than the SHR; however, this was not always the case. There was some tendency for city police departments to record more murders than the SHR, but the pattern is not consistent.

One variable, victim-offender relationships, shows a consistent pattern of underreporting for city police departments as compared to SHR data. The distributions of victim-offender relationships for city police and SHR data are given in Table 2.

As shown in Table 2, among the three types of victim-offender relationships, the city police consistently record more stranger murders than the SHR. For six of the seven cities, (excluding Dallas) the agreement ratios were smaller than for either of the other two types of victim-offender relationships.

For the individual cities the agreement ratios ranged from .07 in Oakland to .97 in Dallas. In other words, while the Oakland SHRs only reported about 7 percent of the stranger murders, the Dallas SHRs reported almost 97 percent of them.

Table 2

Victim-offender relationships as reported by seven city police departments (PD) and SHR (1978)

City	PD Freq.	SHR Freq.	Agreement Ratio
Philadelphia			
Within Family	46	40	.87
Friends & Acquaintances	138	147	.94
Strangers	106	52	.49
Unknown	72	114	1.58
TOTAL	362	353	.98
Newark			
Within Family	13	10	.77
Friends & Acquaintances	32	32	1.00
Strangers	28	21	.75
Unknown	29	46	1.59
TOTAL	102	109	1.07
St. Louis			
Within Family	27	20	.74
Friends & Acquaintances	92	68	.74
Strangers	37	17	.46
Unknown	51	105	2.06
TOTAL	207	210	1.01
Memphis			
Within Family	16	23	1.44
Friends & Acquaintances	68	64	.94
Strangers	23	12	.52
Unknown	9	15	1.67
TOTAL	116	114	.98
Dallas			
Within Family	44	39	.89
Friends & Acquaintances	95	78	.82
Strangers	63	61	.97
Unknown	31	54	1.74
TOTAL	233	232	1.00
Oakland			
Within Family	11	10	.91
Friends & Acquaintances	51	18	.35
Strangers	14	1	.07
Unknown	22	67	3.04
TOTAL	98	96	.98
Ashton			
Within Family	19	19	1.00
Friends & Acquaintances	38	32	.84
Strangers	21	12	.57
Unknown	12	25	2.08
TOTAL	90	88	.98

While agreement for the stranger murder category is less than agreement for the other two categories, the greatest agreement for family murders occurred in Dallas, Oakland and Ashton. For the within family type, the ratios ranged from a low of .74 in St. Louis to a high of 1.06 in Ashton (excluding Memphis). For unknown reasons, the Memphis SHR reported many more family murders than city police.

In terms of agreement ratios, Table 2 illustrates that for three cities, murders of friends and acquaintances had the highest agreement ratios. For Philadelphia, the SHR reported slightly more murders of friends and acquaintances than by the police (1.06). For the remaining cities, the SHR reported as few as 35 percent of the murders of friends and acquaintances in Oakland to as many as 97 percent of these murders in Newark. The SHR uniformly reports a larger number and more unknown relationships than the police. The range in agreement was from 1.58 in Philadelphia to 3.04 in Oakland. In an analysis of Chicago Police Department records and SHRs for the years 1976-1981, Riedel (1987) found that stranger homicides were also underreported.

It appears that the underreporting of stranger homicides in Memphis is the result of a reporting lag between local police departments and the UCR. In the original study of this problem, Riedel (1981) used a computerized data base of all homicides in Memphis from 1974-1978 and compared the distribution of victim-offender relationships with a similar distribution from the SHR. The pattern of agreement among the three victim-offender categories was similar to that reported in the seven cities and Chicago.

Riedel (1981) also found that stranger homicides took a longer time to clear by the identification and arrest of one or more offenders in Memphis in comparison to other types of victim-offender relationships. Because of the longer time, when SHRs were completed by police departments each month, the victim-offender relationship information was not available and the relationship was recorded as "unknown." These records were then forwarded to the UCR. If an arrest was made later, the victim-offender relationship was recorded in police records, but an updated report was not forwaded to the UCR.

1.4.2 Missing Values

Probably because of funding reductions in recent years, researchers are using secondary data and official statistics more frequently. This has led to more concern with the problems of missing cases and missing values in these data sets (Raymond, 1986; Little and Rubin, 1987).

However, for researchers who are interested in studying patterns of murder, the concern is one of unbiased reporting rather than a complete count.

In other words, the variable may be incompletely reported, but that does not mean that what is available is reported in a biased fashion.

Williams and Flewelling (1987) have developed an interesting and useful approach to the problem of missing data in the SHR. The authors developed three alternative rate calculation procedures to take account of missing values, using a sample of 83,007 incidents of murder and nonnegligent manslaughter in the U.S. from 1980 through 1984. Only murder and nonnegligent incidents that involved one offender and one victim were used. The geographic areas included 168 cities with more than 100,000 people, their respective metropolitan areas (N = 125), the 50 states, and nine geographic regions.

The first rate calculation procedure, which accounted for non-reported cases in the SHR, is a ratio of the number of victims reported on Return A to the number of victims reported in the SHR. The adjusted counts are derived by multiplying the unadjusted counts in the SHR by the weighting factor.

The second and third rate calculation procedures developed by Williams and Flewelling focused on victim-offender relationships, although other offender characteristics could be used. The second procedure extrapolates from the known composition of a category of victim-offender relationship to the unknown one. Thus, if 40 percent of the known events involve stranger murders, the 40 percent of the unknown cases are added to the calculation of the adjusted rate of stranger murders.

The difficulty with the second approach is that it assumes that the distribution of known characteristics is the same as the distribution of unknown or missing values. Because proportionately more of the unknown cases involve stranger murders, the adjusted rates tend to overestimate the rates of murder among family members of friends and acquanintances and underestimate the rates of stranger murders.

To address this issue, Williams and Flewelling developed a third procedure in which an additional variable, circumstances of the offense, was added to the calculations if it was related to the victim-offender relationships. This variable indicated whether the murder was felony-related. The effect of the procedure was to adjust family and acquaintance murders downward and stranger murders upward, as theoretically expected.

After constructing unadjusted, adjusted, and circumstance adjusted rates, the authors calculated bivariate correlations among the three types of rates for the cities, metropolitan areas, and states. The correlations for the three methods were high, ranging from a low of $r = .936$ to a high of $r = .996$.

The authors also used percent poor and percent black in a regression analysis to determine if parameter estimates were altered by the estimation procedures. The correlations changed to some extent; however, the greatest changes occurred in the expected directions for the origin (a) and the regression coefficient (b). The authors concluded that:

To the extent that an investigator's analytical purpose is to determine the absolute amount of change in rates of family, acquaintance, or stranger homicide associated with changes in theoretically relevant variables, these findings suggest that the use of an adjustment procedure is necessary. Moreover, descriptive statistics pertaining to the absolute and relative amount of specific types of homicide are affected in important ways by the adjustment procedures used (e.g., the absolute and relative amount of stranger homicide becomes higher than family homicides). The circumstance adjustment procedure appears most appropriate because it uses an extensive range of data in the SHR to guide the adjustment process, and analyses using the resulting rates reveal predictable empirical patterns. Nonetheless, if an investigator's purpose is merely to determine patterns of association (i.e., direction, significance, or magnitude of an association), then the choice among the rate calculation procedures is not so consequential (Williams and Flewelling, 1987: 20-21).

1.4.3 Problems of Classification

In addition to a reporting lag, the SHR is hampered by a lack of knowledge concerning the validity of its classification categories. In one of the few studies of its type, Loftin (1986) compared the homicide circumstances classification for the SHR to a classification generated by examining narrative summaries of each of 196 cases from the files of the Baltimore City Prosecuting Attorney and the Public Information Office of the Baltimore Police Department. An initial inspection of the two classifications indicate a high degree of consistency. The Baltimore SHR classified 14.3 percent of the homicide circumstances as robbery while Loftin's coders classified 17.3 percent of the homicide circumstances as robbery. However, when the cases are grouped and cross-classified, 42 cases were classified as robbery-circumstance in one or both of the studies, but only 20 of them were so classified in both studies. If the three categories are considered (robbery, not robbery, and undetermined), the two classifications agreed in only 93 out of 196 cases; only a 47 percent agreement.

Loftin (1986) concluded that the classification of robbery-related homicides was not very reliable. He suggests that there are three problems with the SHR classification. First, categories used by the SHR are mutually exclusive which forces coders to place a case in only one category when, logically, it could be placed in two or more. Second, there are no clear rules for coding cases with ambiguous motives. Third, the SHR coders placed many more cases in the "undetermined" category than did the coders used by Loftin. The failure to use an appropriate "other-than-robbery" category can have a major impact on studies of the correlates of robbery-murder.

Loftin, Kindley, Norris and Wiersema (1987) extended the analysis of classification to an examination of victim-offender relationships. In developing and testing the utility of a classification based on attributes of the victim and of the offender, Loftin, et al., used homicide and SHR cases from the earlier study. Forty of the Baltimore homicides were classifed as stranger homicides by either the SHR or attribute classification, but only 16 (40 percent) were classified as homicides with stranger involvement by both classification approaches.

1.4.4 SHR Summary

Evaluation of the research comparing SHRs to police department records on murder suggest the following conclusions. First, with respect to missing cases, the comparisons suggest that the SHR reports the majority of cases. In comparisons of the seven city data and Chicago, the agreement with respect to the total number of cases was very high. These results are, however, based on comparisons in large cities; the amount of agreement in rural areas and small towns is unknown.

Second, in comparing distributions of variables, with one exception, the nature of the relationship between the two data sets is unclear. While there is a tendency for city police to record more cases than the SHR, there is no clear pattern. Furthermore, with respect to the amount of discrepancy, there are large variations among cities.

Third, there is substantial evidence that stranger murders are underreported in the SHR. The difficulty is that they are not underreported by any consistent amount. The research suggests, however, large variability across cities and over time in the same city. In the seven cities noted previously, the number of stranger murders reported by the SHR may be incorrect by as little as 3 percent (Dallas) or as much as 93 percent (Oakland). In Chicago, depending on the year, the SHR may report as many as 95.1 percent (1978) or as few as 60.0 percent (1980) of them.

Fourth, given this pervasive problem of missing values, the alternative method of rate calcaluation using information about the circumstances proposed by Williams and Flewelling is important. The construction of circumstance-adjusted-rates is more important in determining the absolute amount of change in offender variables than in descriptive studies or studies attempting to determine the magnitude or direction of association.

Finally, the SHR appears to have errors and problems of classification. The research by Loftin and his associates indicates a considerable lack of agreement between the classification used by the UCR and that constructed by the authors. The author's recommendations hopefully, will be closely examined in the revision of the UCR currently underway (Poggio, Kennedy, Chaiken and Carlson, 1985).

2. The National Center for Health Statistics (NCHS)

Unlike the UCR Program, homicide data from the Vital Statistics Division of the NCHS is part of a nationwide collection of mortality data. The death registration system, as well as the fetal-death reporting system of the U.S. encompasses the 50 states, the District of Columbia, New York City (which is independent of New York State for the purpose of death registration), Puerto Rico, the Virgin Islands, Guam, American Samoa and the Trust Territory of the Pacific Islands (NCHS, 1985). In this discussion, the U.S. refers to the 50 states and the District of Columbia.

Information on mortality, including homicide, is collected through the use of a standardized death certificate which is completed by a medico-legal officer, such as a medical examiner, in the case of a violent death. The death certificate, or a state approved variation which contains relevant NCHS information, is then given to the funeral director who gives the certificate to the local registrar and secures a burial permit. The local registrar, who may be the county health officer, verifies the completeness and accuracy of the death certificate, makes a record of it and sends it to the state registrar. The state registrar reviews it for incomplete or inconsistent information, makes a copy and forwards a copy to the National Office of Vital Statistics. There, coders prepare the case according to categories given by the *International Classification of Diseases* and enter the case into the national mortality data published as Vital Statistics of the United States (National Office of Vital Statistics, 1954).

The death certificates received by NCHS are submitted by states who are members of the death registration area. To be admitted to this area, each state agency must demonstrate that the data submitted represent at least 90 percent of the events that occurred. Because NCHS assumes complete coverage since 1933, no estimates are used and all published data is considered final and not subject to revision (Cantor and Cohen, 1980; National Office of Vital Statistics, 1954).

While all states have adopted laws that require the registration of deaths, NCHS maintains on-going quality control measures to examine and analyze demographic and medical items on the death certificates, as well as coding errors. By 1985, national officials concluded "that over 99 percent of the births and deaths occurring in this country are registered" (NCHS, Technical Appendix, 1985: 13).

2.1 Definition and Classification

The classification categories of homicide used by NCHS are established by the *International Classification of Diseases* (ICD), a publication of the

World Health Organization which supports a world wide vital statistics reporting system. This classification is revised decennially in a meeting of participating nations. The various ICD causes of death are given three digit codes and, in recent revisions when more detail is needed, four digits are used.

Since the series of homicide data examined here began in 1933, classification categories are governed by the fourth through the ninth revision of the ICD. Table 3 summarizes the major categories used in each revision.

What makes general comparisons of NCHS and FBI definitions difficult is that the ICD versions of homicide are expressed solely in terms of the classification categories-which vary every ten years.

One major source of incompatibility between the two series is that prior to 1949, NCHS classified justifiable homicides under the category of "other means." Since most justifiable homicides involve legal intervention by police and legal executions, comparisons with the murder and nonnegligent series of the FBI are difficult because police killings and executions cannot be extrapolated from the NCHS series. However, beginning in 1949, separate categories were established for legal interventions and executions. Cantor and Cohen suggest that the latter changes "allow comparison of these two homicide indicators with, what appear to be, roughly equivalent definitions" (Cantor and Cohen, 1980: 125-126).

Examination of Table 3 indicates that the one category which remains identical through the various revisions is homicide in which the cause of death was a cutting or piercing instrument. Causes of death by homicide that were classified as "other or unspecified means" in early revisions sometimes acquired separate codes in later revisions. For example, homicides by poisoning became a separate category in 1949.

Beginning with the eighth revision, several other new categories were introduced: homicides due to fights, brawls or rape, and corrosive and caustic substances were listed as a cause distinct from poisoning. Hanging and strangulation and late effects of injuries which led to the victim's death, as well as pushing the victim from high places were also added.

For the ninth revision (See Table 3) explosives and firearms were distinguished as to type. In addition , a new category, "Child battering and other maltreatment" was added. In one sense, the addition of this category is reminiscent of the "Infanticide" category that was used from 1930 through 1948. However, this new category is a more legally specific category and the four digit codes request additional information in order to determine whether the act was was done by parents, other specified or unspecified persons.

2.2 NCHS Data Set Variables

Unlike the UCR Program, NCHS data contain no information on the offender. While NCHS reports time and location information, it is limited to

Table 3

Homicide-cause-of-death categories showing ICD revisions (3 digit codes)*

1930-1938 4th (1940)**	1939-1948 5th (1940)	1949-1957 6th (1948)	1958-1967 7th (1957)	1968-1978 8th (1967)	1979- 9th (1977)
Firearms	Firearms	Firearms and Explosives	Firearms and Explosives	Firearms and Explosives	Firearms and Explosives
Cutting or Piercing Instruments	Cutting or Piercing Instruments	Cutting or Piercing Instruments	Cutting or Piercing Instruments	Cutting or Piercing Instruments	Cutting or Piercing Instruments
Other Means	Other Means	Other Means	Other and Unspecified	Other and Unspecified	Other and Unspecified
Infanticide (Under 1 year)	Infanticide (Under 1 year)			Fight, Brawl, Rape	Fight, Brawl, Rape
				Corrosive or Caustic Substance	Corrosive or Caustic Substance
		Poisoning	Poisoning	Poisoning	Poisoning
				Hanging and Strangulation	Hanging and Strangulation
				Drowning	Drowning
				Pushing from High Places	
					Child Battering and Other Maltreatment
				Late Effects of Injury	Late Effects of Injury

*Four digit codes were not used in coding homicides prior to 1979.
**"Three digit codes for 1930-1938 period (4th revision) was taken from the fifth revision manual. According to the Bureau of the Census (1940), "No changes have been made in the classification of deaths from homicide" (p. 50).

victim characteristics. Also unlike the UCR, there is a three-year lag in making the NCHS data available to users. The UCR information on 1986 crimes was available mid-1987. The most current homicide statistics available from NCHS in 1987 are from the calendar year 1984.

The NCHS documentation of each variable and each reporting year is detailed and extensive. The sex, age and race of the homicide victim is recorded. The age reported is the age on the death certificate as of the last birthday. Homicides are also classified by the race of the victim: white, black, Indian, Chinese, Japanese and other races. Beginning in 1979, the additional categories of Filipino and other Asian or Pacific Islander were used to classify the homicide victim. NCHS has consistently made a distinction between classifications of race and ethnicity, although it does not provide an ethnicity classification. Thus, the "white category includes, in addition to person reported as white, those reported as Mexican, Puerto Rican, Cuban and all other Caucasians" (NCHS, Technical Appendix, 1985: 5).

Information is given for the place of residence of the victim and the place of the incident's occurrence, SMSAs, metropolitan and non-metropolitan counties, and for urban and for rural areas. Before 1970, homicide victims who were nonresidents of the U.S. were classified by place of death in the residence data. Beginning in 1970, these victims were not included in the residence data. Because these nonresident United States victims were always classified in the place of occurrence data, but not place of residence, beginning in 1970, the total number of homicides by place of occurrence will always be slightly larger than the total number of homicides by place of residence. The month in which the homicide occurred has been regularly reported for the NCHS series. The date of death was first made available in the 1972 data (NCHS, 1985).

2.3 Intrasystem Comparisons of the NCHS

Reviewing the research on the NCHS reporting system must proceed differently from that done in examining the UCR. The small body of available research examines problems at either the national or the local level. National level research focuses on problems that exist from the time the death certificate leaves the possession of the local registrar to the time the results appear in annual editions of vital statistics. Research on local problems examines the classification of homicides at the local level.

Decennial revisions of the ICD raise questions of comparability between the homicide series of different revisions (NCHS, 1964, 1965, 1975, 1980). To determine the effect of classification revisions, NCHS uses comparability ratios. Comparability ratios are based on dual coding of a single set of death certificates. For example, to construct comparability ratios for the seventh and eighth revisions, a sample of death certificates coded by the classification categories of the seventh revisions is coded by the classification categories of the eighth revision. This procedure is done for a sample of deaths for one seventh revision year and for each of the major cause of death categories (Israel and Klebba, 1969).

The ratios are obtained by dividing the numbers of deaths assigned to particular cause of death category according to the eighth revision, by the number of deaths assigned to the most nearly comparable causes under the seventh revision. The resulting ratios measure the net effect of changes in the classification, changes in rules for selecting the underlying cause of death, and changes in procedures used by NCHS.

These comparability ratios can be used by researchers to correct the series from the previous revision to make it comparable to that given by the later revision. For example, Israel and Klebba show how the asthma rate decreased from 2.0 to 1.4 in the 1967 seventh revision data when multiplied by the comparability ratio of.696.

At the national level, there were two isolated events which had an impact on NCHS homicide data. First, in 1964, approximately 6,000 deaths registered in Massachusetts were not received by NCHS. NCHS indicates that figures for this year for the U.S. and the New England Division were "somewhat affected." Second, data on deaths for 1972 were based on a 50 percent sample of all deaths occurring in the 50 states and the District of Columbia. The sample design and estimates of the errors are given in the technical appendices for 1972 (NCHS, Technical Appendix, 1985).

No matter how carefully the data are treated at the state and national level, the accuracy and utility ultimately depend on classification of the cause of death by the medical officer completing the death certificate. Highly critical of the NCHS procedure at the data collection stage, Sherman and Langworthy (1979) point out several significant flaws.

First, they point out the poor quality of medical diagnosis at the time of death. They cite a study by Moriyama, Baum, Haenszel and Mattison (1958) which indicates that 39 percent of a Pennsylvania sample of death certificates was based on "sketchy" diagnostic information. Another study was done by James, Patton and Heslin (1955) of 1,889 autopsied deaths in Albany, New York. The authors reviewed clinical information, autopsy protocols and laboratory reports and concluded that 57 percent of the homicide and suicide deaths could have been misclassified as to the circumstances of the death (Sherman and Langworthy, 1979).

It is difficult to disagree with Sherman and Langworthy largely because so little is known about the general quality of medical certification. In reviewing an annotated bibliography of 128 cause of death validation studies from 1958-1980, the authors concluded:

The most striking finding is that so little is known about the quality of medical certification and its effect on diagnostic statistics in general and on national cause-of-death statistics in particular. Apparently no country has a well-defined program for systematically assessing the quality of medical certifications being reported on death certificates or for measuring the error effects on the level and trends of cause-of-death statistics (NCHS, 1982: iii).

None of the 128 studies focused on homicide. In addition, an extensive computerized literature search by the author uncovered no material on the quality of death certification for homicides beyond what is reported here.

Sherman and Langworthy (1979) contend a second flaw is that there is "apparently widespread lack of the coroners' awareness of, support for, and legal obligation to comply with the system's request for the full information necessary to code the causes of death according to ICD categories" (p. 548). In a telephone interview with the authors, the then chief medical examiner of New York City claimed that most of his colleagues around the country are generally "turned off" by the ICD categories, particularly where stigma may result from the use of the categories. In another interview, a board-certified forensic pathologist indicated that individuals with his qualifications should be more aware of ICD categories.

A third flaw pointed out by Sherman and Langworthy (1979) is that the instructions for completing the standard death certificate are vague. While it is especially true in trying to distinguish a civilian-caused homicide from a death caused by legal intervention, the subject of the Sherman and Langworthy study, the implication is that the statement holds for other kinds of homicides as well. In response to how the injury occurred, a very small space is made available on the death certificate. In addition, the handbook on death registration for medico-legal officers urges users to be complete in their reporting while "using as few words as possible" (p. 549).

2.4 NCHS Summary

It is clear that the mortality reporting system of NCHS, which includes homicides, is much simpler than that of the UCR. With state bureaus of vital statistics enforcing death and birth registration requirements and with complete reporting since 1933, it is a system which is probably about as well and simply organized as could be expected for such a heterogeneous collection of people, jurisdictions and states.

From the researchers viewpoint, the addition of four digit categories in the ninth revision of the ICD contributes much to the utility of the NCHS dataset. The major advantage is that criminal justice researchers can now manipulate the three and four digit categories to create a data series which more closely approaches the requirements of specific criminal law and criminological categories.

The availability of comparability ratios affords the research user the opportunity to evaluate the effect of various revisions on a lengthy homicide series. A review of the comparability ratios for the total number of homicides over the many revisions suggests that changes in classification have had a minimal effect on the series. However, most of the comparability ratios have been limited to assessing the effect of revisions on the total number of homicides; very little information is available on the changes in classification with respect to three or four digit codes.

The most serious criticism of the NCHS data is the limited reliability and validity of death certifications. Other than one or two studies and some anecdotal evidence, of limited utility, there is no adequate empirical research. The quality of death certifications is a particularly critical issue, because no matter how sophisticated the remainder of the NCHS reporting system becomes, death certifications are the initial essential input. Without validity and reliability at this point, all other efforts have little value.

3. Intersystem Agreement: NCHS and UCR

The present section examines the amount of agreement between the NCHS and the UCR at the national and state or local levels. Despite the fact that police departments generally have long term cooperative relationships with the offices of medical examiners or coroners, neither of their national reporting counterparts have capitalized on that relationship to establish case identifiers that would be common to both reporting systems. Thus, like comparisons between police department and SHR data there is no way to compare, on a case-by-case basis, homicides reported to NCHS by a coroner or medical examiner to homicides reported by the police to the UCR. With respect to studying intersystem agreement, researchers are left with aggregate comparisons defined by time and location.

3.1 National Comparisons

In comparing Return A, FBI estimates, and SHR figures to NCHS figures, there are two problems. First, there is a problem of comparability in terms of specific reporting areas. The UCR receives reports from law enforcement agencies while NCHS receives reports from county level medical examiners or coroners. The jurisdiction of law enforcement agencies, except for county Sheriffs, does not always coincide with the county level jurisdiction of NCHS data. While it is possible in some instances to make the two data sets comparable with respect to reporting agencies, it requires detailed knowledge of the boundaries of the law enforcement reporting agency and how that knowledge can be matched with county level data. For national and state comparisons, this issue is not a problem.

The second problem, that of similarity in definition, has been alluded to in earlier sections. NCHS reports data on homicides, which include justifiable homicides. While homicide data are available, most of the research using data from the UCR has used murder and nonnegligent manslaughter. While a major category of justifiable homicides, police killings and executions, can be removed from the NCHS data series beginning in 1949, at best, the results represent only general comparability. This general comparability may be adequate for nationwide comparability studies, but represents a problem if smaller geographical units are used. It is possible that NCHS data may be made more comparable to the murder and nonnegligent manslaughter category beginning in 1979 because of the addition of four digit codes. However, no research examining that problem has been done.

One of the earliest studies of the agreement between homicides as reported by the UCR and the NCHS was done by Hindelang (1974). He compared murder and nonnegligent manslaughter and NCHS annual totals for the nation from 1935 through 1970. In examining the graph of rates for the two series, Hindelang concluded that agreement between the two series from 1940 through 1970 was "generally good. Indeed the similarity in the shapes of the curves is striking" (p. 3).

> Overall, the data ... suggest that CHS and UCR are in reasonably close agreement with respect to estimates of homicide rates in the period for which data from both sources are available; to the extent that one lends credence to the CHS results, credence is also lent to the UCR homicide results (p. 5)

Cantor and Cohen (1980) did a more extensive investigation of the agreement between UCR data and the NCHS data. For all intersource comparisons, Cantor and Cohen used the national murder and nonnegligent manslaughter estimates available from the Office of Management and Budget (OMB). Estimates from the annual UCR reports were not comparable before and after 1958.

From 1949, when the authors were able to eliminate police killings from the NCHS series, to 1973, comparisons of the two series indicated close agreement. However, in the period from 1960 through 1963, the two indicators moved in opposite directions for reasons that were unknown to the authors. They recommend that any analysis which is primarily concerned with that time period be conducted with both indicators to assess the effect of discrepant trends in those years.

Assessing the amount of agreement for the entire series (1933-1975) raises many more problems. In order to examine the entire series for both data sources, Cantor and Cohen used the NCHS series which included police killings; these data were compared with the OMB estimates of murder and nonnegligent manslaughter. They found that the correlations between the two series varied from .85 to .98 depending on whether the 1933-1970, 1936-1975 or 1933-1975 periods was selected. The correlation was affected most dramatically by whether either the 1933-1935 or 1970-1975 period was excluded from the entire series. With the former period removed, the correlation for 1933-1975 is increased from .92 to .98. When the 1970-1975 period is eliminated, the same correlation drops from .92 to .85.

To demonstrate the different results that would be obtained with independent variables, the authors intercorrelated the two series with such explanatory variables as percentage of homicides cleared by arrest, percentage of resident population between the ages of 15-24, and the unemployment rate. They found different results depending on the time period and, sometimes, the homicide series analyzed. They further indicated that the point in time at which the analysis begins and ends may substantially effect the results of the analysis and strongly recommended that researchers consider the time frame under study in planning the analysis. Cantor and Cohen (1980) further suggest that a critical evaluation is particularly important in studies which depend on the analysis of homicide time series data of the deterrent effect of the death penalty.

Using data from a previous project of nationwide homicide patterns (Riedel and Zahn, 1985), the author examined the amount of agreement between FBI estimates, Return A counts, SHR counts, and NCHS counts of homicides. Legal intervention and execution homicides were excluded from NCHS series and murder and nonnegligent manslaughters were used for the FBI series. Figure 1 gives the rates of each measure by reporting year. Table A in the appendix gives the frequencies and rates for each measure.

The differences in the rates for FBI estimates and NCHS data are small and they parallel one another closely. The curves for SHR counts and Return A counts also cluster together, but are some distance from the other two rates. In addition, Figure 1 indicates a very close relationship between Return A and SHR rates after 1974.

To explore the amount of agreement in more detail, agreement ratios were calculated for each year of the series and a mean agreement ratio was calculated for a series of comparisons. For example, SHR frequencies were divided by FBI estimates for each of the eleven years. The mean of the series range and difference between the highest and lowest annual agreement ratio is given in Table 4.

Table 4 indicates that, with one exception, the highest mean agreement ratio is for the comparison of FBI estimates for murder and nonnegligent

Figure 1

Homicide Rates in the United States (1968-1978) According to Four Sources

Graph showing rates per 100,000 population from 1968 to 1978 for NCHS Counts, FBI Estimates, Return A Counts, and SHR Counts.

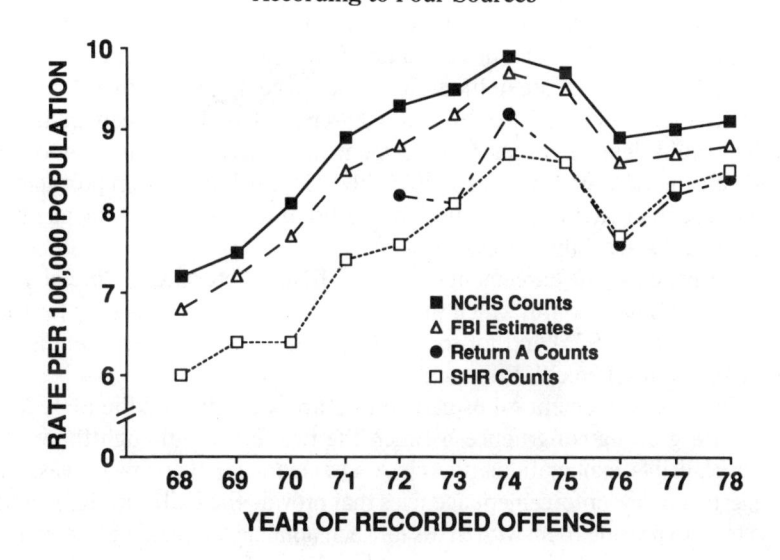

Table 4

Mean agreement ratios comparing four sources for the total number of homicides (1968-1978)

	SHR vs. FBI Est.	SHR vs. Return A	SHR vs. NCHS	NCHS vs. FBI Est.	NCHS vs. Return A	Return A vs. FBI Est
X̄ (agreement) N = 11	.89	.99[a]	.86	.97	.89[a]	.92[a]
Range	.83-.97	.92-1.01	.79-.94	.95-.98	.89-.93	.89-.96
Diff	.14	.09	.15	.03	.03	.08

[a]N = 7

manslaughter with NCHS counts of homicides for the eleven year period; the FBI estimates account for .97 of the homicides reported by NCHS. Given that NCHS data probably contain some justifiable homicides, this result suggests that there is very close agreement between the national series. The range of agreement ratios ranges from .95 in 1968 to .98 in 1975.

According to Table 4, the highest mean agreement ratio is for the comparison between Return A counts and SHRs (.99). There are, however, several reasons to believe this mean agreement ratio may be higher than would be the case if data were available for the entire eleven year series. First, examination of the annual agreement ratios derived from the data in Table A indicate that the lowest agreement ratios are always found earlier in the series, whereas the highest are found late in the series. Thus, in comparing Return A counts to SHRs, the series from 1968-1971 would probably have low agreement ratios which would depress the mean agreement ratio. Second, unlike any other comparison, there are three years (1976-1978) in which the SHR reports more homicides than Return A which serves to bring the mean agreement ratio closer to 1.00 (see Table A).

Nevertheless, the agreement between SHR and Return A is impressive. It is the only comparison in which the total numbers agree completely for two years (1973 and 1975) and for four of the remaining five years, there is no more than a five percent difference.

The high agreement ratios between Return A counts and the SHR data suggest a growing congruence between the two forms. Although there are other plausible explanations, the close agreement for these two measures suggests that law enforcement agencies that provide the UCR with Return As also tend to provide them with SHRs for each homicide. Consideration of this point, along with the research reported earlier which found that the total number of cases reported by the SHRs agreed well with those recorded by the large city police departments, suggests that most underreporting of homicides may be occurring in rural areas and small towns.

There is more agreement between FBI estimates and the NCHS data than between FBI estimates and other measures within the UCR. According to Table 4, the mean agreement ratio for the SHR data and FBI estimates is .89, while for Return A counts and the FBI estimates, the mean agreement ratio is .92. As with the comparison between Return A counts and the NCHS data, the latter mean agreement ratio may be lower than reported here.

3.2 State and City Comparisons

The only study of comparisons between homicide measures reported by the UCR and the NCHS at both the state and city level was done by Sherman and Langworthy (1979). Rather than focusing on homicide or murder, these authors examined homicides committed by police officers.

To determine whether NCHS measures could be used as a measure of police killings of civilians, the authors used thirteen jurisdictions for the years 1970-1976 and gathered comparable data on police homicides from NCHS data and police generated sources. The latter included data reported by the police to statistical analysis centers, data from SHRs, and data compiled by the police. The jurisdictions were two heavily urban states (California and New Jersey), six less urban states (Alaska, Nebraska, Oregon, South Carolina, Vermont and Wisconsin), and five New York city counties.

In nine of the thirteen counties, the death counts from police-generated data exceeded those compiled by the NCHS. The authors found that 51 percent of the police homicides were underreported by NCHS; the latter number held not only for the total, but also for the heavily urban and less urban clusters of jurisdictions.

According to NCHS national data, the jurisdictions used accounted for 25 percent of all deaths by legal intervention from 1971-1975. Considering the amount of underreporting, and the fact that some years were omitted in some jurisdictions, the authors conclude that the total national incidence of police homicides was about 26 percent higher than reported by the NCHS. Sherman and Langworthy (1979) also concluded that NCHS data cannot be used to measure the national incidence of police homicides. Since the police generated data does not cover the entire country, it is clear, the authors suggest, that the number of police homicides nationwide are simply unknown.

The authors also attempted to determine whether available data sources could be used to measure the relative incidence of police homicide from one city to another or one police department to another. To address this question, NCHS data and a combination of several sources of police killings were used. Information was complied on the latter alternative source of police homicides, as well as the NCHS, for a total of 133 city-years from 36 jurisdictions of over 250,000 population. The correlation between the two data sources was .64 for the raw data; when the death counts are standardized by population, the correlation drops slightly to .53. As the authors point out neither correlation accounts for even half the variance.

While the data were not accurate enough to measure relative incidents from city to city, similarities in the pattern of relative incidents make it possible to use either data set as a measure of the pattern of variation in police homicides in relation to a set of independent variables. To examine that possibility, the authors developed measures of theoretically relevant independent variables. Among the cluster of community characteristics, they included such variables as population density, gun density, unemployment and suicide rates, violent index crime and UCR homicide rates. The cluster of police organizational structure variables included such variables as geographic decentralization, span of control and self regulation. Examples of police organizational policy variables were disciplinary formalism measures and disciplinary pressure measures.

The seventeen measures were correlated with the two measures of police homicides. Despite the diversity of procedures employed with the data, the researchers found that the two data sources generated similar results. The alternative data sources produced stronger correlations and most were in the theoretically predicted direction. The authors concluded that the two measures can be used to gauge patterns of variation in police homicide rates (Sherman and Langworthy, 1979).

Focusing on homicide in the seven cities mentioned earlier in the chapter, Riedel and Zahn (1983) compared the number of homicide cases reported by the police department to that recorded by the medical examiner in each of the seven cities. In general, the degree of agreement was high with five of the seven cities having a 95 percent or better agreement figure for the total number of homicides.

> In six of the cities, more cases were reported as homicides by the medical examiners offices than by the police departments. In Philadelphia, for example, 18 of 21 discrepancies were those reported by the medical examiners as homicide; in Ashton, all 20 were medical examiner cases, with 12 of those 20 being hit and run cases and eight being victims (or their remains) found in areas of police jurisdictional dispute. Regarding the use of cars in homicide, a pattern similar to that of Ashton prevailed in Dallas; the medical examiner reported 13 more cases of homicide than did the police department, with 12 of those 13 being motor vehicle deaths. In general a review of the discrepant cases showed more cases of homicide being reported by medical examiners' offices than by police departments and that the bases for differences in determination were primarily differences in jurisdictional definitions; some differences in the evaluation of arson cases; and differences in the evaluation of hit and run cases ... In general, the degree of agreement was high with five of the seven cities having a 95 percent or better agreement figure for the total number of homicides (p. 105).

Data from police departments and medical examiners offices were also compared for victim's sex, race, age and victim-offender relationship. The agreement for victim's sex was very high, ranging from 99.5 percent in Philadelphia to 100.0 percent in the other six cities.

The agreement on race between the two local sources ranged from 75.6 percent in Ashton to 100.0 percent in St. Louis. In general, discrepancies in the area of race occurred in the coding of Hispanics, Mexicans or Puerto Ricans. In Newark, over half of the discrepancy on this variable occurred because the police department coded the victim by the specific ethnic group while the medical examiner coded the victims race as "other races."

For victim's ages, when the criteria of agreement included differences of ages by only one year, the range of agreement was from 80.1 percent in Newark to 99.0 percent in Ashton. Five of the seven cities had 90 percent or higher agreement.

Not surprisingly, the poorest agreement occurred for victim-offender relationships. The range was from 52.2 percent in Ashton to 80.6 percent in

Newark. No data was available on this variable from the medical examiner's offices in St. Louis.

The reasons for the poor agreement on the relationship variable are a result of the medical examiner's concern for the victim and lack of data on him or her. Subsequent investigation and apprehension of the offender is the concern of the police department. Consequently, whatever data on victim/offender relationships are available at the *time* of the event is what finds its way ito in the medical examiner's files. In support of this view, agreement was high between offices on domestic slayings for which offenders are quickly apprehended. It was poor for stranger and acquaintance slayings, which require more time to clear by arrest (Riedel and Zahn, 1983).

3.3 Intersystem Summary

Research on national, state and city comparisons of the amount of intersystem agreement between homicide measures used by the UCR and NCHS data support the following conclusions.

There is greater agreement between the two series with recent data in contrast to older data. This is true not only for comparisons of FBI estimates and NCHS counts, but also for comparisons of Return A counts and SHR counts with FBI estimates and NCHS measures. While it is difficult to give an answer which would be appropriate for all uses and occasions, it appears that with respect to a report of total homicides from the UCR, data prior to 1960 will present greater difficulties than data from that point to the present. From 1960 onward, many of the revision problems that characterized early estimates were resolved and the agreement with NCHS data appears to be very high.

For the NCHS, the data appears to be usable beginning in 1949 when police killings and executions were given separate codes. However, with regard to specific variables, this data generally has less utility because it is limited to the victim and some of the cause-of-death categories were not refined until 1979.

There is a kind of schizophrenic character to the results of national comparisons. On the one hand, very close agreement between FBI estimates and NCHS data are found; on the other hand, much lower agreement occurs between FBI estimates and other measures of murder and nonnegligent manslaughter. SHR counts and Return A counts, for example, seem to agree very well with each other from 1974 to 1978, but neither agree closely with FBI estimates. There is something paradoxical about a reporting system in which intersystem measures agree better than intrasystem measures.

The problem seems to reside in the agencies that do not report to the UCR. What is needed is a more careful examination of which agencies are not reporting, or are underreporting, to the UCR. A more careful review of these agencies's practices would allow us to assess both their relative contributions to the number and character of homicides and whether additional efforts should be made to bring them into the reporting system.

With respect to the intersystem comparison at the state and local levels, it appears that the NCHS seriously underreports police homicides. The research by Sherman and Langworthy (1979) indicates that the NCHS may underreport police homicides by as much as 51 percent.

Comparisons of case completeness and variable completeness at the level of city police departments and county medical examiners offices indicate a high level of agreement between the two organizations. Most of the discrepancies in the total number of homicides were small and occurred because of jurisdictional disagreements and conflicts over the definition of the crime. For specific variables, such as the victim's sex, race and age, the agreement was generally high. The lack of agreement for victim-offender relationships was mainly for stranger relationships for which information is more difficult to collect and less important to medical examiners.

For the researcher who is examining variations in homicides or police homicides, the results are encouraging. The efforts of Cantor and Cohen (1980) to relate variations in homicide to independent variables and those of Sherman and Langworthy (1979) with police homicides indicate that FBI estimates and NCHS data provide similar results. Of course, as both sets of authors indicate, they have not included all possible independent variables, nor, in Cantor and Cohen's case, did they consider how the two dependent variables behave with other than national level data. In light of Cantor and Cohen's study many cautionary statements about the time period covered by a proposed analysis, it is important that the researchers attempting to use either FBI homicide data or NCHS data examine very carefully how the two reporting systems behave in the time period and at the geographical level of aggregation needed.

4. Summary

Perhaps the most unequivocal conclusion that can be made about the two nationwide homicide data sets is that both provide, consistent with their definitions, a reasonably accurate count of the annual number of homicides for approximately the past 25 years. While an accurate national count of homicides may extend back to 1949 for NCHS, the research does seem to indicate that their count of legal intervention homicides substantially underreports the number of police homicides.

When questions of variable completeness are considered for SHRs, it is clear there is a substantial amount of disagreement between national and city police sources. Whether a similar pattern of disagreement exists for national and local NCHS sources is unknown because of an absence of research.

Where the concern focuses on whether the data can be used for studying variations in the offense, the results are somewhat more positive. However, the available research is limited. Cantor and Cohen's analysis, Sherman and Langworthy's results and Williams and Flewelling's comparisons of rates suggest that the two data sets may have considerable research utility without being complete with respect to the number of cases or variables. However, the research by Loften and his associates indicates that there may be numerous classification errors.

Considering the enormous amount of resources that have been expanded over the years to obtain a complete record of the most highly reported offense, murder or homicide, the record of achievement for either reporting system cannot be described as enviable. Where the major claim for success rests in only being able to count reasonably accurately the number of times the event occurs nationally in a time period, it appears to this author that the expenditure of resources has been disproportionate to the amount of achievement.

The single greatest problem for both reporting systems, as well as research criminologists, has been the unwillingness to focus research on the basic first step-how the murder or homicide is initially reported at the level of reporting officer or medical examiner. There is very little research at the local level with respect to how judgments are made with respect to the SHR, how reports of investigating officers are transferred to SHRs, the qualifications of police personnel who do this task or how recording inconsistencies are resolved. Neither data set is going to be better than the quality of the data at this first step.

In reviewing the two nationwide homicide reporting systems, the reader may be more impressed with the simplicity and rigorous detail of the NCHS reporting system in comparison to the UCR. However, the two reporting systems operate with different sets of constraints and confront slightly different reporting problems.

As an organization, the NCHS has expended more resources on resolving the problems of their reporting system, especially at the state and national level. But that is, after all, part of the major mission of NCHS as an organization. The UCR, on the other hand, is a rather small part of a much larger organization that is devoted to the practice of nationwide law enforcement. In other words, given the greater amount of resources available to the NCHS, more quality and completeness of data should be expected for the NCHS than for the UCR.

In addition, the data collection and reporting tasks of the two reporting systems cover different problems. NCHS is primarily concerned with collecting information on the age, race, sex and cause of death of the homicide victim.

One of the most important sources of victim information for the NCHS—the dead human body—is the most available and is sometimes the only indication that a homicide has occurred.

Data collection problems for the UCR are more difficult. While information is available on the victim, the UCR also collects additional and detailed information about the offender, who may or may not be available. Since murder and nonnegligent manslaughter clearance rates are about 75 percent, about 25 percent of the offender information will be missing at the time of the event and, frequently, for some period thereafter.

The well-organized NCHS reporting system is impressive. The system entails mandatory reporting at the state level for all 50 states. The organization of reporting from local medical officers to the state level is well defined; only one form is completed; classification categories are relatively clear and are periodically updated. Returns are carefully monitored, and great care is taken in assembling the final collection of homicide data.

On the other hand, for the UCR, only part of the reporting agencies fall under a mandatory system, several forms need to be completed, classification categories have only recently been clarified, and there is no well-developed system of monitoring returns and updates. Given the considerations that have been discussed, what is surprising is not that the NCHS data are of high quality, but that the FBI homicide data are as good as they are.

Finally, in recent years, the UCR has become an organization that is more open to the requests and suggestions of researchers. In its responsiveness to requests and criticisms, the UCR has recognized that criticisms that go unanswered by the reporting organization tend to be self-reinforcing and lead to stereotypes.

In working with the research community, the UCR currently follows practices similar to the NCHS, an organization that has had a long and successful history of working with researchers. In part, the greater sophistication of NCHS data stems from a recognition that making data available to researchers is not a one-way street; because researchers make extensive and detailed use of the data, they find deficiencies which are not apparent to the more casual user. Thus, cooperation with the research community pays dividends to the reporting organizations by making them aware of shortcomings and problems that they otherwise would not have found.

Appendix

Table A

**Homicide victim counts and rates according to four sources
United States, 1968-1978**

	FBI Estimates		Return A		SHR		NCHS	
Year	Count[a]	Rate[b]	Count[a]	Rate	Count[c]	Rate	Count[c]	Rate
1968	13,648	6.8	—[d]	—	11,955	6.0	14,336	7.2
1969	14,590	7.2	—	—	12,918	6.4	15,123	7.5
1970	15,810	7.7	—	—	13,039	6.4	16,550	8.1
1971	17,630	8.5	—	—	15,322	7.4	18,403	8.9
1972	18,520	8.8	17,258	8.2	15,832	7.6	19,372	9.3
1973	19,509	9.2	17,123	8.1	17,123	8.1	20,120	9.5
1974	20,600	9.7	19,570	9.2	18,632	8.7	21,138	9.9
1975	20,510	9.5	18,642	8.6	18,642	8.6	21,013	9.7
1976	18,780	8.6	16,605	7.6	16,821	7.7	19,293	8.9
1977	19,120	8.7	18,033	8.2	18,300	8.3	19,746	9.0
1978	19,555	8.8	18,714	8.4	18,941	8.5	20,232	9.1

[a] FBI murder and nonnegligent manslaughter Return A counts and estimates are taken from annual editions of the UCR (1968-1978).
[b] Civilian population is taken from *Statistical Abstract of the United States*, 1986, p. 5.
[c] SHR and NCHS counts taken from homicide projects tapes (Riedel and Zahn, 1985).
[d] Data on Return A counts were not available in the UCR for 1968-1971.

Part III

The Past and the Future

10

Measurement in Criminology and Criminal Justice: A Brief 20-Year Retrospective

Robert M. Figlio

In discussing the content of this chapter the task could be viewed as one of simply reviewing the area of measurement in criminology over the last 20 years from several perspectives: the development of parameter estimates for various forms of delinquency and criminality using officially recorded offense data, self-report scales and the National Crime Survey (NCS), longitudinal birth cohort studies, the evaluation of criminal justice system effectiveness from various statistical and methodological positions, and the surveying and scaling of public attitudes about crime and its severity. This approach would produce a series of statements such as: This is what we thought we knew in the late sixties and this is what we think we know now. These "think we knows" would then be repeated for the research and measurement areas with which one's familiarity would vary depending upon experience and interest. This straightforward exposition would condense in a short exposition of the conclusions from several studies and the periodic reviews of the field. Nothing would be said about what should have been done or what ought to be done, only what, from one or another's perspective, has been accomplished.

In preparation for this ex post facto documentary, some remarks made by Bayley in an address to the Academy of Criminal Justice Services in 1978 seem appropriate to consider:

> ... we researchers in criminal justice are often our own worst enemies. We talk too much about what we are doing and how we are doing it. We are distractingly self-conscious. We emphasize tribal differences that are intelligible only to ourselves. Paraphrasing Aristotle, give me an intelligent researcher looking at questions that are both topical and theoretically interesting and I will move the criminal justice world. Give me, however, twenty researchers who spend their time talking about the problems of criminal

justice research, and I will show you a group of people who won't be able to move in out of the rain. (Hagan, 1982, p. 6).

This rather sour view of commissions, committees and many panel discussions is either too glib, true, untrue, bitter, appropriate or some combination of all of the above, depending on which position in any of several relevant continua you, the researcher, funding agency, practitioner or just plain observer-critic, lie. Certainly, many scholars and practitioners have, during the last 20 years of involvement with commissions, committees, groups and researchers, felt at one time or another in agreement with most or all of these perceptions.

1. Planning the Research

In 1982, The John D. and Catherine T. MacArthur Foundation undertook a study program which involved approximately forty researchers, some of whom are represented in this collection, to discuss and examine the various merits and weaknesses of several proposals for large-scale prospective longitudinal studies of delinquency and crime. These proposals underwent an extensive peer review process, which ultimately eliminated some twenty applications, leaving three to be considered for further assessment. All of the applicants were invited to a meeting to discuss these works, along with the study panel who convened the gathering, and the board and representatives of the foundation which was to consider funding the work. By the end of a three-day meeting, the various competing perspectives, ideologies, research agenda and personalities had so clouded the issues that no consensus as to the goals of the research, its character and method was apparent. None of the three proposals was ever discussed, (the primary reason for holding the conference), and the meeting was adjourned with the only conclusion being that someone would write a summary of the discussion, including a consideration of the approaches of the three proposals with some additions from the remainder of those which had not survived the review process.[1]

Unfortunately, the board members of the foundation were somewhat disenchanted with the field as represented by the discussion and no further research was funded. As a result, a great loss was sustained at that time by the discipline because of the importance of the work that has yet to be undertaken, by the many researchers who have invested—in some cases—several years of preparations, and by the field of criminal justice research as a whole because of its self-generated appearance of confusion, internal jealousies and lack of concern for the greater good.

Why was the conference convened? Why, well into the eighties, was another longitudinal cohort study being considered for massive funding? What were the data, analyses and policy issues? Why, almost twenty years after the President's Crime Commission began its deliberations, were issues being addressed so similar to those that are about to be outlined here that one might think the interim period had not been lived, so that the criminological research community as viewed from the outside, must have appeared as a group of Rip Van Winkles?

Of course the situation was not so simple as implied above nor was the discussion unenlightened. In fact the meeting reflected the frustration of a discipline that felt itself on the verge of significant breakthroughs largely because of the magnitude and strength of the work which had been accomplished during the period from 1965 to the mid-eighties.

2. Modern Criminology Develops

Twenty years ago, the President's Commission on Law Enforcement and Administration of Justice (1967a, 1967b) released its report begun two years earlier under the all-encompassing title of *The Challenge of Crime in a Free Society*. This seminal work, which stands as a landmark in the development of criminology and criminal justice, concluded by saying:

> The Commission's recommendations must be implemented through a strategy for change involving all levels of government, private groups, and every American citizen. Control of crime requires three very basic emphases: Preventing delinquency before it ever becomes a matter for the criminal justice system to deal with; providing agencies of justice with adequate resources; and pushing forward the search for better knowledge about crime and how best to handle it ... The role of the Federal Government must be to lead and coordinate change through providing financial and technical assistance and support of research ... (p 301).

From these words began, from a measurement point of view, modern criminology and the pathway along which the discipline has traveled to date. Interestingly enough, the authors of one of the Task Force reports of the series, *Crime and Its Impact*, must have felt a sense of "deja vu," as one often does when "taking stock," when in Chapter 10 of that report they recall:

> Over 30 years ago a distinguished Commission appointed by the President of the United States to study crime and propose measures for its control reported serious deficiencies in essential information at the national level. Calling "accurate data ... the beginning of wisdom," the Wickersham Commission recommended development of a "comprehensive plan" for a "complete body of statistics covering crime, criminals, criminal justice, and penal treatment"

at the Federal, state and local levels and the entrusting of this plan at the Federal level to a single agency.

Had this recommendation been adopted, the present Commission would not have been forced in 1967 to rely so often on incomplete information or to conclude so frequently that important questions could not be answered. Given the importance of sound data to both crime control and public understanding, it is hard to believe that such basic facts as the trend of juvenile delinquency, the percent of crimes committed by professional criminals, or the likelihood of recidivism are beyond the capacity of our present statistical resources ... There are no national and almost no state or local statistics at all in a number of important areas: the courts, probation, sentencing, and the jails ... There is no reliable measure of the extent of organized crime and no satisfactory test for police performance. In short the United States is today, in the era of the high speed computer, trying to keep track of crime and criminals with a system that was less than adequate in the days of the horse and buggy. (The President's Commission on Law Enforcement and Administration of Justice, 1967b, p. 123).

To ameliorate this state of data and measurement affairs, the Commission suggested ten goals of a statistical program which, if undertaken, would lead to, among other benefits, "safe streets:"

1. Inform the public and responsible governmental officials as to the nature of the crime problem, its magnitude and its trend over time.

2. Measure the effects of prevention and deterrence programs, ranging from community action to police patrol.

3. Find out who commits crimes by age, sex, family status, income, ethnic and residential background and other social attributes in order to find the proper focus of crime prevention programs.

4. Measure the workload and effectiveness of the police, the courts and the other agencies of the criminal justice system, both individually and as an integrated system.

5. Analyze the factors contributing to success and failure of probation and parole, and other correctional alternatives for various kinds of offenders.

6. Provide criminal justice agencies with comparative norms of performance.

7. Furnish baseline data for research.

8. Compute the costs of crime in terms of economic injury inflicted upon communities and individuals, as well as assess the direct public expenditures by criminal justice agencies.
9. Project expected crime rates and their consequences into the future for more enlightened government planning.
10. Assess the societal and other causes of crime and develop theories of criminal behavior. (The President's Commission on Law Enforcement and Administration of Justice, 1967b, p. 123-124)

To these and other operational ends the Omnibus Crime Control and Safe Streets Act of 1968 created the Law Enforcement Assistance Administration (LEAA) and in 1970, to supervise the collection of the above named data, the National Criminal Justice Information and Statistics Service (NCJISS). Over the years, because of critical reviews, political influences and the resulting changes in emphases, these agencies have been divided, transformed and modified into what now are known as the Office of Justice Programs including the National Institute of Justice (NIJ), the Bureau of Justice Statistics (BJS), the Office of Victims of Crime (OVC), the Office of Juvenile Justice and Delinquency Prevention (OJJDP), the Bureau of Justice Assistance (BJA), and their various subdivisions.

It is important to pause here to point out that the creation of the Office of Law Enforcement Assistance of the Department of Justice and the involvement of the Institute for Defense Analyses, from which have come many creative efforts, was from the outset a political act following from the perceived need to reduce crime, even if the work was not particularly or obviously political in its intent. As a result, the report and recommendations of the Panel, upon retrospect, appear to be extraordinarily optimistic with regard to the promise of crime reduction through the application of the methods of operations research and the resulting systemic reforms, and lacking in the various argumentative biases which rapidly followed in the footsteps of the Panel's work during the succeeding years. For those individuals among the research community who have worked in the shadow of and support from this set of agencies, the review of their histories reveals political involvement, confrontation and the need for the preparation of complex annual justifications by researchers and agency personnel for the continuance of what, as viewed from most prospectives, has been a series of high quality research programs promoted and supervised by a largely apolitical and competent government staff. ("Apolitical," here refers to the lack of value impingement by these agencies on individual research efforts, not necessarily on the choice of the kind of research which was and is supported.)

As Walker pointed out in his "Reexamining the President's Crime Commission" in 1978: "The creation of LEAA (even the name is significant) was

Congress's way of saying 'support your local police' in an election year. Thus, it is hardly surprising that LEAA immediately became a vast pork barrel for local police departments. LEAA encountered immediate and continuing criticism for overemphasizing the police at the expense of other agencies and for spending too much on hardware" (Walker, 1978, p. 11).

Parenthetically, the Task Force on *Crime and Its Impact* noted that in 1967 the budget estimates for major Federal statistical programs totalled 124 million dollars. Of that amount the Bureaus of the Census and Labor Statistics utilized over $15 million and twelve other programs spent more than $2 million each per year on statistical work while the Federal budget for all criminal justice system statistical expenditures was less than $800,000 (The President's Commission Law Enforcement and Administration of Justice, 1967b). In 1976 the National Advisory Committee on Criminal Justice Standards and Goals (1976) reported that although the total expenditure for research and development in the Federal Criminal Justice System was about six times greater than in 1969 (as a result of the research program of LEAA administered under the National Institute of Law Enforcement and Criminal Justice), the total outlay for this category was still, in its maximum year, only 0.4% of the total criminal justice system expenditure. At the same time the research and development component of the budgets of education, agriculture and health were .3%, 1.0% and 4.6%, respectively. These values can be put into perspective by comparison to the average of 2.0% for large manufacturing concerns (National Advisory Committee on Criminal Justice Standards and Goals, 1976). In addition, this relatively modest increase was being offset somewhat by a reduction in private foundation support for basic criminological research and the retreat of the National Institute of Mental Health (NIMH) from funding strictly crime-related projects. Further, a large proportion of the research and development money was being absorbed by police-related research programs which bore upon operational effectiveness, and crime and civil disobedience control during that period.

In this context it should be remembered that a major component of the Commission's work centered about the need for further *research on a wide variety* of criminological issues.

It might be asked what bearing does this discussion have on the assessment of the state of the art and science of measurement today? Quite a bit, especially in terms of the *kinds* of research which are now deemed relevant and appropriate to fund and on the whole research climate of criminology.

The LEAA block program grants to states to aid in crime control operations were designed to have an evaluation component as an integral part of any experimental or intervention program. Thus, the early enthusiasm for program development in treatment, corrections, police and general criminal justice system operations spawned a concurrent involvement of a new cadre of participants in the rapidly growing field of "evaluation technology." A journal was published and a massive handbook on evaluation techniques appeared on the scene from the pens of the sociologists at the University of Southern California (Klein and Teilmann, 1980).[2]

However, much of the program monies were never spent on the evaluation of projects. In Philadelphia, for example, the $1.5 million Police Cable TV project allocated only $3,000 for the three-member evaluation team composed of a law professor, electrical engineering professor, and a criminologist. This team was to assess the technical adequacy of the equipment, the legal ramifications of using a television booking and charging system and the efficiency of the operation from an overall criminal justice system view. The interesting finding of that evaluation was that the increase in the efficiency of the police in charging, booking, and presentation of the defendant before the court by use of a cable TV system for a preliminary hearing was insignificant because the overwhelming factor in prisoner processing time was the availability of a magistrate or judge to hear the case (Haber, Spritzer and Figlio, 1977).

Thus, as a result of court backlogs and judicial inefficiency due to excessive absences and other work-related difficulties, any improvements in police processing times were relatively unimportant. The final multimillion dollar Cable TV booking system would thus have a minimal impact on its stated purpose, the reduction of prisoner processing time.

The point here is that money which at the outset was in principle allocated to evaluative research remained in the other "hardware" categories. The effect of this corruption of the Commission's intentions was the production of a spate of poorly thought-out and evaluated programs. Due to the legislative and scholarly predisposition toward crime control rather than prevention already gaining momentum in the late sixties, even less money and talent were expended on the prevention of juvenile and adult criminality and intervention evaluations than on operational studies of the criminal justice system.

The work of Lipton, Wilkes, Martinson, Wilson, Von Hirsch, and in an unintended way that of the American Friends Service Committee Report, *Struggle for Justice*, and other liberal writers sounded the death knell for rehabilitative and correctional interventions.[3] Just as researchers learned to perform valid and reliable evaluations and experimental designs, funding shifted away from those areas most amenable to the application of this, for criminology, new technology. Concurrent with the rise in funding came a proliferation of criminal justice programs in universities around the country whose graduates sought to enter this new growth industry.

3. New Directions

This shift from proactive crime prevention to reactive crime control has had a profound effect on the kinds of data collected and, more importantly, the uses to which these materials are put. The goals of crime control and prevention through deterrence by threat of incapacitation do not necessarily require a completely different set of data and measurement procedures; but the needs of constraint certainly affect the direction and emphases of collection and research efforts. This statement does not imply that the quality of the work was or is affected by this state of affairs. In fact, the crime control perspective has produced a wealth of high quality data and innovative analytical perspectives. The data specificity required by modeling of the criminal justice system has sharpened the focus on variable delineation and measurement validity and reliability. Such clarity of problem definition and measurement integrity previously had never existed in criminology.

From the point of view of this collection, the "new criminology" is that body of work which we have seen develop during the last twenty years, and is characterized by: careful definition of variables, concern with the measurement issues of validity, and reliability, the awareness of error terms and of statistical artifacts, the development and utilization of categorical data analytic techniques, and the refinement of multivariate techniques of all types. No specific mention of those areas which have been traditionally called theory is made here, because embedded in all of the above is a conceptual scheme whose manifestation exists inextricably bound with variable selection and even with the method by which one looks for interrelationships among these indicators of our "unmeasured" concepts.

However, all of this discussion must be cast within an ideological framework which has had a direct impact on the research issues which have been addressed. Nonetheless, had we chosen to follow different ends, the means would have been the same: large-scale survey research, national level approaches to the gathering and dissemination of data and information, and the production of computer-based, sophisticated analytical schemes.

In 1977 the LEAA and NCJISS produced a Program Plan for Statistics 1977-1981 (U.S. Department of Justice, 1981). In that plan was a reiteration of some of the goals of the Crime Commission, but with more focus, that is, the review of prior years' works and outline of specific program goals and projects. In fact, this rather small volume set the tone for several years of work for LEAA, NIJ, and OJJDP. In the words of the report:

> "This is a plan for the total statistics program of LEAA. Although the plan will be the particular concern of NCJISS, it has implications for other LEAA offices. Accomplishment of the objectives will contribute substantially to other aspects of the LEAA program." (p. 1)

In this program is the specific goal of guiding national policy, through the collection of various data. Again, there appears a restatement of the Commission's objectives, a review of the Wickersham Commission's goals, and a mention of the National Advisory Commission on Criminal Justice Standards and Goals (1976) referred to earlier. The authors of this program state:

> "The goals of the LEAA criminal justice statistics program are the purposes for which the data are used, *not the statistical series or reports produced*" (p. 10) (emphasis added).
>
> "Nationwide criminal justice statistics should and must permit the public and Federal and State, and local agencies concerned with crime to assess the crime that occurs, its nature, and the effectiveness of methods to alleviate it... They should support the planning, management, implementation and evaluation of efforts to improve these systems" (pp. 7-8)

In addition, the report noted that the "LEAA statistics program should contribute substantially to providing the following information:

1. The nature and extent of crime and criminal behavior and the direction and amount of change in criminal activity.
2. The degree of seriousness ascribed by the public to a wide range of violations of the law, based on the perception of harm caused by such violations.
3. The correlation of crime with economic, social and demographic phenomena.
4. The nature of criminal victimization and the characteristics of victims and offenders.
5. The attitudes, opinions and perceptions of the public concerning the impact of crime and the response of criminal justice systems to criminal behavior.
6. The characteristics of accused persons and offenders entering and being processed by criminal justice systems at all levels of government.
7. The administration of justice at Federal, State and local levels in terms of volume, rate and time involved in the processing of cases and persons.
8. The extent of operational and informational linkage of the components of criminal justice systems involved in the processing of cases and persons.
9. The characteristics of detained, sentenced, and released prisoners—including those sentenced to capital punishment—and the opera-

tion and administration of the Federal, State and local institutions that hold prisoners.

10. The expenditures, manpower and facility resources, financing sources and total operational costs of criminal justice systems at all levels of governments.

11. The number and characteristics of criminal justice agencies and their employees at all levels of government.

12. The impact of crime on this society in terms of the total direct and indirect costs and the implications for other public policies and programs."

Additionally the authors note:

> "data about crime and criminal justice are vital to intelligent decision-making concerning crime, criminals and society's response to crime. It is essential that these data describe the linkage of law enforcement, prosecution, adjudication, and correctional functions in their dealings with crime and criminals. It is critical that these data describe the extent of recidivism and the relation of recidivism to prior actions of the criminal justice system" (U.S. Department of Justice, 1981, p. 7-8).

In these statements of goals are the embodiment and operationalization of the title of Chapter 12 of *The Challenge of Crime in a Free Society:* "Research—Instrument for Reform."

These goals all address scholarly and policy-relevant issues which, if realized, would definitely broaden and deepen our understanding of certain kinds of criminal behavior and the response of the criminal justice system to these illegal acts. But what is missing from this list of objectives? Unfortunately, quite a number of additional scholarly and policy-relevant items among which are:

1. A concern for the etiological examination of delinquency and criminality.

2. A concern for the social-structural correlates of behavior.

3. An awareness that the whole topic area of corrections and rehabilitation was and is not a settled issue and should be further studied and evaluated.

4. An awareness of the magnitude and need for research in the area of corporate and governmental crime—large-scale social system misbehavior.

In general, the recommendations of the plan display an ideological orientation which had been growing rapidly in the late sixties, reached its youthful vitality in the seventies and has blossomed into full maturity in the eighties. The intellectual harvest of that perspective is now being reaped in our inability to support studies of the causes of delinquency and crime in terms relevant to social systemic dysfunction, and in our cynicism about governmental and managerial misconduct, and especially in our general preoccupation with incapacitation, especially "selective."

On the other side of the coin, despite the direction in which our society is moving in this area and the selective manner in which our research has been interpreted and used, there is no doubt that we have progressed in an empirical sense more in the last twenty years than in the entirety of prior social science research in this area. This volume evidences the magnitude and depth of this recent work.

Without the centralized agencies, now NIJ, BJS and OJJDP, as envisioned by the President's Commission, there would be no NCS, improved Uniform Crime Reports and large-scale surveys of crime and delinquency. The survey of national victimizations is the single most important criminal justice indicator ever developed, with the exception of the Uniform Crime Reports. These two surveys give us complementary and multiple perspectives on the state of the nation's crime experience and provide the basis for several additional studies.

For example, the NCS was the vehicle for the National Survey of Crime Severity (NSCS), a study of the perceptions of over 50,000 Americans about the relative seriousness of over 200 different kinds of criminal behavior.

The NSCS is being used in many jurisdictions as a component for prosecutorial decision-making and as an element in seriousness-based mandated sentencing programs. These perceptions, when added to an incidence-based measure enable the production of a metric which has utility for research in many areas of criminal behavior and allows the conversion of categorical injury violations into a measure having comparable interpretive potential across all types of criminal behavior (Wolfgang, Figlio, Singer and Tracy, 1985).

Twenty years ago the life-time probability of an individual being arrested, convicted, or punished was unknown. Offender prevalence and incidence rates were speculatively estimated from cross-sectional data. Long-term funding has permitted, through data derived from several longitudinal studies, the estimation of: criminal career lengths, the timing between offenses, the probabilities associated with offense switching and specialization, the delinquency and criminal dropout potential or desistance rates, age at onset probabilities and the links which may exist between early and later delinquency and criminal behavior. Uniformities in various parameters based on these longitudinal studies are beginning to appear and fill the holes in estimation models.[4]

4. Self-report Studies: The Third Major Indicator

The John D. and Catherine T. MacArthur Foundation in collaboration with NIJ has recently begun a major initiative to develop a whole new series of longitudinal studies which will incorporate earlier work in this area with experimental interventions. This program will:

> "In addition to its primary task of designing a coordinated and integrated set of longitudinal cohort studies, including where possible assessment of the effects of experimental interventions, the program will serve a number of supportive functions. Those include efforts to initiate or support development and maintenance of archives of longitudinal data on crime and delinquency; development of a larger network of longitudinal researchers by forging links with other disciplines in which longitudinal efforts have been more fully elaborated; sponsorship of secondary analysis of existing longitudinal sets; and development of a central repository for written materials concerning longitudinal research on criminological or related subjects" (Castine Corp. Memo, 1988, p. 8).

This initiative permits the commencement of the work which earlier in this decade, as mentioned previously, was so haltingly begun.

Self-report studies, the third major, but as yet less developed, crime indicator, have been combined with official data in ways which have, in some instances, confirmed conclusions about delinquent behavior and, in other instances, raised doubts about preconceptions regarding the extent and character of criminal behavior in the U.S. Earlier studies using official records were severely criticized by those who saw systematic bias in police reporting practices, especially when delinquency estimates from early self-report studies produced such divergent conclusions. But more recent work indicates that the two data sources are convergent, although both have errors and both are complementary (Kitsuse and Cicourel, 1963; Elliot and Ageton, 1980; Hindelang, Hirschi and Weis, 1979).

Serious officially recorded delinquents tend to underreport their police contacts and a liberal interpretation of a self-report scale can make delinquents or criminals of almost all individuals. In addition, it is now known that institutionalized felons commit many more offenses than could have been estimated from their official arrest records or from other delinquency self-report studies.

This work is crucial in its impact on the probable effects of various intervention and/or incapacitation strategies.

In short, we now have a much better set of estimates of many of the parameters of interest in the *Program Plan for Statistics* than was available even as short a period as five years ago. These data have been gathered and assessed at great monetary and personal expense. The extent and intensity of this effort cannot be overestimated, as many readers are well aware. The persistence of researchers and of NIJ, BJS, OJJDP and NIMH directors and project monitors has been enormous, especially in light of our society's cyclicly pulling back from its commitment to the resolution of social problems.

However, we are far from a resolution of the problem of criminal behavior. Our mandated sentencing practices, habitual offender programs, and increased police budgets have filled our prisons to the extent that over four times as many offenders are locked up in jails and prisons now than in 1977 (Bureau of Justice Statistics Bulletin, 1986; U.S. Dept. of Justice, 1986). The predicted commensurate drop in the crime rate has not occurred and recent proposed recidivism models address only the potential incapacitative effect as a function of a base line prevalence rate for the population, the likelihood of recidivism given certain earlier predisposing factors of questionable value for sentencing guidance, and the average age of criminal career burn-out (See Avi-Itzhak and Shinnar, 1973; Blumstein, Cohen, Roth and Visher, 1986). The best predictor of criminal behavior is still prior criminality or delinquency, and the best causal model does not explain more than 25 to 30 percent of the variation in delinquent behavior (Elliot and Ageton, 1983). Delinquents are likely to have delinquent peers and a prior record of delinquency. That is perhaps an oversimplified reduction, but not too far from the research supported evidence.

However, many of the parameters of delinquency have been estimated in terms of quantity, quality, seriousness, persistence and demography. Sophisticated recidivism models now exist that proscribe crime control incapacitation strategies. We have studies showing that "nothing works" and "everything works" and we have evidence that we really do not yet know enough to support either position, except to say that, perhaps, some things work and some do not.

5. Large-scale, Long-range Efforts

What then is necessary for us to do as we reach the end of the incapacitation debate? The basic causal questions leading to prevention must now be addressed with renewed vigor. The American crime and incapacitation rates are among the highest in the world. Our population is not biologically more predisposed to criminal behavior than are other populations. Increasing prison capacity may relieve crowding, but it is doubtful that such an expenditure will reduce crime rates.

We must not retreat from the goals of the President's Crime Commission. The results of long-term research efforts are just beginning to be felt, but in ways which will aggravate the problem rather than reduce it. Our studies have shown that many people do commit delinquencies and criminal acts, and a small percentage commit an extraordinary number of these illegal deeds. Our problem now is to research causal mechanisms through large-scale efforts equivalent to other assaults on problems of national urgency. Recent revelations of crimes in high places are astonishing, alarming, and for sociological criminologists at least, not unexpected. We must broaden our theoretical and empirical armament to make our approach more egalitarian. The limits of the control of "street crime" have been reached; we must now look elsewhere for explanation.

In this brief essay the work discussed has been over-simplified and has underrepresented the course of events, the work, and the conclusions. But social action is a complex of interacting forces and in a summary such as this, one does justice to none of them. However, some concerns about the recent ideological and political trends in our field should be mentioned from a data-based research perspective and this collection offers an opportunity, as we look back over twenty years, to review some of these impressions.

11

Alternative Futures in Measuring Crime

Benjamin H. Renshaw III

What emerges from a reading of this volume is the multiplicity of persons and professions whose disciplines, career aspirations, and professional recognition derive from the conduct of major criminal justice statistical series and surveys. For all of these persons—whether involved in the field capture, processing, initial local analysis, policy interpretation, archiving, secondary analysis, publication, technology research and development or national policy formulation—the future of these large statistical enterprises is of consuming importance. As one who has been intimately involved over the last decade in the design and redesign of national criminal justice statistics programs, this is a set of ruminations on the institutional, organizational, budgetary and intellectual futures of these programs.

1. Closing the Circle on the Uniform Crime Reports (UCR) and the National Crime Survey (NCS)

As pointed out by Steve Schlesinger in his Preface to this volume, the extensive redesigns of the two preeminent national indicators of crime and victimization have just been concluded. The traditional Uniform Crime Reporting program has been transformed into the National Incident-Based Reporting System (NIBRS) with final specifications released by the Federal Bureau of Investigation (FBI) in the summer of 1988. The previous summary reporting mode has been replaced with incident reports containing fifty-two data elements describing the victims, offenders, arrestees and circumstances of the crimes. The traditional eight Index or Part I crimes have been expanded to twenty-two crime categories (Group A) made up of forty-six discrete offenses. NIBRS provides more detailed linkages (1) to connect victims, offenders, and arrestees to the criminal incident, and (2) to connect victims to the offenses committed against them. Expanded victim-offender relationship data are provided. The much criticized "hierarchy rule" has been eliminated, since in

NIBRS the twenty-two major categories plus eleven less serious (Group B) offenses occurring in an incident are to be reported. A new scoring category of crimes against society has been added to the traditional crimes against persons and property. Special attention within NIBRS has been given to drug/ narcotic offenses; distinctions are made by type of criminal activity (using, buying, cultivating, possessing, distributing), by suspected drug type (sixteen categories), and in the estimated quantity of the seized drug or narcotic. Finally, expanded quality assurance standards and measures will be incorporated in the new national incident system; FBI/UCR staff will assist state UCR programs and local agency respondents in quality control measures. Numerous other alterations have been made, but those noted above are the most critical to the research and analysis field. Funding the initial study and providing funds to states now implementing NIBRS, the Bureau of Justice Statistics (BJS) has supported the Federal Bureau of Investigation's efforts to have UCR again be a system of real analytic utility to local law enforcement. Throughout the course of the UCR redesign, the FBI has shown appreciation for the interests and analytic concerns of the academic research community. (For these and other interested parties the NIBRS is explained in a three volume set, the first of which—"Data Collection Guidelines"—sets forth the new analytic potential in the FBI data after the first redesign in over fifty-five years. Federal Bureau of Investigation, U.S. Department of Justice, July 1988.)

Beginning in 1979, a similar extensive evaluation was made of the National Crime Survey (NCS) administered by the Bureau of Justice Statistics. Critical improvements were made in: (1) the screening strategy to help people remember and report victimizations by means of a more comprehensive screening procedure; (2) the expansion of victimization data through use of initial interview data previously eliminated due to their unbounded nature; (3) the change in the threshold for reporting series crimes from three to six incidents to define more clearly the intractable problem involving events where victims have been victimized so often they cannot remember details of specific incidents; (4) the stratification of the NCS sample by a composite crime index developed from the UCR; (5) the consideration of a full person-based longitudinal design which would follow persons interviewed who had experienced victimizations regardless of where they moved within the United States and seek attitudes on the performance of the criminal justice system; (6) the commitment to expanded use of computer-assisted telephone interviewing in data collection to improve data quality; (7) the use of direct interviews with respondents down to the age of twelve, (8) the expansion of information concerning victim behavior (interaction between victims and offenders) and life-style variables (circumstance under which victimization is more or less likely to occur); and (9) more frequent utilization of supplements to acquire data on issues not part of the on-going administration of the victimization survey, but of interest to the Department of Justice and the research community (Bureau of Justice Statistics, U.S. Department of Justice, 1988).

While, for both Bureaus, the completion of the redesign efforts is a watershed with a new stability and continuity established within both UCR and NCS, the choices and policy options will continue to be examined. Especially in the National Crime Survey there will be continued testing of data collection instruments, and critical implementation issues, such as splicing, to be addressed. However some suggestions for change must necessarily be resisted, even if unsuccessfully, on the grounds of methodological purity. In two instances pressures from Capitol Hill resulted in changes in the two series which have caused problems for the sponsoring agency. For example, several years ago arson was added to the UCR crime index through the strong interest of a single United States Senator, despite the FBI's strong protestations of the difficulties of adding such incidents to a law enforcement series. More recently BJS has been directed by statute to do more in the NCS on the subject of family violence, despite the enormous difficulty of eliciting responses on such incidents during an interview conducted in a family setting. But both sponsoring agencies recognize that the two redesigns were resource constrained. As a result, we expect advocates of specific data elements, collection methodologies, and analytic options to continue to press their cases for inclusion in UCR or NCS. Annual and other forums to address user interests would seem to be imperative.

But by far the greatest imperative is to maintain multiple national measures of crime and the response to crime. If the genesis of the UCR in the early nineteen thirties, at least in part, lay in the frustration of police chiefs that newspaper reporters could start crime waves, and if the genesis of the NCS in the early seventies, at least in part, stemmed from the frustrations of social scientists with the extent of crime not reported to police chiefs, then both the law enforcement and academic community must continue to demand both a thermometer and barometer of the extent of crime. In a field where any set of observations has inherent weaknesses, we must maintain multiple series as a check and as a means of calibration. The measurement of crime warrants such diversity.

How serious a nation feels about a problem is reflected best by what it is willing to spend to measure and understand it; good data will not assure sensible policy, but it is certainly the *sine qua non* of understanding the dimensions of problems, formulating options, and monitoring outcomes. Thus, even in the most difficult budget environments, we must press for a multiplicity of efforts emphasizing the real consistency in findings, moving toward more complete specifications within and coordination among various data sets, and explaining definitions and formats for working with both UCR and NCS data bases.

And if all else fails even try humor. In the early days of the first Reagan Administration I had the opportunity, while acting as the Director of BJS, to brief then Attorney General William French Smith on the full range of our statistical programs. At the very end of the briefing the Attorney General came back to the issue of why both NCS and UCR were needed, the issues of offenses measured, scope, costs, and kinds of information produced. Specifically he asked about the failure to measure homicides in the NCS. Always seeking to interject a light touch in our normally esoteric explanations I instantly responded, "Homicide victims are notoriously poor respondents to Census Bureau interviewers." The Attorney General did not laugh. Better forget humor.

2. Filling the Gap by Understanding What Happens After Arrest and Victimization

The Uniform Crime Reports, the National Crime Survey, the National Center for Health Statistics homicide data, and the Censuses of Prisons and Surveys of Inmates, given their scope and continuity as national data bases, surely merit the attention given them in this volume. Yet, for the future of measuring crime, the ability to track the movement of the cases and persons accused of criminality is the single most policy-relevant statistical activity for a national statistical agency. Over the years, in responding to a myriad of requests for data, our greatest frustration has been the inability to answer such basic questions as "What happened to people arrested for robbery in the United States?"

Four consequential efforts and data bases aimed at understanding felony case processing, sentencing outcomes, movement of adult offenders at the state level, and the flow of Federal cases and offenders are underway under our auspices. Not treated directly in this volume, these data bases must evolve into nationally representative data bases if we are to integrate front-end law enforcement data with the downstream components of prosecution, adjudication and corrections, particularly probation.

2.1 Prosecution of Felony Arrests

Using a subset of the data generated by the prosecutor management information systems (PROMIS), BJS in the mid-1970s established a statistical series describing the prosecution of adult felony arrests in urban prosecutors' offices (Prosecution of Felony Arrests, 1982). Starting with thirteen jurisdictions (twelve cities and one state), agencies participating expanded to over forty offices as more district attorneys used second and third generation management information systems that generated the data of interest to us—cases diverted, rejected after screening, dismissed in court, pled guilty, acquitted, convicted after trial, disposed by probation or incarceration, and with elapsed time from arrest to disposition. Moving now from a case study type of report into a full statistical series derived from an urban national sample of the two-hundred largest jurisdictions, the series can approach being nationally representative; the series will, however, maintain individual jurisdiction data for a substantial number of jurisdictions, with emphasis on key disposition rates for a dozen crime types. Other goals include annual estimates, descriptive information on how prosecutors operate and keep records, and special surveys on such issues as plea (or charge or sentence) bargaining practices and the use of continuances and delays. The felony case processing project has depended on the active participation of urban prosecutors in the interpretation of their highly idiosyncratic case processing practices.

2.2 Sentencing Outcomes

BJS sentencing studies, compiled over the last four years, have developed a methodology for collecting felony sentencing data from felony courts and have collected such data for three years, the most recent data collection year being 1986. Beginning with eighteen jurisdictions, the study has used a limited number of variables (15 to 24), clear operational definitions and counting rules, a variety of data sources as well as courts, no philosophical predispositions, and has been responsive to local legal environments; it has been a retrospective study as opposed to using a tracking perspective. Focusing on the use of different kinds and degrees of sanctions, the study has been able to analyze the impact on sentencing patterns of such factors as crime severity, determinate v. indeterminate sentencing systems, the number of conviction offenses and the use of bargaining v. full trials. Currently with one-hundred jurisdictions, the goal for 1988 is to collect sentencing data in three-hundred jurisdictions that are representative of the United States. In a policy arena that includes preoccupation with sentencing guidelines and the necessity of updating criminal history records with disposition data, the future outputs of the study will include jurisdiction-specific data (annually), national average data (perhaps every five years), and the prospect for cohort studies. Both research and new statistical series from a representative sample could reach probation and case-aging issues.

2.3 State Offender-Based Transaction Statistics (OBTS)

The least advanced of the tracking data bases is the OBTS. Proceeding from the Law Enforcement Assistance Administration (LEAA) effort to automate criminal history records, OBTS was to be a statistical derivative of computerized criminal history records always assuming (and it was to prove to be a huge assumption) that accurate and complete disposition data were available for each specific charge. The formal national OBTS program was implemented in 1983 when data pertaining to 1980 dispositions were collected. Participation by the states is entirely voluntary with fifteen states covering 46% of the Nation's population currently providing data. The critical impediment to adequate state transaction data is the quality of criminal history records: either failure to automate, selective (incomplete) recording of either or both arrests and dispositions, or records consisting solely of "free text" without any conversion options. Since criminal histories are the linchpin of every consequential crime control strategy (career criminal programs, selective incapacitation, sentencing reform) and therefore of vital importance more to individual states than to the Federal government, such indifference is incomprehensible. But without retrenchment and reform of individual state criminal histories, with particular attention to adjudicatory dispositions, OBTS cannot become a national statistical program; it can of course continue to provide valuable insights into the functioning of criminal justice systems in the participating states. One prospect here, as with other case processing data bases, is for offender tracking studies focusing on drug offenders.

2.4 Federal Integrated Data Base

Commencing in the early 1980s, a Federal statistics program was established within BJS. Linking data from the Federal Bureau of Investigation, the Executive Office for the U.S. Attorneys, the Administrative Office of the U.S. Courts, the Bureau of Prisons and the U.S. Parole Board. Collected annually, this series permits the tracking of cases and offenders from prosecution through adjudication, sentencing and corrections. The Federal integrated data base was launched, ironically, after a decade in which the Federal government had encouraged and assisted states and localities in developing comprehensive transaction data, but had not moved to create a comparable series; this despite the fact that all but one of the cooperating agencies reported to the Attorney General of the United States. The key ingredient at the inception of the series was the full cooperation of the FBI, whose unwillingness to participate had doomed previous efforts to link Department of Justice data bases going back to the manual records of the 1960s. Future objectives for the Federal program are (1) to expand the data on Federal investigations and arrests, (2) to acquire data and conduct analyses on a modified real-time basis, and (3) to analyze data on case movement, backlogs and workload in the context of Department of Justice budgetary submissions, policy changes in Federal criminal procedures, shifts in crimes committed and characteristics of accused persons entering the Federal system.

Perhaps the assertion that began this section, specifically that the ability to track cases and people is the single most policy-relevant task that a national statistical agency can perform. For those that regard only methodologically sophisticated national surveys as "bred to the purple" and find data derived from operational files, whether manual or automated, to be soft, shaky and squishy will be particularly offended. Let me therefore seek eminent if ancient support for my view. Felix Frankfurter opened a study which he and Roscoe Pound directed in 1921-22 of the administration of criminal justice in Cleveland, Ohio with the following words: "The inquiry had two aims: first, to render an accounting of the functioning of this system, to the fullest extent that social institutions are as yet adapted to statistical appraisal; and, second, to trace to their controlling sources whatever defects in the system the inquiry disclosed." The then Professor of Administrative Law and the then Dean of the Harvard Law School placed at the heart of their "scientific study," the examination of 3,236 case records of "individual offenders" who passed through the Cleveland courts in 1919 and of 1,322 "prisoners in the workhouse" whose sentences were terminated during six months of 1920. In the intervening years many lawyers and social scientists have followed the methodological precedent of Pound and Frankfurter, recognizing the enormous diagnostic power of processing or transaction data in understanding the "defects" of our present-day, but often little-changed, criminal justice systems.

Improvements in criminal justice simulation modeling, combined with the ability to tie caseflow to the resources required at each stage of the criminal justice system, gives us the remarkable power to anticipate the downstream impact and either shift or generate the capability to respond. Much has changed in the nearly twenty years since such simulation models were really a technique in pursuit of a data base. A future that combines quantum improvements in the quality of automated criminal histories with the capacity to monitor the flow of cases in urban centers, state aggregates, and the Federal system is a future "devoutly to be wished."

3. Creating a Future Between Tensions and Opportunities

Before turning to prospects, visions and opportunities it seems necessary to examine several tensions that could constrain statistical enterprises in the next decade.

3.1 Monitoring the Future-Five Tensions

First and foremost of these tensions is the spectre of cutbacks in criminal justice series and surveys in the face of the macro-budget environment of massive Federal budget deficits. If such cutbacks should come in the form of across-the-board reductions, statistical agencies with relatively fixed budgets—as compared with agencies with more discretionary room—have only two choices in responding: first, if the across-the-board cuts are relatively minor (less than 5%), budget cuts can be absorbed without termination of full series or programs; after that level, meat-axe cuts so damage the integrity of all major statistical series that full programs must be ended to maintain the continuity and quality of the remaining programs.

Statistical triage is the result. And the pain—as when I recommended the temporary termination of the National Crime Survey following the National Academy of Sciences' critique in the late seventies—is considerable and far reaching. Even those highly critical of an existing statistical series will fight to the death for its continuation if the alternative is a politically uncertain future attempt to reestablish a discontinued effort. When these statistical programs are housed in an agency, such as the Department of Justice, where across-the-board cuts will fall directly on personnel because of the labor-intensive character of such agencies (litigators and investigators), resistance is further weakened. Economic events of the 1990s will impact on the major long-term programs described here; if the research and academic community is to participate in these choices they must understand the constraints of those functioning in a non-beneficent Federal fiscal environment.

Another considerable tension results from the time required to launch or reshape major statistical programs and the time-frame imperatives of elected officials on Capitol Hill and newly-appointed political executives. New political leadership wants immediate results, or, at a minimum, immediate credit for new programs or new configurations of the old; they are highly impatient with the statistical bureaucracy whom they view as dealing with time frames that only geologists comprehend. Pressures to modify existing series and to find resources for new initiatives are always present in the early years of a new administration. Adapting long-range statistical series by means of supplements and maintaining a stable of competent profit and non-profit organizations to implement short-term exploratory surveys and studies are a de-minimus response.

(A strange mirror image of the last point is when the Federal policy-making apparatus in both the executive branch and on Capitol Hill tolerates a set of national indicators that are seemingly inadequate to measure a problem. Uncritical acceptance of the state of our national measures with relation to drugs is the norm, and it has continued largely unchanged over the past decade. Without a full statement of the extent of my indictment, in general there is enormous dissatisfaction with the coverage and quality of statistics that monitor the extent of drug use, the consequences of use and problems of distribution, retail street transactions, demand for treatment services, and price/purity numbers as a measure of enforcement effectiveness. The 1986 and 1988 versions of Federal drug legislation left these flaws and gaps in our national intelligence concerning drugs largely unaddressed. One emerging data base of importance, however, is the Drug Use Forecasting [DUF] work of the National Institute of Justice, conducting urine analysis of arrestees in twenty or more American cities. National Institute of Justice, U.S. Department of Justice, 1988; Wish, 1987.)

Another tension with relation to on-going research and statistical activities and the political program environments in which they operate is the "two language problem." Those engaged in advocating improvements in the administration of justice, research and statistical initiatives, and crime control interventions largely speak the language of the social sciences learned in years of Ph.D study; those responsible for implementing improvements and making the connection between research and statistical findings and concrete reforms speak a language derived from years of law school study. (Occasionally one may find a judge with an undergraduate engineering degree who sees a caseflow diagram in terms of electrical circuits, but such happy days are few, and concomitantly, Capitol Hill staff rejoice in the presence of an English-speaking sociologist or criminologist.) Whether associated with the use of statistical evidence in courts or simply communicating the importance of data for statutory choices, the tension is there. Every academic who hopes to change or influence public policy should provide a clear explanation of the implications of his or her work for criminal justice reform. Arguably, policy oriented bodies and officials demand a third language from both lawyers and social scientists; it consists entirely of quick, concise bottom-line sentences.

Related to the budget environment difficulties is the tension between demonstrating the value of numbers for public decisions and the assessments that policy officials will increasingly make as to whether to continue a particular statistical series. Serious evaluations of the cost/benefit ratios with respect to data series are difficult to do and are seldom done, but there is an increasing disposition to hold the larger series and surveys discussed in this volume to a higher level of performance. Those who do so proceed from the notion that statistical programs are not an end in themselves, but exist primarily to drive criminal justice policy formulations. To justify continuation of both annual and periodic series, statistical agencies are asked to identify specific decisions and policy choices and show that the numbers have had a consequential impact on the decision. This is a hard standard, rather equivalent to validating simulation models by making predictions that years later prove to be accurate, but such report cards can be anticipated. Again, a passing grade in the Department of Justice, the Office of Management and Budget, and the Congress will require a new dialogue within the legitimate iron triangle of (1) the law enforcement and research community, (2) executive branch officials responsible for the statistical programs, and (3) key Capitol Hill staff.

Finally there is the future possibility of non-cooperation with any of the series discussed here. Whether resistance should come from respondents to the victimization surveys, from inmates giving self-reports on prior criminality or drug use, or from a limited number of police agencies, there are few choices. One would require the imputation of values (with all the attendant methodological questions), the other, creation of some kind of incentive to induce cooperation, possibly (but not probably) economic. No solution is offered, only the admonition to monitor and respond quickly at the slightest indication of a real diminution in response rates.

3.2 Marketing the Future-Six Opportunities

With the "five tensions"—an obligatory set of political realities recorded—let us turn to the possibilities for halcyon days, the opportunities for persons concerned with all aspects of criminal justice numbers to flourish.

Implicit in my earlier plea for maintaining multiple series associated with law enforcement, case processing and sentencing/correctional outcomes is the need to examine data derived from various sources for comparability and consistency of findings. My experience (and the chapter examining UCR homicide and National Center for Health Statistics numbers) suggests a consistency of findings that is at once both surprising and reassuring. To the extent that researchers use consistent formats made possible by comparable definitions of crimes and ethnic/racial groups, rich analyses can be developed, for instance, on victim-offender relationships. Testing for comparability and consistency and accomplishing calibrations of data is an open field of endeavor.

Movement to theory-driven data collection efforts is another opportunity. This is asserted in full realization that statistical programs cannot bear the entire empirical orientation or knowledge-generating function in criminal justice for the Federal government; clearly there are research (NIJ and NIC) and assistance agencies also involved. Bob Figlio's paper points to the opportunity for greater integration of the research community and Federal agencies, citing "the persistence of researchers and of NIJ, BJS, OJJDP and NIMH directors and project monitors" in sustaining programs aimed at social/statistical concerns.

The Federal executive branch can do much more, however, to integrate research (NIJ) and statistics (BJS) with the operational data bases and program evaluations generated by the Bureau of Justice Assistance (BJA) and the Office of Juvenile Justice and Delinquency Prevention (OJJDP). While these are agencies most familiar to me (including eight months as Acting Director of BJA) the same imperative should drive the analytic efforts of operational agencies such as the FBI and DEA. Integration would mean not just a listing of statistics, but identification of hypotheses concerning crime control interventions that could be tested in operational settings by specification of data to be collected. Through a quiet, careful examination by agency leadership of such possibilities when annual program plans and budgetary commitments are made, a genuinely heuristic hypothesis-testing focus could be established in the research and development cycle associated with crime control policy.

Broadening the number of users of data will continue to be both an objective and an opportunity. The BJS archive at the University of Michigan will be one instrumentality to serve this aim. Others will be the BJS Justice Statistics Clearinghouse and the recently established Data Center and Clearinghouse for Drugs and Crime, both located in Rockville, Maryland. The archive will continue to serve the university researcher primarily but also others seeking computer access to full data sets. The two clearinghouses will aid a broader cross section of media, state and local researchers, and private organizations seeking everything from a single number or publication to tailored policy analysis pieces. Issues associated with computer applications and technology bear on both institutions. To expand use the archive can consider distribution of subsets of data on diskettes, codebooks offering more complete specification of data sets and other means of improving access and facilitating transfer. Microcomputers offer ease of analysis after downloading of complete or partial data sets. Through the Archive and Clearinghouses an awareness and focus on users will be maintained with effective feedback on how various data bases are used in public information, policy formulation and a variety of analytic constructs.

Among analytic opportunities is the examination of both aggregate and individual data bases in order to maintain distinctions that emanate from these data. In a volume treating large aggregate data bases, the perspective to be gained from focusing on individual offenders and the longitudinal sequence in criminal activity must be emphasized. Clearly, as Al Blumstein has taught, the crime rate is a function of the size of the criminal population and the individual offender's propensity to offend, or lambda (the 11th letter of the Greek alphabet assumes the meaning of annual crimes per criminal) (Blumstein and Cohen, 1987). Studies of criminal cohorts are essential to assigning ranges to lambda. Several analyses are possible and need to be differentiated. Age peaks in arrest specific rates in the aggregate are steep; individual rates are much flatter, suggesting a different arrival and departure sequence in the criminal justice system.

As suggested earlier, the analytic potential of the National Crime Survey (NCS) has been much enhanced. Two opportunity areas seem worth highlighting. First is opening the NCS to the use of supplements which would allow researchers to add ideas prior to data collection and not be limited exclusively to secondary analysis. This provides a massive data collection instrument within which to examine new theoretical perspectives. The opportunity to place such supplements on the NCS has already been opened to the research community through a joint BJS/NIJ competitive procurement. Currently a supplement dealing with school crime has been added to NCS and will reach over 14,000 children between the ages of twelve and eighteen in the first six months of 1989. As a clear rule, supplements that involve simply adding questions to the existing instrument are far easier to handle than those that must be incorporated or integrated into the questionnaire. A second shift in the NCS much discussed in the redesign was increasing the longitudinal focus in the series by following all those moving from households in the original sample, the prime concern of which was with movers who were victims of crime and whose subsequent disability, victimization and treatment by the criminal justice system is of great policy relevance. Because of issues involving separation of cross sectional and longitudinal weights, the chance to scrutinize a full longitudinal file is a way off; however, a longitudinal supplement in the near future is under consideration.

Opportunities for analysis of the redesigned Uniform Crime Reports are equally extensive. Besides the points made earlier, various conundrums associated with the UCR have been solved, including the age by race, by sex and victim-offender relations issues. Since the final data specifications of the new UCR were issued by the Federal Bureau of Investigation only in recent months, the research community should study the data collection requirements for new analytic possibilities (See Federal Bureau of Investigation, 1988). But perhaps the greatest opportunity contained in the new UCR is for a new relationship between law enforcement, the media and the community. Embedding the new UCR data requirements in a new generation of law enforcement management information systems will speed the implementation of this system across the nation. UCR data as a statistical series will then have many if not all of the data elements contained in sophisticated operational crime analysis programs. Public access packages, providing a further subset of crime analysis data, will permit citizens and citizens groups involved in crime prevention to know the crime patterns in a neighborhood, without in any way impinging on on-going investigations. People will have a far more accurate view of the risks they face in various life-style situations. Media, particularly newspapers, can disseminate this easier-to-understand information broadly within a community. But active feedback of crime data by police to citizens will provide the quid-pro-quo for active assistance provided by citizens to police in crime control efforts (See Spelman, 1988 for an excellent exposition of the benefits of the new UCR.)

For the myriad of professions and people concerned with measuring and controlling crime, the last twenty-five years has a dominant message. Investment in research, statistics, and improvements in the administration of justice has not kept pace with similar investments in the economic, health, energy, and arts fields, yet the measures of public safety, and their direction, have been of greatest concern to the American public over the same period. While the investment has moved proportionally downward, the negative indicators have moved exponentially upward. In criminal justice this situation can only change when those with an empirical orientation to measurement align themselves with those with an operational focus on enforcement. Clearly the future offers improved computer technology, data standardization, new survey techniques, shared data and shared instruments, and a special concern for the full range of users of each major statistical series. What must follow is a full and more vigorous dialogue between all those whose work manifests a desire to use measurement in criminology for improvements in criminal justice, since indifference to either measurement or operational advances limits our professional and personal advancement.

Notes

Chapter 2

1. The voluntariness of the current UCR is open to some question. Maltz (1977: 37) argues that the UCR should no longer be considered purely voluntary since many states have passed laws requiring that UCRs be submitted by local police agencies to state agencies. These state-level "UCR Programs" then forward the data to the FBI.

2. See Federal Bureau of Investigation, 1984: 33-38, for a description of the hierarchy system of offense classification.

3. For a discussion of this problem in the context of homicide classification, see Loftin, Kindley, Norris, and Wiersema, 1987.

4. This is the view that motivated joint sponsorship of the UCR's Redesign Project by the Bureau of Justice Statistics (which oversees the National Crime Survey) and the Federal Bureau of Investigation, and recommendations to coordinate joint reporting of results (Poggio, et al., 1985: 157, 160-161, 181).

5. ICPSR is a membership organization consisting of over 300 colleges and universities in the United States and around the world. Each institution pays annual membership dues which entitles its faculty, staff, and students to receive ICPSR services free or at a nominal cost. The primary feature of the ICPSR is its data archive. Particular to the discussion here is the National Archive of Criminal Justice Data formerly the Criminal Justice Archive and Information Network (CJAIN) project, which maintains the National Criminal Justice Data Archive. During the last ten years the CJAIN staff has assembled a large collection of criminal justice-related data collections, including a fairly extensive collection of Uniform Crime Reporting Program data sets. Data assembled by CJAIN are distributed on magnetic tape without charge to individuals affiliated with the ICPSR member institutions. Researchers not located at ICPSR member institutions are assessed a modest charge for access, based on the size of the data collection requested. Requests for data should be addressed to:

   National Archive of Criminal Justice Data, ICPSR, Room 4263
   P.O. Box 1248
   Ann Arbor, MI 48106

6. The data were provided in packed binary fields with large and variable record lengths probably because it was the most efficient way to archive huge files. At that

time, however, software and hardware capable of dealing with these formats were not widely available.

7. Due to confidentiality restrictions, identification of each respondent's place of residence is not available in the NCS. This limits analysis of areal aggregations of NCS data to primary sampling units (PSUs) or segments as defined by the Census Bureau's sampling methodology. Some would say that the NCS is valueless for small area analysis.

8. Contact: Chief, User Services Unit, Uniform Crime Reporting Section, Federal Bureau of Investigation, Gallery Row Building, Washington, DC 20535.

9. These materials are also available from ICPSR.

10. The UCR master data files that are distributed by ICPSR are collectively known as ICPSR Study 9028.

11. We use the term "complex" structure in the sense that the file is not "rectangular" (i.e., having a fixed number of records per case with each record representing the same type of observational unit). See the discussion of complex file structures in the SPSS User's Guide (SPSS Inc., 1986: 191-218) for more information.

12. Other SHR data collections representing victims, offenders, and incidents are discussed below.

13. There are "age by gender" tabulations and separate race/ethnic origin totals for each offense. Age by race or race by gender breakdowns are not collected.

14. Indeed, the microcomputer revolution has demonstrated, if nothing else, that (with good software design) complicated procedures can be masked to such a degree that the user is not likely to be threatened or overwhelmed by the computer. On the contrary, easy-to-use software probably explains a great deal of the personal computer's tremendous success.

15. OSIRIS is a collection of data management and statistical analysis programs developed by the Survey Research Center, Institute for Social Research, University of Michigan.

16. SPSS^x is a registered trademark of SPSS, Inc., Chicago, Illinois.

17. ICPSR does not currently distribute data on microcomputer diskettes or magnetic media other than reels of 9-track tape. A subsequent chapter discusses how UCR data can be analyzed using a microcomputer. However, while the microcomputer may be useful for managing and analyzing UCR subsets, it is not yet very convenient for dealing with large files such as the archival UCR data sets. In fact, unless one has a very large (and fast) microcomputer hard disk and/or a very limiting mainframe or mini-computer environment, it would not make sense to manipulate the complete UCR data files on a microcomputer, given that one could, under these circumstances, feasibly transfer the data from the tapes in the first place. Personal computer technology is changing rapidly, however, and we believe that the microcomputer may well be worth considering as data storage and interchange standards adapt to improvements in the technology.

18. This file is created by OSIRIS to store variable label, column location, and code value information for an associated data file, but is not itself a part of the data.

19. SAS is a registered trademark of the SAS Institute, Cary, N.C.

20. UCR files distributed by ICPSR are rectangularly structured (i.e., each logical record has the same length and variables are located in the same relative positions on the record from one case to the next). Many programming languages and statistical software programs provide methods for reading raw data in fixed formats.

21. According to the FBI, the total number of police agencies active in the Uniform Crime Reporting Program represented approximately 98 percent of the total population in 1980 (Federal Bureau of Investigation, 1981). This suggests that considerable efforts have been made to secure participation.

22. Although "crimes actually reported" (not estimated), have been distinguished from estimated totals since 1959.

23. A detailed written description of the actual algorithm used by the FBI was requested but was not available. Instead, an oral description of the technique was provided. The source of this information is conversations with UCR officials initiated by the authors in the fall of 1983.

24. The data, obtained in 1983, might have been an updated version of the data used to produce the 1980 CIUS in accordance with standard UCR policies. Although this could not be confirmed, two facts support the hypothesis. First, the total number of cases differs between the two sources. The computer-readable file contains data on 15,553 agencies; CIUS reports 15,544. Second, the computer-generated totals differ from the published counts, even for states in which every agency submitted complete reports.

25. It is not clear exactly what they meant by this since the topic is not elaborated in the report.

26. Hierarchical modeling techniques such as those currently under development by statisticians (see Lehoczky, 1986 for an introduction to this method as applied to criminal careers) might be adapted to estimate data for small geographic areas based on distributions of data from other areas that reported more fully.

The authors would like to thank Colin Loftin and Charles Wellford for their thoughtful comments on drafts of this chapter.

Chapter 5

1. For a more current and authoritative discussion of the long-term changes in the NCS see Taylor (forthcoming) and Biderman, Carter, Lynch, and Martin (1986).

2. Spanish-speaking interviewers are available for Spanish speaking persons. Respondents who speak other languages are interviewed by proxy if possible.

3. See Taylor *op. cit.* note 1 for more current information on the long-term redesign.

4. The Police Foundation and the Police Executive Research Forum conduct periodic surveys of police practices, but they include a very small proportion of police organizations in the nation. Plans are underway to expand this data collection as part of the Bureau of Justice Statistics (BJS) Law Enforcement Management and Administration Statistical Series. All of these efforts collect data at the department level. There are no existing data sets that collect incident-level data on police service of the type available in the new NCS.

Chapter 6

1. The author wishes to acknowledge the thoughtful comments provided by Diana Call of the U.S. Census Bureau, Government's Division and of Larry McGinn, U.S. Bureau of the Census, Demographic Surveys Division.

2. In all, there are currently six national surveys and censuses series. In four separate series, data are collected for prisons, prisoners, jails and jail inmates. A fifth series, the Annual Jail Survey, conducted in those years when the full Jail Census is not done, provides estimates of the jail population and jail characteristics based on a sample of jails. A sixth series, Children in Custody, done with the Office of Juvenile Justice and Delinquency Prevention, provides facility and resident characteristics for juveniles housed in public and private juvenile correctional, detention, and shelter facilities. In addition, a survey of juveniles housed in long-term state-operated juvenile correctional facilities was recently completed. The results of this experimental survey, which focuses on criminal, demographic and drug history characteristics, were published in *Survey of Youth in Custody, 1987.*

3. The Survey of Inmates of Adult State Correctional Facilities hereafter will be referred to as the Survey.

4. The Census of State Adult Correctional Facilities hereafter will be referred to as the Census.

5. This focus includes the annual count of prison inmates, probation counts, capital punishment, admissions and releases, and special reports on recidivism done in conjunction with the State Branch of BJS.

6. Because of delays in conducting the most recent Survey, data for this Survey were weighted to the inmate count done in December 1986, rather than to the 1984 Census.

7. More specifically, in the 1974 Census, a jurisdictional approach was used, and in the 1979 and 1984 Censuses, a custody approach was used. In a jurisdictional approach, inmates are counted based upon whose jurisdiction they are under, not where they are housed. Thus, in the 1974 Census, State prison inmates were included even if they were housed in a local correctional facility. On the other hand, in a custody

approach, inmates are counted in terms of where they are housed, rather than in terms of whose jurisdiction they are under. Thus, in both the 1979 and 1984 Censuses, inmates under State jurisdiction but housed in a local correctional facility were not included.

8. In 1974, as a first step in developing the design, all institutions were stratified by number of prisoners into five groups: 0-19, 20-199, 200-399, 400-899, and 900+. All institutions with an estimated population of 900+ were automatically included in the sample. Prisoners in these institutions were sampled at a rate of one in eighteen. Institutions in the remaining four strata were sorted within stratum by: type of institution (adult prison, community correctional center, work release center, prison or road camp, reception or pre-release center, and other types of facilities), region (Northeast, North center, South, and West), and specific size of institution. Institutions were selected from stratum I (size of 0-19 inmates) at one in eighteen, from stratum II (size of 20-199 inmates) at one in six, from stratum III (size of 200-399 inmates) at one in 3.6, and from stratum IV (size of 400-899 inmates) at one in two. Prisoners were selected from each of these non-self-representing strata at a ratio of one in one, one in three, one in five, and one in nine, respectively. These sampling procedures assured an estimated sample of roughly 200 institutions, and an overall sampling rate of about one in eighteen for all prisoners. (U.S. Department of Justice, 1976: 13-17).

In 1979, a sample of 215 facilities was selected. From these facilities a total of 12,000 inmates, 9,500 males and 2,500 female inmates were chosen for interviews. Women inmates were oversampled to enable analyses by sex of inmates and to produce reliabilities of no larger than a five percent coefficient of variation of estimates of ten percent subpopulations of male inmates, and a ten percent coefficient of variation for estimates of ten percent subpopulations for women inmates.

The sample selections produced for the 1986 Survey paralleled those used in 1979. Women inmates were oversampled to allow for meaningful analyses by sex. In order to attain coefficients of variation of roughly 5.4 percent for women and 4.3 percent for men for estimates of ten percent subpopulations for male and female inmate samples, respectively, and to maintain roughly the same proportion of men to women in the sample (i.e., 3.8) as was used in 1979, approximately 15,000 inmates were sampled nationwide. This figure included 11,875 men and 3,125 women.

9. Five characteristics were noted. These included: perimeter, towers, patrols, surveillance and detection devices, and inmate housing. For each of these characteristics, administrators were asked to describe their facility by checking the box that best described the facility. For instance, for the characteristic of inmate housing, administrators were asked to determine if the facility generally had single cells/rooms, single cells/rooms and dormitories, or dormitories only. These characteristics were devised in cooperation with the National Institute of Corrections staff.

10. Rated capacity refers to the number of inmates the facility may house as determined by State or other officials. Design capacity refers to the number of inmates the facility is architecturally designed to house without crowding by, for example, double bunking.

11. Incidents included riots, food fasts, strikes by inmates, escapes, and fires set by inmates.

12. Expenditure data were collected from the State Department of Corrections for all State-operated corrections facilities in the State rather than from each individual facility.

13. Academic programs included basic adult education, secondary education, special education such as programs for inmates with learning disabilities, and college courses taught both within and outside the facility. Counseling programs included psychological, psychiatric, or therapeutic programs, employment programs that prepare inmates for re-entry into the community, parenting programs, and other programs specified by the facility administrators.

14. Prison industry jobs were defined as those jobs that focus on reducing the cost of operating state institutions and agencies, and on productivity or profits. These jobs included the production and distribution of goods for state institutions and agencies, such as furniture making or repair, shops for decals, machinery, engraving or other uses, making license plates, textiles, or farming. Prison maintenance jobs included prison labor to care for inmates or for the upkeep of the facility, such as food service, laundry or dry cleaning, construction, or maintaining the grounds and gardens. Vocational training jobs were defined as programs redesigned to provide inmates with a skill rather than to enhance productivity or profit. These programs included such areas as auto repair, sheet metal shop, drafting, or data processing. The definitions for each of these types of programs was devised using the American Correctional Association's *Manual of Correctional Standards* (1966).

15. Items regarding the nature of the relationship between the offender and the victim were drawn from the National Crime Survey. These items included the number of victims, their age, sex, race, and relationship to the offender, and whether the offender thought the victim had used drugs or alcohol, or both just prior to the offense. These items were selected for two reasons. First, the items in the National Crime Survey have been used for several years with great success; thus, pre-testing the validity of these items was unnecessary. Second, use of these items would allow comparisons of the characteristics of offenders from the victim's perspective and characteristics of the victims from the offender's perspective for similar types of crimes at about the same point in time.

16. Data users will note, however, that despite the intent to include victim data only for offenses against persons where the victim is more readily identifiable, the public use tape includes victim information for property crimes for some records. Inclusion of victim data for these records reflects the interviewer's limited understanding of the difference between person and property offenses, and points up a flaw in the training materials. Errors include, for instance, calling burglary or larceny a violent crime. However, the data for property victims was retained on the tape for the interested user. In any case, since the purpose of the victim data is to highlight victim-offender relationships for violent crimes, the user is cautioned to control for the nature of the offense in analyzing data pertaining to victims.

17. Recent research, however, suggests that the alcohol itself may not be the deciding factor in stimulating aggressive behavior. McAndrews and Edgerton (1969), for

instance, examined the validity of the disinhibition assumption across several cultures in terms of the societal context within which drinking occurs and its relationship to aggression. Their results indicate that the alcohol in and of itself was not the determining factor in generating aggressiveness, but that the cultural context within which the drinking occurs shapes the behaviors associated with the drinking.

Taking the social context approach one step further, Donovan and Marlatt (1980) found that when one expects to drink alcohol, consumption of a liquid heightens aggressive tendencies. Subjects in his study were randomly assigned to groups wherein they either expected or did not expect to receive alcohol, and then actually did or did not receive it. From their findings, the authors concluded that the American culture has built up an expectation that alcohol consumption leads to aggressiveness and has developed an acceptance of this response to alcohol consumption.

Based on this kind of information, Heath (1981) proposed a practical application of the social cultural context of drinking. He noted that understanding the norms of the population regarding acceptance of drinking and concomitant behaviors is important in developing programs to assist problem drinkers in coping with their own behaviors as they relate to drinking is an important element of this approach.

These studies suggest the importance of understanding the social context within which drinking usually occurs among offenders, and the context wherein drinking occurs just prior to the crime. The social milieu itself may foster criminal behaviors because of the acceptability of aggressive responses to drinking.

18. The results showed that nearly one-third of the inmates had been drinking very heavily just prior to the commission of the offenses for which they had been incarcerated at the time of the interview; about 20 percent said that they had drunk very heavily in the year prior to the current incarceration; 16 percent had at some time been enrolled in an alcohol treatment program (Kalish and Masamura, 1983a: 1). In addition, roughly 60 percent of the offenders incarcerated for violent crimes, and 68 percent of those incarcerated for property crimes had been drinking very heavily immediately preceding the current offense (Kalish and Masamura, 1983a: 3). Heavy drinkers in the year prior to the current crime tended to be white, male, divorced, unemployed, and to have at most, a high school education (Kalish and Masmura, 1983a: 2).

19. Although the 1979 Survey obtained information of frequency and quality of drinking, it did not tap binge drinking. However, this information would be useful to determine if the current offense had been committed during a period of such heavy drinking.

20. The item used asked inmates to assess if they felt "relatively sober," "feeling good," "pretty loaded," or "pretty drunk." However, individual differences in the perception of "drunkenness" may flaw this measure. A more objective measure is the Blood Alcohol Concentration (BAC). To determine usual drinking patterns, one obtains the quantity of alcohol consumed, the number of hours over which the person had been drinking, and the individual's weight at the time the drinking occurred. This information may then be compared with the estimated BAC for the day of the offense to determine whether drinking on the day of the offense was typical of usual drinking patterns. The 1986 Survey attempted to include all these elements. However, since some inmates

have been incarcerated for several years, their assessment of factors such as their weight may be in error. Thus, the utility of these data is limited.

21. Recent research suggests a correlation between drug use and crime. Studies in Baltimore, California, and Harlem show increased crime with more drug use. Ball, et al. (1983) found that over a nine year period, the crime rate of 354 black and white heroin addicts dropped with less narcotics use, and rose with active narcotics use. Similarly, Anglin and Speckart (1984) compared crime in the year before and the first year after addiction among 753 white and Hispanic addicts admitted to methadone maintenance programs in California between 1971 and 1978. Results indicated that between 21 percent and 30 percent more persons were involved in crimes during the first year after addiction, arrests increased substantially, and the number of days that addicts were engaged in crimes increased markedly after their first addiction.

In a study of behaviors and economic effects of heroin among 201 street heroin users in Harlem between 1980 and 1982, Johnson, et al. (1985) found that daily users reported the highest crime rates. There were 209 nondrug crimes per year for daily users, as compared with 162 among regular users (i.e., those who used heroin three to five days a week), and 116 among those who used heroin sporadically (i.e., those who used heroin two days or less per week). Daily heroin users committed about twice the number of robberies and burglaries as regular users, and about five times as many as irregular users.

Whether there is a causal connection between the use of drugs and crime and in which direction the causal arrow points is uncertain. There is some indication that involvement in crime may precede drug use. Greene (1983) found that most arrested addicts began their criminal involvement before they began using drugs. However, a complete understanding of the myriad of factors that affect criminal behaviors, such as environment, motivation, social and economic pressures, and carefully conceptualized and methodoligically sound research. McBride and McCoy (1982), for instance argue that longitudinal research is required to assess the complexities of the relationship between drugs and crime.

22. Results showed that nearly one-third of all state prisoners had been under the influence of an illegal drug at the time of the current offense; more than half had taken an illegal drug in the month prior to the current offense; and more than 75 percent had used illegal drugs at some point in their lives (Kalish and Masamura, 1983b: 1).

23. In the RAND Study of the reliability of prisoner self-reports, Marquis (1981) found that inmates did not deny convictions. Rather, convictions were sometimes coded in the wrong category (Marquis, 1981: 78).

Chapter 7

1. The National Science Foundation now requires a signed agreement from new grantees, before a formal award is made, that data will be archived within eighteen months of completion of the grant period.

2. Examples of journals which now require public access to data on which articles were based include *Public Opinion Quarterly* and the *American Journal of Sociology*. The National Science Foundation is now implementing a policy which requires intent to archive data collected under its auspices as a precondition of an award.

3. The Inter-university Consortium for Political and Social Research is based upon a membership of colleges and universities who pay an annual fee which entitles individual students and faculty members routine access to archival resources without additional charge. The costs of access to the resources of the Criminal Justice Archive for individuals at nonmember institutions who are Department of Justice grantees are covered by the BJS grant.

4. The National Institute of Justice has supported both summer research fellowships and a small grants program based upon secondary analysis. Sometimes the research focus of the programs has been left to the interests of the applicants, and sometimes the agency has attempted to steer applicants to research areas in which it has a current interest.

5. The Criminal Justice Archive at the ICPSR publishes a listing of sources of computer-readable criminal justice data entitled The *Directory of Criminal Justice Data Collections in the United States* which contains information about the holdings of a number of other archival operations as well.

6. A review of the basic data files shows the approximately 98 percent of all the self-reported victims reported four or fewer incidents in their semiannual interview. The maximum number of incidents reported in any interview by a respondent is thirteen.

Chapter 8

1. The article of Krasnoff (1986) in *PC Magazine* reviews flat file data bases for the IBM PC family and compatibles. Most of the microcomputer magazines will report on performance and features of popular software including data base software and are good places to begin comparing products.

2. IBM PC, PC/AT and Personal System/2 are registered trademarks of International Business Machines Inc.; Apple II and Apple Macintosh are registered trademarks of Apple Computer Inc.; VAX is a registered trademark of Digital Equipment Corporation; MS DOS is a trademark of Microsoft Corporation; SAS, SAS/BASE, SAS/STAT and SAS/FSP are registered trademarks of SAS Institute, Inc.; SPSS is a registered trademark of SPSS, Inc.; dBASE III is a registered trademark of Ashton-Tate, Inc.; and Lotus Symphony is a registered trademark of Lotus Development Corporation.

3. A good source of reviews and information on statistical and data analysis programs for microcomputers are the "Statistical Computing Software Reviews" and "New Developments in Statistical Computing" sections of the *The American Statistican* and reviews in *Computational Statistics & Data Analysis*. Many other professional journals also report on microcomputer software relevant to their specific fields.

4. Taylor (1986) gives a further discussion of microcomputer security along with several product reviews.

5. Articles by Addelson (1986) and Derfler (1986) discuss microcomputer links with mainframes.

6. See the May 1986 issue of *Byte* for a discussion of optical disk technology as applied to microcomputers.

7. This example is taken from the 1985 Workshop on *Analytical Techniques and Use of Large Data Bases in Criminal Justice* hosted by the Department of Experimental Statistics and Department of Criminal Justice, Louisiana State University, Baton Rouge, LA.

Chapter 9

1. Information on homicides is collected by means of an Age, Sex and Race of Persons Arrested form, Return A form and SHR form. The first two are described below; the SHR and FBI estimates based on Return A are described in the chapter by Schneider and Wiersema in this volume.

> *Age, Sex, and Race of Persons Arrested:* As the name of this form implies, aggregated information on the age, sex, and race of arrested offenders is collected monthly on this form. Prior to 1976, it was the only available information on homicide arrest. Beginning in 1976, offender information was collected on the SHR.
>
> *Return A-Monthly Return of Offenses Known to the Police:* All offenses, including murder and nonnegligent manslaughter, are reported to the police on this form. The form distinguishes between reported and unfounded homicides and UCR with the total number of homicides per month for a given reporting agency.

2. Information on changes in the SHR codes was taken from coding guides provided by the UCR Program as well as discussions with the personnel of that program.

Chapter 10

1. The work summarizing this report may be found in the authoritative publication by Farrington, Ohlen and Wilson (1986).

2. The Evaluation Quarterly, Sage Publications, Beverly Hills (1977) and Klein and Teilmann's (1980) handbook.

3. See Radzinowicz and Wolfgang (eds.) (1977) p. 3-44 and p. 335-410 for relevent excerpts or the work of these writers and the American Friends Service Committee (1971).

4. The large-scale data bases developed by Delbert Elliot and his colleagues and known as the National Youth Survey, the work by Lyle Shannon and his colleagues in Racine and Madison, Wisconsin, the work by David Farrington in the United Kingdom and that of Marvin Wolfgang and his colleagues in Philadephia have been primarily responsible for the advances in knowledge during recent years in this area. The reader is referred to Farrington, Ohlen and Wilson (1986) for a discussion of these and other studies and their data bases and to the June 22, 1988 announcement from the Program on Human Development and Human Behavior, Castine Corporation, Maine.

References

Chapter 2

Beattie, R. H. 1960. Criminal Statistics in the United States. *Journal of Criminal Law, Criminology, and Police Science, 51,* 49-65.

Biderman, A. D. and A. J. Reiss. 1967a. On Exploring the 'Dark Figure' of Crime. *Annals of the American Academy of Political and Social Science, 374* 1–15.

Biderman, A. D. and A. J. Reiss, 1967b. *Reporting on a Pilot Study in the District of Columbia on Victimization and Attitudes Law Enforcement.* Washington, D.C.

Black, D. 1970. Production of Crime Rates. *American Sociological Review, 35,* 733-748.

Bureau of Justice Statistics. 1984. *Criminal Victimization in the United States, 1982.* Washington, DC: Government Printing Office.

Decker, S. H. 1977. Official Crime Rates and Victim Surveys: An Empirical Comparison. *Journal of Criminal Justice, 5,* 47-54.

Dodge, R. W., and A. G. Turner. 1971. Methodological Foundations for Establishing a National Survey of Victimization. Paper presented at the National Meeting of the American Statistical Association, Social Sciences Section.

Federal Bureau of Investigation, 1984, *Age-Specific Arrest Rates,* 1965-1983. Washington, D.C.: Uniform Crime Reporting Program.

Federal Bureau of Investigation. 1986. *Age-Specific and Race-Specific Arrest Rates for Selected Offenses, 1965-1984.* Washington, D.C.: Uniform Crime Reporting Program.

Federal Bureau of Investigation. 1981. *Crime in the United States, 1980.* Washington, D.C.: Government Printing Office.

Federal Bureau of Investigation. 1985. *Population-at-Risk Rates and Selected Crime Indicators.* Washington, D.C.: Uniform Crime Reporting Program.

Federal Bureau of Investigation. 1984. *Uniform Crime Reporting Handbook.* Washington, D.C. Government Printing Office.

Fox, J. A. and G. L. Pierce. 1978. Uniform Crime Reports: Supplementary Homicide Reports, 1976-1983 [codebook and machine readable-data files]. Northeastern

University, Boston, MA [producer]. Inter-university Consortium for Political and Social Research, Ann Arbor, MI [distributor].

Helwig, J. T. (ed.) 1985a. *SAS Introductory Guide*. Third edition. Cary, N.C.: SAS Institute.

Holsti, O. R. 1968. Content Analysis. Ch. 16 (pp. 596-692) in *Handbook of Social Psychology*, Volume 2, Research Methods (2nd ed.), G. Lindzey and E. Aronson, eds., Reading, Mass.: Addison-Wesley Pub. Co.

Hoover, J. E. 1966. *Uniform Crime Reporting Handbook*. Washington, D.C.: Government Printing Office.

Kitsuse, J. I. 1962. Social Reaction to Deviant Behavior: Problems of Theory and Method. *Social Problems, 9*, 274-256.

Kitsuse, J. I., and A. V. Cicourel. 1963. A Note of the Uses of Official Statistics. *Social Problems, 11*, 131-139.

Law Enforcement Assistance Administration. 1974. *Crime and Victims: A Report of the Dayton-San Jose Pilot Survey of Victimization*. Washington, D.C.: National Criminal Justice Information and Statistics Service.

Lehoczkey, J. P. 1986. Random Parameter Stochastic-Process Models of Criminal Careers. Pp. 380-404 in *Criminal Careers and Career Criminals, Volume II*, A. Blumstein, J. Cohen, J. A. Roth, and C. A. Visher (eds.). Washington, D.C.: National Academy Press.

Loftin, C., K. Kindley, S. L. Norris, and B. Wiersema. 1987. An Attribute Approach to Relationships between Offenders and Victims in Homicide. *Journal of Criminal Law and Criminology, 78(2)*, 259-271.

Maltz, M. D. 1975. Crime Statistics: A Mathematical Perspective. *Journal of Criminal Justice, 3*, 177-194.

Maltz, M. D. 1977. Crime Statistics: A Historical Perspective. *Crime and Delinquency*, 32-40.

Mead, B. 1929. Police Statistics. *Annals of the American Academy of Political and Social Science, 194*, 74-85.

National Commission of Law Observance and Enforcement. 1931. *Report on Criminal Stastics*. Washington, D.C.: Government Printing Office.

Poggio, E. C, S. D. Kennedy, J. M. Chaiken, and K. E. Carlson. 1985.*Blueprint for the Future of the Uniform Crime Reporting Program: Final Report of the UCR Study*. Washington, D.C.: Department of Justice.

Pierce, G. L., W. Bowers, J. Baird, and J. Heck. 1981. Uniform Crime Reports: National Time-Series Community-Level Database, 1967-1980 [codebook and machine-readable data files]. Center of Applied Research, Northeastern University, Boston,

MA [producer]. Inter-university Consortium for Political and Social Research, Ann Arbor, MI [distributor].

Reiss, A. J. 1967. Measurement of the Nature and Amount of Crime, in President's Commission on Law Enforcement and Administration of Justice, *Studies in Crime and Law Enforcement in Major Metropolitan Areas*, Field Survey III. Volume I, Section. Washington, D.C.: Government Printing Office.

Reiss, A. J. 1969. Crime Against Small Business: A Report on the Small Business Administration. *U.S. Senate Document 91:* 14, 91st Congress, 1st Session, April 3.

Riedel, M. and M. A. Zahn. 1987. Trends in American Homicide, 1968-1978: Victim-level Supplementary Homicide Reports [codebook and machine-readable data file]. Southern Illinois University, Carbondale, IL [producer]. Inter-university Consortium for Political and Social Research, Ann Arbor, MI [distributor].

Robison, S. M. 1966. A Critical View of the Uniform Crime Reports. *Michigan Law Review, 64,* 1031-1054.

SAS Institute. 1985. *SAS User's Guide Basics. (Version 5 edition).* Cary, N.C.: SAS Institute.

Schneider, V. and B. Wiersema. 1985. Estimating Crime: The Impact of Imputation in the Uniform Crime Reports. Paper presented at the Annual Meeting of the American Society of Criminology, San Diego, California.

Seidman, D. and M. Couzens. 1974. Getting the Crime Rate Down: Political Pressure and Crime Reporting. *Law and Society Review, 8(3),* 457-493.

Shulman, H. M. 1966. The Measurement of Crime in the United States. *Journal of Criminal Law, Criminology, and Police Science, 57,* 483-492.

Skogan, W. 1976. Crime and Crime Rates, in Wesley Skogan (ed.), *Sample Surveys of the Victims of Crime.* Cambridge, MA: Ballinger Publishing Company.

Skogan, W. G. 1975. Measurement Problems in Official and Survey Crime Rates. *Journal of Criminal Justice, 3,* 17-32.

Skolnick, J. H. 1966. *Justice Without Trial: Law Enforcement in Democratic Society.* New York: John Wiley & Sons.

SPSS, Inc. 1986. *SPSS^x User's Guide, Edition 2.* Chicago: SPSS, Inc.

Turner, A. G. 1972. *Methodological Issues in the Development of the National Crime Survey Panel: Partial Findings.* Washington, D.C. National Criminal Justice Information and Statistics Service.

U.S. Department of Justice, Federal Bureau of Investigation. 1984. *Uniform Crime Reports, 1980. Part I: Offenses Known and Persons Arrested* [machine-readable data set]. (2nd ICPSR edition). Washington D.C.: U.S. Department of Justice. [producer]. Ann Arbor: Inter-university Consortium for Political and Social Research [distributor].

Wheeler, S. 1967. Criminal Statistics: A Reformulation of the Problem. *Journal of Criminal Law, Criminology, and Police Science, 58*, 317-324.

Wolfgang, M. 1968. Urban Crime, in J. Q. Wilson, *The Metropolitan Enigma.* Cambridge, MA: Harvard University Press.

Wolfgang, M. 1962-1963. Uniform Crime Reports: A Critical Appraisal. *The University of Pennsylvania Law Review, 3,* 708-738.

Chapter 3

Abt Associates, Inc. 1984. *On the Future of the Uniform Crime Reporting Program.* Proceedings of the Belmont Conference: January 25-28, 1984, Elkridge, Maryland). Draft.

Chaiken, Jan M. and Yoshio Akiyama. 1985. *The Uniform Crime Reporting Study: 1984 Survey of Law Enforcement Agencies.* Cambridge, Massachusetts: Abt Associates, Inc.

Federal Bureau of Investigation. 1987. *Redesigned Uniform Crime Reporting Program: Implementation and Automated Data Capture Specifications.* Draft.

Federal Bureau of Investigation. 1939. *Ten Years of Uniform Crime Reporting: 1930-1939.* Unpublished manuscript. For greater detail, see: Rossman, Henry H., Emily L. Roueich and Eugene C. Poggio. *The Uniform Crime Reporting System of the Federal Bureau of Investigation: An Outline of Issues Raised in the Research Literature.* (Working Paper) Cambridge, Massachusetts: Abt Associates, Inc.

International Association of Chiefs of Police (IACP). 1976. *The IACP-UCR Audit/ Evaluation Manual.* Gaithersburg, Maryland.

Kincaid, Stephen C. 1985. Oregon UCR Crime Statistics, July 1984. Personal Communication contained in *Blueprint for the Future of the Uniform Crime Reporting Program*, p. 86.

Lejins, Peter P., Charton F. Chute and Stanley R. Schrotel. 1958. *Uniform Crime Reporting—Report of the Consultant Committee.*

Poggio, Eugene C., Stephen D. Kennedy, Jan M. Chaiken and Kenneth E. Carlson. 1985. *Blueprint for the Future of the Uniform Crime Reporting Program.* (Final Report of the UCR Study) Cambridge, Massachusetts: Abt Associates, Inc.

Tully, Edward J. 1986. The Near Future: Implications for Law Enforcement. *FBI Law Enforcement Bulletin* 58, pp.1-9.

Chapter 4

Alexander, Charles H. 1987. Use of NCS for Estimation. Paper presented at the Workshop on the Design and Use of the National Crime Survey. University of Maryland.

References

Biderman, Albert D. and Albert J. Reiss, Jr. 1967. On Exploring the 'Dark Figure' of Crime. *The Annuals of the American Academy of Political and Social Science*, 374 (Nov.): 1-15.

Block, Richard and Carolyn R. Block. 1980. Decisions and Data: The Transformation of Robbery Incidents Into Official Robbery Statistics. *Journal of Criminal Law and Crimimology*, 71 (4): 622-636.

Block, Richard and Wesley G. Skogan. 1984. *The Dynamics of Violence Between Strangers: Victim Resistance and Outcomes in Rape, Assault, and Robbery*. Final Report. Evanston, IL: Center for Urban Affairs and Policy Research, Northwestern University.

Boggs, Sarah L. and John F. Galliher. 1975. Evaluating the Police: A Comparison of Black Street and Household Respondents. *Social Problems* 22 (Feb.): 393-406.

Bureau of Justice Statistics. 1987. *Criminal Victimization in the United States, 1985*. Washington, D.C.: Government Printing Office.

Dodge, Richard W. and Harold R. Lentzner. 1978. Patterns of Personal Series Incidents in the National Crime Survey. Paper presented at the annual meeting of the American Statistical Association, San Diego, CA.

Garofalo, James. 1977. *Public Opinion About Crime: The Attitudes of Victims and Nonvictims in Selected Cities*. Law Enforcement Assistance Administration. Washington D.C.: Government Printing Office.

Garofalo, James and Michael J. Hindelang. 1977. *An Introduction to the National Crime Survey*. Law Enforcement Assistance Administration. Washington, D.C.: Government Printing Office.

Gottfredson, Michael R. 1986. Substantive Contributions of Victimization Surveys. *In* Michael Tonry and Norval Morris (eds.), *Crime and Justice: An Annual Review of Research*, Vol. 7, pp. 251-287. Chicago: University of Chicago Press.

Hindelang, Michael J. 1976. *Criminal Victimization in Eight American Cities*. Cambridge MA: Ballinger.

Hindelang, Michael J., Travis Hirschi, and Joseph G. Weis. 1981. *Measuring Delinquency*. Beverly Hills, CA: Sage Publishing.

Inter-University Consortium for Political and Social Research. 1987 *National Crime Surveys: National Sample, 1979-1985 (Revised Questionaire)*. Ann Arbor, MI: ICPSR.

Laub, John H. 1987. *A Critical Assessment of National Juvenile Justice Data Collection Efforts Relating to Juveniles as Victims of Personal Crimes*. Working Paper. Albany, N.Y.: Hindelang Criminal Justice Research Center, State University of New York.

Lehnen, Robert G. and Albert J. Reiss, Jr. 1978. Some Response Effects in the National Crime Survey, *Victimology* 3 (1-2): 110-124.

Lynch, James P. 1986. Routine Activity at Work and the Risk of Personal Victimization. Paper presented at the annual meeting of the American Society of Criminology, Atlanta, GA.

National Academy of Sciences. 1972. *America's Uncounted People.* Washington D.C.: National Academy of Sciences.

Nelson, James F. 1984. Compound Poisson Models of Criminal Victimization Reported in a Police Data Set. Paper presented at the annual meeting of the American Society of Criminology, Cincinnati, OH.

Paez, Adolfo L. and Richard W. Dodge. 1982. *Criminal Victimization in the U.S.: 1979-80 Changes, 1973-80 Trends.* Bureau of Justice Statistics. Washington, D.C.: U.S. Department of Justice.

Penick, Bettye K. Eidson and Maurice E.B. Owens III, eds. 1976. *Surveying Crime.* Washington, D.C.: National Academy of Sciences.

Reiss, Albert J., Jr. 1967. *Studies in Crime and Law Enforcement in Major Metropolitan Areas*, Vol. 1, Sect. 1, President's Commission on Law Enforcement and Administration of Justice. Washington, D.C.: Government Printing Office.

Sellin, Thorsten. 1931. The Basis of a Crime Index. *Journal of Criminal Law and Criminology* 22 (Sept.): 335-356.

Shenk, Fred and William McInerney. 1981. Analytic Limitations of the National Crime Survey. *In* Robert G. Lehnen and Wesley G. Skogan (eds.), *The National Crime Survey: Working Papers*, Vol. 1, pp. 70-75. Bureau of Justice Statistics. Washington, D.C.: Government Printing Office.

Skogan, Wesley G. 1981. *Issues in the Measurement of Victimization.* Bureau of Justice Statistics. Washington, D.C.: Government Printing Office.

Sparks, Richard F. 1982. *Research on Victims of Crime: Accomplishments, Issues, and New Directions.* National Institute of Mental Health. Washington, D.C.: Government Printing Office.

Sparks, Richard F. 1981. Surveys of Victimization - An Optimistic Assessment. *In* Michael Tonry and Norval Morris (eds.), *Crime and Justice: An Annual Review of Research*, Vol. 3, pp. 1-60. Chicago: University of Chicago Press.

Turner, Anthony G. 1984. An Experiment to Compare Three Interview Procedures in the National Crime Survey. *In* Robert G. Lehnen and Wesley G. Skogan (eds.), *The National Crime Survey: Working Papers*, Vol. 2, pp. 49-53. Bureau of Justice Statistics. Washington, D.C.: Government Printing Office.

Turner, Anthony G. 1972. *San Jose Methods Test of Known Crime Victims.* Law Enforcement Assistance Administration. Washington, D.C.: Government Printing Office.

Whitaker, Catherine J. 1986. *Crime Prevention Measures.* Bureau of Justice Statistics. Washington, D.C.: Government Printing Office.

Wolfgang, Marvin E., Robert M. Figlio, Paul E. Tracy and Simon I. Singer. 1985. *The National Survey of Crime Severity*. Bureau of Justice Statistics. Washington, D.C.: Government Printing Office.

Woltman, Henry F. and John M. Bushery. 1984. Results of the NCS Maximum Personal Visit/Maximum Telephone Interview Experiment. *In* Robert G. Lehnen and Wesley G. Skogan (eds.), *The National Crime Survey: Working Papers*, Vol. 2, pp. 20-48. Bureau of Justice Statistics. Washington, D.C.: Government Printing Office.

Chapter 5

Biderman, Albert D., et al. 1967. *Report on the Pilot Study in the District of Columbia on Victimization and Attitudes Toward Law Enforcement*. Report to the President's Commission on Law Enforcement and the Administration of Justice, Washington, D.C., Government Printing Office.

Biderman, Albert and Albert J. Reiss. 1967. On Exploring the 'Dark Figure' of Crime, *The Annals*, vol. 374.

Biderman, Albert, David Cantor and Albert J. Reiss, Jr. 1982. A Quasi-Experimental Analysis of Personal Victimization Reporting by Respondents in the National Crime Survey. Joint Statistical Meetings of the Social Survey Section of the American Statistical Association, Cincinnati, OH.

Biderman, Albert, J.P. Lynch and J. Peterson. 1983. Why the NCS Diverges from UCR Trends: The Contributions of Differences in Definitions and Procedures. Paper presented at the Annual Meetings of the American Society of Criminology, Denver, CO.

Biderman, Albert, D. Carter, J. Lynch and E. Martin. 1986. *Final Report of Research and Development for the Redesign of the National Crime Survey*. Washington, D.C. Bureau of Social Science Research.

Cantor, David. 1984. *Segment Cluster and Longitudinal Aggregation*, Item 104 in SCDD:CSRC, Washington, D.C. Bureau of Social Science Research, Inc.

Greenberg, Stephanie, W.M. Rohe and J.R. Williams. 1981. *Safe and Secure Neighborhoods: Physical Characteristics and Informal Territorial Control in High and Low Crime Neighborhoods*. Research Triangle Park, N.C. Research Triangle Institute.

Lavange, Lisa and Ralph Folsom. 1985. *Development of an NCS Error Adjustment Model: RTI Final Report for the NCS Redesign Project*. Research Triangle Park, N.C. Research Triangle Institute.

Lynch, James P. 1987. Routine Activities and Victimization at Work. *Journal of Quantitative Criminology*, vol. 4.

Lynch, James P. and Albert D. Biderman. 1984. Cars, Crime, and Crime Classification: What the UCR Should Tell Us But Doesn't. Paper presented at the American Society of Criminology Meetings, Cincinnati, OH.

Lynch, James P. and Albert D. Biderman. 1982. *The Case for Including Vandalism in the Near Term Redesign.* Item 121 in SCDD: CSRC, Washington, D.C., Bureau of Social Science Research, Inc.

Lynch, James P. and Albert D. Biderman. 1983. Changes in Police Organizations and the Divergence of the NCS and UCR. Paper presented at the Annual Meetings of the American Society of Criminology, Denver, CO.

Lynch, James P. and Albert D. Biderman. 1984. A Preliminary Discussion of Core and Supplement Format in the Redesigned NCS. Washington, D.C., Bureau of Social Science Research, Inc.

Lynch, James P. and Albert D. Biderman. 1981. *Recommendations of the Crime Survey Research Consortium.* Washington, D.C., Bureau of Social Science Research, Inc.

Martin, Elizabeth. 1982. *NCS Supplement: Life Activities.* Washington, D.C., Bureau of Social Science Research, Inc.

Penick, Bettye K. E. and Maurice Owens. 1976. *Surveying Crime: Report of the Panel for the Evaluation of the National Crime Survey.* Croton-on-Hudson, Hudson, N.Y.

Reiss, Albert J., Jr. 1982. *Victimization Productivity in Proxy Interviews,* Report No. 3, Institute for Social and Policy Studies, Yale University: New Haven, CT.

Skogan, Wesley. 1976. Citizen Reporting of Crime: Some National Panel Data. *Criminology,* vol. 13, pp. 35-49.

Taub, Richard, Garth Taylor and Jan Dunham. 1981. Neighborhoods and Safety. in Dan Lewis (ed.) *Reactions to Crime.* Beverly Hills, CA: Sage Publications.

Taylor, Bruce. 1984. *BJS Conclusions on Near-term Implementation.* Washington, D.C., Bureau of Social Science Research, Inc.

Taylor, Bruce. Forthcoming. *Redesign of the National Crime Survey.* Washington, D.C., U.S. Department of Justice, Bureau of Justice Statistics.

Whitaker, Catherine. 1986. *Crime Prevention Measures.* Washington, D.C., Bureau of Justice Statistics.

Chapter 6

National Criminal Justice Information and Statistics Service. *Advance Report: Census of State Correctional Facilities—1974, National Prisoner Statistics Special Report.* Washington, D.C.: (1975)

American Correctional Association, *Manual of Correctional Standards,* 1966. Washington, D.C.: The American Correctional Association.

References

Anglin, M. D. and G. Speckart. 1984. *Narcotics Use and Analysis: A Confirmatory Analysis.* Los Angeles: UCLA, unpublished manuscript.

Armor, D. J. and J. M. Pollich. 1982. Measurement of Alcohol Consumption, in *Encyclopedia Handbook of Alcoholism*, E. Mansell Pattison, ed. New York: Gardner Press, 72-80.

Ball, J. C., J. W. Shaffer and D. N. Norco. 1983. Day to Day Criminality of Heroin Addicts in Baltimore: A Study in the Continuity of Offense Rates, *Drugs and Alcohol Dependence*, 12: 119-142.

Barton, W.I. 1980. Drug Histories and Criminality: Survey of Inmates of State Correctional Facilities, January 1974, *The International Journal of the Addictions*, 15(2): 233-258.

Baunach, P. J., 1985. *Mothers in Prison.* New Brunswick: Transaction, Inc.

Beck, A. J., S. A. Kline and L. A. Greenfeld. 1988. *Survey of Youth in Custody, 1987.* Washington, D.C.: Bureau of Justice Statistics.

Bonfanti, M. S., Felder, M. Loesch and N. Vincent. 1974. "Enactment and Perception of Maternal Role of Incarcerated Mothers." Masters Thesis, Louisiana State University.

Bureau of Justice Statistics. 1982. *Prisons and Prisoners.* Washington, D.C.: Bureau of Justice Statistics.

Cantwell, M. 1979. *Profile of State Prison Inmates: Sociodemographic Findings From the 1974 Survey of Inmates of State Correctional Facilities.* Washington, D.C.: National Criminal Justice Information and Statistics Service.

Cantwell, M, and W. T. Masamura. 1981. *Veterans in Prison.* Washington D.C.: Bureau of Justice Statistics.

Census of State Adult Correctional Facilities 1984: Codebook. Ann Arbor: Criminal Justice Archive and Information Network, 1986.

1984 Census of State Adult Correctional Facilities. 1987, Washington, D.C.: Bureau of Justice Statistics.

Collins, J. J. 1981. *Drinking and Crime.* New York: The Guilford Press.

Conrad, J. 1967. *Crime and its Correction.* Berkeley: University of California Press.

Donavan, D. and G. A. Marlatt. 1980. Assessment of Expectancies and Behavior Associated with Alcohol Consumption. *Journal of Studies on Alcohol*, 41(11): 1153-1185.

Dubose, D. 1975. Problems of Children Whose Mothers are Imprisoned, New York: Institute of Women's Wrongs, mimeographed.

Gardner, R. 1982. Prison Population Jumps to 369,725, *Corrections Magazine*, 8(3): 6-14.

REFERENCES

Gettinger, S. 1979. Addicts and Crime. *Police Magazine*, 2(6): 35.

Gettinger, Steven. 1983. The Prison Population Boom: Still No End in Sight, *Corrections Magazine*, 9(3): 6-11, 47-48.

Greene, B. T. 1982. Examination of the Relationship Between Crime and Substance Use in Drug/Alcohol Treatment Population. *International Journal of the Addictions*, 16(4): 627-645.

Greenfeld, L. A. 1987. *Prisoners in 1986*. Washington, D.C.: Bureau of Justice Statistics.

Gropper, B. 1985. Probing the Links Between Drugs and Crime. *National Institute of Justice Reports*. Washington, D.C.: National Institute of Justice.

Heath, D. 1981. Determining the Social Cultural Context of Alcohol Use. *Journal of Studies on Alcohol* Supplement, 9:9-17.

Innes, C. 1986. *Population Density of State Prisons: Special Report*, Washington, D.C.: Bureau of Justice Statistics.

Innes, C. 1988. *Profile of State Prison Inmates 1986*. Washington, D.C.: Bureau of Justice Statistics.

Johnson, B., P. Goldstein, E. Preble, J. Schmeidler, D. Lipton, B. Spunt and T. Miller. 1985. *Taking Care of Business: The Economics of Crime by Heroin Abusers*. Lexington: Lexington Books.

Kalish, C. and W.T. Masamura. 1983a. *Prisoners and Alcohol*. Washington, D.C.: Bureau of Justice Statistics.

Kalish, C. and W. T. Masamura. 1983b. *Prisoners and Drugs*. Washington, D.C.: Bureau of Justice Statistics.

Langan, P. A. and L. A. Greenfeld. 1983. *Career Patterns in Crimes: Special Report*. Washington, D.C.: Bureau of Justice Statistics.

Langan, P. A. and L. A. Greenfeld. *The Prevalence of Imprisonment: Special Report*. Washington, D.C.: Bureau of Justice Statistics.

Marquis, K. H. 1981. *Quality of Prisoner Self-Reports: Arrest and Conviction Response Errors*. Santa Monica: RAND Corporation.

Miller, B. A. and J. W. Welte. 1986. Comparisons of Incarcerated Offenders According to Use of Alcohol/Drugs Prior to Offense. *Criminal Justice and Behavior*, 13(4): 366-392.

Miller, R. E. 1984. Nationwide Profile of Female Inmate Substance Involvement. *Journal of Psychoactive Drugs*, 16(4): 319-326.

McAndrews, C. and R. Edgerton. 1969. *Drunken Comportment: A Social Explanation*. New York: Aldine.

McGowan, B. and K. Blumenthal. 1978 Why Punish the Children?: A Study of Children of Women Prisoners. Hackensack: National Council on Crime and Delinquency.

Minor-Harper, S. 1982. *Prisoners in 1981.* Washington, D.C.: Bureau of Justice Statistics.

Montilla, R. and N. Harlow. 1979. *Corrections Facilities Planning.* Lexington: D.C. Heath Company.

Nesbitt, C. 1983. Public Correctional Policy on the Purpose of Corrections. *Corrections Today,* 45(6): 66-72.

Palmer, T. 1976. Martinson Revisited. In Matthew Mattlin, Ed. *Rehabilitation, Recidivism, and Research,* Hackensack: National Council on Crime and Delinquency, 41-62.

Piercy, D. 1984. Violence: The Drug/Alcohol Patient, In James T. Turner, ed. *Violence in the Medical Care Setting,* Rockville: Aspen Systems, Inc., 123-151.

Sherman, M. and G. Hawkins, (1981) *Imprisonment in America,* Chicago: University of Chicago.

Stanton, A. 1980. *When Mothers Go to Jail.* Lexington: D.C. Heath Company.

Sullivan, R. 1973. The Economics of Crime: An Introduction to the Literature, In L.J. Kaplan and D. Kessler, eds. *An Economic Analysis of Crime,* Springfield: Charles C. Thomas, 15-23.

von Hirsch, A. 1976. *Doing Justice: The Choice of Punishments.* New York: Hill and Wang.

Watters, J. K., C. Reinarman, and J. Fagan. 1985. Causality, Context, and Contingency: Relationships Between Drug Abuse and Delinquency. *Contemporary Drug Problems,* 12(3): 351-373.

U.S. Department of Justice. 1976. *Survey of Inmates of State Correctional Facilities, 1974: Advance Report.* Washington, D.C.: National Criminal Justice Information and Statistics Service.

Zalba, S. 1964. *Women Prisoners and Their Families.* Sacramento: State of California Department of Social Welfare and Department of Corrections.

Chapter 7

Clubb, Jerome M., Erik W. Austin, Carolyn L. Geda and Michael W. Traugott. 1985. Sharing Research Data in the Social Sciences, *In* Fienberg et al eds. *Sharing Research Data.* Washington: National Academy Press, pp. 39-88.

Fienberg, Stephen E., Margaret E. Martin and Miron L. Straf, eds. 1985. *Sharing Research Data.* Washington: National Academy Press.

Gerbner, George and Larry Gross. 1976. Living with Television: The Violence Profile. *Journal of Communication,* vol. 26, no. 1, pp. 173-199.

REFERENCES

Hirsch, Paul M. 1980. The 'Scary World' of the Nonviewer and Other Anomalies: A Reanalysis of Gerbner et al.'s Findings on Cultivation Analysis. *Communication Research*, vol. 7 no. 4, pp. 403-456.

Marks, Judith A. and Michael W. Traugott. 1980. Data Resources and Services from the Criminal Justice Archive and Information Network. *In* J. Raben and G. Marks, eds. *Data Bases in the Humanities and Social Sciences*. Amsterdam: North Holland.

Miller, Warren E. 1976. The Less Obvious Functions of Archiving Survey Research Data. *American Behavioral Scientists*, vol. 19, no. 4, pp. 409-418.

Schneider, Victoria W., Karen M. McCurdy and Julie S. Drucker. Replicating Results from Published Reports. Is it Possible? The Case of Victimization in the District of Columbia. Paper presented at the Annual Meeting of the American Society of Criminology, October 29-November 1, 1986. Atlanta, GA.

Schneider, Victoria and Brian Wiersma. Estimating Crime: The Impact of Imputation in the Uniform Crime Reports. Paper presented at the Annual Meeting of the American Society of Criminology, November 13-17, 1985. San Diego, CA.

Traugott, Michael W. 1981. Archival Data Resources. *Research on Aging*, vol. 3, no. 4, pp. 487-501.

Chapter 8

Aarons, R. 1986. Q&A: A Data Base with a Smart Interface. *PC Magazine* 5(5), 185-188.

Addelson, R. 1986. Emulating the 3278. *PC Tech Journal* 4(2), 48-63.

Baran, N. M. 1986. Software Reviews: Symantec Corp's Q&A and Ansa Software's Paradox. *Computer Language* 3(8), 102-110.

Date, C. J. 1981. *An Introduction to Data Base Systems, Third Ed.* Addison-Wesley Pub. Co., Reading, 574 pp.

Derfler, F. J., Jr. 1986. Micro to Mainframe: Making the Right Connection. *PC Magazine* 5(9), 116-124.

Donlan, T. G. 1986. No TEMPEST in a Teapot: Hacking is No Longer Child's Play. *Barron's*, September 29, pages 14, 53.

Efron, B. 1979. Computers and the Theory of Statistics: Thinking the Unthinkable. *Society for the Industrial and Applied Mathematics Review* 21, 460-480.

Hansen, A. 1985. Kermit. *PC Tech Journal* 3(1), 110-123.

Krasnoff, B. 1986. Project Data Base II: Flat-file data bases. *PC Magazine* 5(14), 269-307.

Kryder, M. H. 1987. Data-Storage Technologies for Advanced Computing. *Scientific American* 257(4), 117-125.

Marshall, T., C. Jones and S. Kluger. 1986. The Definicon 68020 Coprocessor, Part I: The Hardware and Operating System. *Byte* 11(7), 120-144.

McCown, R. and H. Clark. 1987. Laser Performance. *PC Tech Journal* 5(9), 100-114.

Rosch, W. L. 1986. Backup Power: When the Juice Stops Flowing. *PC Magazine* 5(15), 181-212.

Stone, M. D. 1986. Fast, Faster, Fastest: 9600-bps Modems Arrive. *PC Magazine* 5(15), 221-230.

Taylor, J. 1986. Protection from Prying Eyes. *PC Magazine* 5(15), 213-219.

Williams, T. 1987. Optical Storage Opens New Applications for System Design. *Computer Design* 26(16), 37-42.

Young, F. W., D. P. Kent and W. F. Kuhfeld. 1987. PROC VISUALS: Experimental SAS Software for Dynamic Hyperdimensional Graphics. *Proceedings of the Twelfth Annual SAS Users Group International Conference,* Dallas, TX, 522-560.

Chapter 9

Beattie, R. H. 1960. Criminal Statistics in the United States. *Journal of Criminal Law, Criminal and Police Science, 51,* 49-65.

Beattie, R. H. 1962. Problems of Criminal Statistics in the United States. In M.E. Wolfgang, L. Savitz and N. Johnston (eds.), *The Sociology of Crime and Delinquency,* (pp. 37-43). New York: John Wiley and Sons, Inc.

Block, C. R. 1984. *Is Crime Seasonal?* Chicago: Illinois Criminal Justice Information Authority.

Bureau of the Census. 1940. Manual of the International List of *Causes of Death* (5th Revision). Washington: U.S. Government Printing Office.

Bureau of the Census. 1986. *Statistical Abstract of the United States, 1986.* Washington: U.S. Government Printing Office.

Cantor, D. and L. E. Cohen. 1980. Comparing Measures of Homicide Trends: Methodological and Substantive Differences in the Vital Statistics and Uniform Crime Report Time Series (1933-1975). *Social Science Research, 9,* 121-145.

Curtis, L. A. 1974. *Criminal Violence: National Patterns and Behavior.* Lexington: Lexington Books.

Federal Bureau of Investigation. 1962. *Crime in the United States—1961, Uniform Crime Reports.* Washington: U.S. Government Printing Office.

Federal Bureau of Investigation. 1985. *Crime in the United States—1984, Uniform Crime Reports.* Washington: U.S. Government Printing Office.

REFERENCES

Federal Bureau of Investigation. 1965. *Uniform Crime Reporting Handbook.* Washington: U.S. Government Printing Office.

Federal Bureau of Investigation. 1974. *Uniform Crime Reporting Handbook.* Washington: U.S. Government Printing Office.

Federal Bureau of Investigation. 1980. *Uniform Crime Reporting Handbook.* Washington: U.S. Government Printing Office.

Gove, W. R., M. Hughes and M. Geerken. 1985. Are Uniform Crime Reports a Valid Indicator of Index Crimes? An Affirmative Answer with some Minor Qualifications. *Criminology, 23,* 451-501.

Hindelang, M. J. 1974. The Uniform Crime Reports Revisited. *Journal of Criminal Justice, 2,* 1-17.

Israel, R. A. and A. J. Klebba. 1969. A Preliminary Report of the Effect of Eighth Revision ICDA of Cause-of-death Statistics. *American Journal of Public Health, 59,* 1651-1660.

James, G., R. E. Patton and A. S. Heslin. 1955. Accuracy of Cause of Death Statements on Death Certificates. *Public Health Reports, 70,* 39-51.

Lejins, P. P. 1966. Uniform Crime Reports. *University of Michigan Law Review, 64,* 1011-1030.

Little, R. J. A and D. B. Rubin. 1987. *Statistical Analysis With Missing Data.* New York: John Wiley and Sons, Inc.

Loftin, C., K. Kindley, S. L. Norris and B. Wiersema. 1987. An Attribute Approach to Relationships between Offenders and Victims in Homicide. *Journal of Criminal Law and Criminology, 78,* 259-271.

Loftin, C. 1986. The Validity of Robber-Murder Classifications in Baltimore. *Violence and Victims, 1,* 191-204.

Moriyama, I. M., W. S. Baum, W. M. Haenszel and B. F. Mattison. 1958. Inquiry into Diagnostic Evidence Supporting Medical Certifications of Death. *American Journal of Public Health, 48,* 1376-1387.

National Center for Health Statistics. 1982. Annotated Bibliography of Cause-of-death Validation Studies: 1958-1980. *Vital and Health Statistics,* Series 2, No. 89, (DHHS Publication No. PHS 82-1363). Washington: U.S. Government Printing Office.

National Center for Health Statistics. 1975. Comparibility of Mortality Statistics for the Seventh and Eighth Revisions of the International Classification of Diseases, United States. *Vital and Health Statistics,* Series 2, No. 55, (DHEW Publication No. HRA 76-1340). Washington: U.S. Government Printing Office.

National Center for Health Statistics. 1965. Comparability of Mortality Statistics for the Sixth and Seventh Revisions: United States, 1958. *Vital Statistics—Special*

Reports, Selected Studies, Volume 51, No. 4, March. Washington: U.S. Government Printing Office.

National Center for Health Statistics. 1964. Comparability Ratios Based on Mortality Statistics for the Fifth and Sixth Revisions: United States, 1950. *Vital Statistics—Special Reports, Selected Studies*, Volume 51, No. 3, February. Washington: U.S. Government' Printing Office.

National Center for Health Statistics. 1980. Estimates of Selected Comparability Ratios Based on Dual Coding of 1976 Death Certificates by the Eighth and Ninth Revisions of the International Classification of Diseases. *Monthly Vital Statistics Report*, Volume 28, No. 11 Supplement, (DHEW Publication No. PHS 80-1120). Washington: U.S. Government Printing Office.

National Center for Health Statistics. 1985. *Vital Statistics of the United States, 1980*, Volume II, Mortality, Part A. Washington: U.S. Government Printing Office.

National Commission on the Causes and Prevention of Violence. 1969. *Crimes of Violence*, Volume 13. Washington: U.S. Government Printing Office.

National Office of Vital Statistics. 1954. *Vital Statistics of the United States, 1950*, Volume 1. Washington: U.S. Government Printing Office.

O'Brien, R. M. 1985. *Crime and Victimization Data*. Beverly Hills: Sage Publications.

Poggio, E. C., S. D. Kennedy, J. M. Chaiken and K. E. Carlson. 1985. *Blueprint for the Future of the Uniform Crime Reporting Program: Final Report of the UCR Study*. Boston: Abt Associates.

Raymond, M. R. 1986. Missing Data in Evaluation Research. *Evaluation and the Health Professions*, 9, 395-420.

Riedel, M. 1981. *Stranger Homicides in and American City*. Paper presented at the meeting of the American Society of Criminology, Washington. November.

Riedel, M. 1987. Stranger Violence: Perspectives, Issues, and Problems. *Journal of Criminal Law and Criminology*, 78, 223-258.

Riedel, M. and M. A. Zahn. 1985. *The Nature and Patterns of American Homicide*. Washington: U.S. Government Printing Office.

Robison, S. M. 1966. A Critical Review of the Uniform Crime Reports. *University of Michigan Law Review*, 64, 1031-1054.

Savitz, L. D. 1978. Official Police Statistics and their Limitations. In L. D. Savitz and N. Johnston, eds., *Crime in Society*, (pp. 69-81). New York: John Wiley and Sons, Inc.

Sellin. T. 1962. The Significance of Records of Crime. In M.E. Wolfgang, L. Savitz and N. Johnston, eds., *The Sociology of Crime and Delinquency*, (pp. 59-68). New York: John Wiley and Sons, Inc.

Sellin, T. 1931. The Bias of a Crime Index. *Journal of the American Institute of Criminal Law and Criminology*, 22, 335-356.

Sherman, L. W. and R. H. Langworthy. 1979. Measuring Homicide by Police Officers. *Journal of Criminal Law and Criminology, 70*, 546-560.

Williams, K. R. and R. L. Flewelling. 1987. Family, Acquaintance, and Stranger Homicide: Alternative Procedures for Rate Calculations. *Criminology, 25*, 543-560.

Wolfgang, M. E. 1963. Uniform Crime Reports: A Critical Appraisal. *University of Pennsylvania Law Review, 111*, 708-738.

World Health Organization. 1948. *Manual of the International Statistical Classification of Diseases, Injuries and Causes-of-Death* (6th revision). Geneva: World Health Organization.

World Health Organization. 1957. *Manual of the International Statistical Classification of Diseases, Injuries and Causes-of-Death* (7th revision). Geneva: World Health Organization.

World Health Organization. 1967. *Manual of the International Statistical Classification of Diseases, Injuries and Causes-of-Death* (8th revision). Geneva: World Health Organization.

World Health Organization. 1977. *Manual of the International Statistical Classification of Diseases, Injuries and Causes-of-Death* (9th revision). Geneva: World Health Organization.

Zahn, M. A. and M. Riedel. 1983. National versus Local Data Sources in the Study of Homicide: Do they agree? In G.P. Waldo, ed. *Measurement in Criminal Justice*, (pp. 103-120). Beverly Hills: Sage Publications.

Chapter 10

American Friends Service Committee. 1971. *Struggle for Justice: A Report on Crime and Punishment in America.* New York: Hill and Wang.

Avi-Itzhak, B. and Shinnar, B. 1973. Quantitative Models in Crime Control. *Journal of Criminal Justice, I*, 185-217.

Blumstein, Alfred, Jacqueline Cohen, Jeffery A. Roth and Christy Visher (eds.). 1986. *Criminal Careers and Career Criminals*, Vols. I and II. Washington, D.C.: National Academy Press.

Bureau of Justice Statistics Bulletin. 1986. *State and Federal Prisoners, 1925-1985.*

Elliott, Delbert S. and Suzanne S. Ageton. 1980. "Reconciling Race and Class Differences in Self-reported and Official Estimates of Delinquency." *American Sociological Review, 45*, 95-110.

Elliot, Delbert S. and Suzanne S. Ageton. 1983. *The Social Correlates of Delinquency Behavior.* Boulder, CO: Behavioral Research Institute, Project Report. No. 30.

Farrington, David, Lloyd E. Ohlen and James Q. Wilson. 1986. *Understanding and Controlling Crime: Toward a Research Strategy.* New York: Spring Verlag.

Haber, Fred, Ralph Spritzer and Robert Figlio. 1977. *Evaluation of the Philadelphia Police Cable TV Report.* Report to LEAA, Washington D.C.

Hagan, Frank E. 1982. *Research Methods in Criminal Justice and Criminology.* New York: The Macmillan Co.

Hindelang, Michael J., Travis Hirschi and Joseph G. Weis. 1979. Correlates of Delinquency: The Illusion of Discrepancy between self-report and Official Measures. *American Sociological Review, 44,* 995-1014.

Kitsuse, John I. and Aaron V. Cicourel. 1963. A note on the Use of Official Statistics. *Social Problems, 11,* No. 2, 131-139.

Klein, Malcom W. and Kathy S. Teilman. 1980. *Handbook of Criminal Justice Evaluation.* Beverly Hills, CA: Sage Publication.

National Advisory Committee on Criminal Justice Standards and Goals. 1976. *Criminal Justice Research and Development, Report of the Task Force on Criminal Justice Research and Development.* Santa Monica, CA: The Rand Corp.

Radzinowicz, Sir Leon and Marvin B. Wolfgang, eds. 1977. *Crime and Justice.* Vol. III. New York: Basic Books.

The President's Commission on Law Enforcement and Administration of Justice. 167a. *The Challenge of Crime in a Free Society.* Washington, D.C.: U.S. Government Printing Office.

The President's Commission on Law Enforcement and Administration of Justice. 167b. *Task Force Report: Crime and Its Impact—An Assessment.* Washington, D.C.: U.S. Government Printing Office.

U.S. Department of Justice., Bureau of Justice Statistics, 1986. *Sourcebook of Criminal Justice Statistics, 1986.*

U.S. Department of Justice. 1980. *Program Plan for Statistics 1977-1981.* Washington, D.C.: Law Enforcement Assistance Administration.

Walker, Samuel. 1978. Reexamining the President's Crime Commission, *Crime and Delinquency, 24,* No. 1.

Wolfgang, M. E. and R. M. Figlio, S. Singer and P. Tracy. 1985. *The National Survey of Crime Severity.* Washington, D.C.: U.S. Government Printing Office.

Chapter 11

Federal Bureau of Investigation, U.S. Department of Justice. 1988. Uniform Crime Reporting—National Incident-Based Reporting System, Vol. 1, Data Collection

REFERENCES

Guidelines; Vol. 2, Data Submission Specifications; Vol. 3, Approaches to Implementing an Incident-Based Reporting System.

Redesign of the National Crime Survey, Bureau of Justice Statistics, U.S. Department of Justice. 1988. NCJ-111457. Also see the BJS Technical Report entitled New Directions for the National Crime Survey March 1989 (NCJ-115571) for a briefer version of the changes made.

Prosecution of Felony Arrests, 1982, Bureau of Justice Statistics, U.S. Department of Justice. May 1988. NCJ-116990. Data for 1986 (NCJ-113248) should be available by the publication date of this volume.

Spelman, William. 1988. Police Executive Research Forum, *Beyond Bean Counting: New Approaches for Managing Crime Data.* Sponsored by the Bureau of Justice Statistics. NCJ-109925.

National Institute of Justice, U.S. Department of Justice. 1988. *Attorney General Announces NIJ Drug Forecasting System*, Research in Action Series.

Wish, Eric D. 1987. *Drug Use Forecasting: New York 1984 to 1986*, Research in Action Series, National Institute of Justice, U.S. Department of Justice.

Blumstein, A. and J. Cohen, 1987, "Characterizing Criminal Careers," *Science*, 237: 985-991.

Contributors

YOSHIO AKIYAMA received a Ph.D. in mathematics/statistics in 1967. He taught mathematics at the University of Minnesota, University of Wisconsin, and Florida State University. Since 1977, he has been affiliated with the National Uniform Crime Reporting (UCR) Program of the FBI and is currently the Chief of the Research and Analysis Unit of the UCR Program. Since 1978 he has been a Professorial Lecturer of Mathematics at the George Washington University, Department of Mathematics. Dr. Akiyama was a Task Force member of the Study of the National UCR Program during 1982-1985 and contributed to the conceptual foundation of the enhanced UCR Program. His criminal justice related publications include: "Murder Victimization: A Statistical Analysis" (FBI Law Enforcement Bulletin, March 1981); "Arson: A Statistical Profile" (FBI Law Enforcement Bulletin, October 1884; Co-author); "An Approach to Interval Estimation in Crime Analysis" (Proceeding of the Criminal Justice Statistics Inc. Conference, Minneapolis, Minnesota; August 1978); "Impact of Age Composition on the Level of Crime" (March 1985, prepared for the California Crime Prevention); "The Uniform Crime Reporting Study: Survey of Law Enforcement Agencies" (Department of Justice, August 1985, Co-author).

PHYLLIS JO BAUNACH is an attorney at Swidler & Berlin, where she practices general litigation and administrative law, and designs and implements computer-based litigation support systems for major litigation. She holds a Ph.D. in Psychology from the University of Minnesota, and has served as director of Surveys and Censuses, Prisons and Jails, at the Bureau of Justice Statistics, U.S. Department of Justice, and as a Research Correctional Specialist at the National Institute of Justice, U.S. Department of Justice, in Washington, D.C. She has taught in the Criminal Justice programs of the University of Minnesota, George Washington University, and the University of Maryland. She has published several book chapters and articles on women and crime, and other topics. For her book, *Mothers in Prison*, she was honored as Young Scholar of the Year by the American Association of University Women Educational Foundation. She is also a co-founder and first chair of the Division of Women and

Crime for the American Society of Criminology, serves on ASC's Executive Board, and is the 1989 ASC Herbert Bloch Award Winner.

ROBERT M. FIGLIO is presently an Adjunct Professor of Legal Studies and Criminology, The Wharton School, University of Pennsylvania and President of CAP Index, Inc. He received his Ph.D. in Sociology from the University of Pennsylvania and has worked as the Principal Investigator on numerous projects examining delinquency in birth cohorts, and analytical and quantitative methods in criminology. He has acted as consultant to state and Federal agencies and has lectured throughout the U.S. and internationally. He has researched and coauthored the following books and monographs, among others, *Delinquency in Birth Cohort, From Boy to Man—From Delinquency to Crime,* and *The National Survey of Crime Severity.*

JAMES GAROFALO is an Associate Professor in the department of Criminal Justice, Indiana University, Bloomington, Indiana. He has been involved in research using the National Crime Survey data since the mid-1970s. His studies in the area of victims of crime are reported in a book and in various monographs, book chapters, and journal articles that he has authored and co-authored.

JAMES P. LYNCH is an Assistant Professor in the Department of Justice, Law and Society at the American University in Washington, D.C. He received his Ph.D. in Sociology from the University of Chicago in 1983 and served as the Project Manager of the NCS Redesign from 1980 to 1985. He has published on crime and justice issues in the *Journal of Criminal Law and Criminology, Law and Society Review, Journal of Quantitative Criminology, Crime and Delinquency, Journal of Research in Crime and Delinquency,* and *Public Opinion Quarterly.* He and Albert Biderman are authors of a forthcoming book from Springer-Verlag, *Understanding Crime Incidence Statistics: Why the UCR Diverges from the NCS.*

DORIS LAYTON MACKENZIE is presently a Visiting Scientist at the National Institute of Justice (NIJ), U.S. Department of Justice and an Associate Professor of Criminal Justice at the Louisiana State University (LSU). She is working at NIJ under an Intergovernmental Personnel Act (IPA) agreement between the Institute and LSU where she holds a joint appointment in the Departments of Criminal Justice and Experimental Statistics. Dr. MacKenzie holds a Ph.D. degree in Psychology from the Pennsylvania State University. Her research has focused on offenders and corrections. Most recently she has studied the effectiveness of shock incarceration. She is director of a multi-site study evaluating shock incarceration programs in six states. She is coeditor of *The*

American Prison: Issues in Research and Policy and has written articles on classification, inmate adjustment, long-term offenders and incarceration rates.

EDGAR BARRY MOSER is Assistant Professor in the Department of Experimental Statistics at Louisiana State University. He has written articles on computer applications of statistics, exploratory and graphical data analysis, and the sampling of wildlife populations. He has taught courses in statistical methods, multivariate statistical analysis, sampling, wildlife biometrics, and computer applications in statistics using the SAS system. He is also a statistical consultant for the Louisiana State University Agricultural Center Experiment Station.

JACK B. PARKER is Dean of the General College at Louisiana State University and former Head of the Department of Criminal Justice. He is a long time advocate of innovative and integrative approaches to criminal justice research and theory building.

BENJAMIN H. RENSHAW is currently the Deputy Director of the Bureau of Justice Statistics of the U.S. Department of Justice. Joining the Department in November 1975 and its Senior Executive Service in July 1979, Mr. Renshaw has been an Assistant Administrator of the Law Enforcement Assistance Administration, Acting Director of the Bureau of Justice Assistance from 1979 to 1982 and Acting Director of the Bureau of Justice Assistance for eight months after the passage of the Anti-Drug Abuse Act of 1986. Prior to coming to the Federal government, he was Executive Director of the Office of Criminal Justice Plans and Analysis of the District of Columbia. Mr. Renshaw's B.S. in Economics and Masters of Governmental Administration are from the Wharton School of the University of Pennsylvania.

MARC RIEDEL is an Associate Professor in the Center for the Study of Crime, Delinquency, and Corrections at Southern Illinois University. He received his Ph.D. in Sociology from the University of Pennsylvania in 1972. Dr. Riedel has done research on racial differences in domestic violence, stranger murders, and the death penalty. He is currently doing research on estimating missing data in secondary datasets.

HARVEY M. ROSENTHAL has a diverse background in social research that has spanned more than thirty years. A sociologist and statistician, he has been with various government agencies at the Federal and city levels, both as a consultant and research administrator, and has a number of publications related to social statistics. Rosenthal has been with the Federal Bureau of Investigation's Uniform Crime Reporting Program since 1976, and before joining UCR, he was affiliated with the MITRE Corporation, where he had responsibility for the direction of research conducted as part of the national level evaluation of the High Impact Anti-Crime Program, for the National Institute of Law Enforcement and Criminal Justice, Law Enforcement Assistance Administration (LEAA), U.S. Department of Justice. Prior to that, he served as the Director of Survey Research for the District of Columbia's Model Cities Program with responsibility for the conduct and administration of Program evaluation research. In the 1960's, Rosenthal was the Chief Statistician of the New York City Department of Correction. Harvey Rosenthal received his graduate training in sociology and statistics at the New York University Graduate School of Arts and Science and the City University of New York.

VICTORIA W. SCHNEIDER is an Archival Assistant Director at the Inter-university Consortium for Political and Social Research (ICPSR), and manages the daily activities of the data archives. She is also co-principal investigator and project manager of the National Archives of Criminal Justice Data (formerly the Criminal Justice Archives and Information Network), sponsored by the Bureau of Justice Statistics, U.S. Department of Justice. Her interests range from studies of victimization such as the National Crime Surveys to work on capital punishment and issues of secondary data analysis.

MICHAEL W. TRAUGOTT is the Director of Resource Development for the Inter-university Consortium for Political and Social Research and the principal investigator on the National Criminal Justice Data Archives project. He is also a Program Director in the Center for Political Studies in the Institute for Social Research at The University of Michigan. He is a political scientist by training, having received his B.A. from Princeton University and his M.A. and Ph.D. from the University of Michigan.

BRIAN WIERSEMA is on the research faculty of the Institute of Criminal Justice and Criminology, University of Maryland at College Park. He is co-director of the Institute's Criminal Justice Data Resource Program, a data archiving project designed to promote secondary data analysis by assisting the National Institute of Justice NIJ acquire, manage, evaluate, and reanalyze data from NIJ-funded research projects. He also serves as coordinator for the summer Workshops on the Design and Use of the National Crime Survey, sponsored by the Bureau of Justice Statistics and the American Statistical Association. In addition to his work with the Uniform Crime Reports and the National Crime Survey, his research interests include violence and its prevention, measurement issues, and computer methods and technology.

Index

Aarons, R., 164
Abt Associates, Inc., 28, 32, 53, 54
Advance Report, 123, 125
Ageton, S. S., 220, 221
Akiyama, Y., 52, 54
Alcohol consumption and criminal behavior, 135-36
Alexander, C. H., 95
American Correctional Association, 120
Anglin, M. D., 136
Archiving of data, 147, 151, 233
Armor, D. J., 136
Attribute Based Crime Reporting (ABCR) system, 57
Avi-Itzhak, B., 221

Bail, 133
Baird, J., 33, 38
Ball, J. C., 136
Baran, N. M., 164
Baum, W. S., 192
Baunach, P. J., 135
Beattie, R. H., 28, 30, 176, 177
Biderman, A. D., 32, 81, 98, 103, 106, 113, 114
Black, D., 26
Block, C. R., 81, 177
Block, R., 81, 89
Blumenthal, K., 135
Blumstein, A., 221, 233
Boggs, S. L., 82
Bonfanti, M. S., 135
Bowers, W., 33, 38
Bureau of Justice Assistance (BJA), 213, 232
Bureau of Justice Statistics (BJS), 25, 78, 80, 82, 86, 88, 91, 96, 213
    crime data collection. *See* National Crime Survey; NCS Redesign effort
    data archiving, 147
    intergovernmental programs, funding for, 6
    Survey of Inmates and Census of Prisons, 119, 128
    UCR Redesign and, 53, 224
Bureau of Justice Statistics Bulletin, 221
Bureau of Labor Statistics, 214
Bureau of Social Science Research, Inc., (BSSR), 97
Bureau of the Census (BOC), 214
    NCS and, 76, 77, 80, 82, 92, 93, 95, 96, 98
    NCS Redesign, 106, 108, 109, 114-15
    Survey of Inmates and Census of Prisons, 119, 126, 127, 129
Burglary, UCR classifications of, 29-30
Bushery, J. M., 95

Cantor, D., 106, 107, 176, 177, 178, 188, 189, 195, 196, 202
Cantwell, M., 119, 135
Career Patterns and Alcohol (1983), 122
Carlson, K. E., 27, 187
Castine Corp., 220
Census Bureau. *See* Bureau of the Census
Census of State Adult Correctional Facilities. *See* Survey of Inmates and Census of Prisons
Census of State Adult Correctional Facilities, 1984: Codebook, 125, 127
Chaiken, J. M., 27, 52, 54, 187
Challenge of Crime in a Free Society, The, 211, 218
Children of inmates, data on, 135
Chute, C. F., 52
Cicourel, A. V., 32, 220
City-County Data Book, 115
Clark, H., 159
Clubb, J. M., 149
Cohen, J., 221, 233

INDEX

Cohen, L. E., 176, 177, 178, 188, 189, 195, 196, 202
Collins, J. J., 135
Computer-readable UCR data, 33-34, 47-48, 52
   aggregation of data, 41-42
   analyses of data made possible by, 34
   estimation of crime with (imputation), 22, 42-47
   management and use of data, 22, 40-47
   master data files
      Age, Sex, Race, and Ethnic Origin of Persons Arrested, 37
      County and City Data Books, 38
      Data Aggregated by Standard Metropolitan Statistical Areas, 38
      Law Enforcement Officers Killed and Assaulted, 37
      National Time Series Community-Level Data Base, 38
      Offenses Known to the Police, 35
      Property Stolen and Recovered, 35-36
      Supplementary Homicide Reports, 36-37, 39
      Trends in American Homicide, 38-39
   preparation of data for analysis, 41-42
   printed UCRs, comparison with, 34
   recoding of variables, 42, 46-47
   structure of files, 40
   subsetting of data, 42, 46
Computers. *See* Mainframe computers; Microcomputers for handling large data bases
Conrad, J., 120
Cost/benefit ratios of data series, 231-32
Couzens, M., 31
Crime and Its Impact, 211-12, 214
Crime in the United States (CIUS), 22, 24, 31, 43, 44, 67
Crime Survey Research Consortium (CSRC), 13
   longitudinal file of NCS data, 106
   members of, 100
   NCS Redesign, 97, 100-101, 108, 109, 110, 112, 113, 114, 116, 117
   Washington Area Metropolitan Survey, 104, 105
Criminal Justice Archive and Information Network (CJAIN). *See* National Archive of Criminal Justice Data
Curtis, L. A., 179

Data bases, criminal justice
   importance of, 10
   limitations of, 10-11
   operational definitions, 10. *See also* specific data bases
Data Center and Clearinghouse for Drugs and Crime, 233
Date, C. J., 158
Decker, S. H., 31
Dodge, R. W., 25, 88, 95
Donlan, T. G., 167
Drug use and criminal behavior, 136
Drug Use Forecasting (DUF) data base, 231
DuBose, D., 135
Dunham, J., 103

Efron, B., 157
Elliot, D. S., 220, 221
Extended analysis of data. *See* Secondary analysis of data

Federal Bureau of Investigation (FBI), 24, 29, 30, 43, 44, 49, 73, 176, 177, 178, 224, 234
   crime reporting program. *See* Uniform Crime Reporting Program; UCR Redesign effort
Federal integrated data base, 228
Felony case processing project, 226-27
Fienberg, S. E., 147
Figlio, R. M., 215, 219
Flewelling, R. L., 185, 186, 187
Folsom, R., 107
Fox, J. A., 39
Frankfurter, Felix, 229
Future of measurement in criminology, 6-7, 16, 221-22
   cost/benefit ratios of data series and, 231-32
   funding issues, 225, 229-30
   integration of research and statistics with operational data bases, 232-33
   microcomputers and, 169-70, 173
   NCS and UCR, developments in, 225-26
   NCS and UCR redesigned programs, analyses of, 233-34
   opportunities for further research, 232-35
   tensions that could constrain statistical enterprises, 229-32
   theory-driven data collection efforts, 232

time-frame imperatives of elected officials and, 230-31
tracking of cases and persons accused of criminality, data base for, 226
"two language" problem, 231
users of data bases, increase in, 233

Galliher, J. F., 82
Gardner, R., 120
Garofalo, J., 79, 94
Geerkin, M., 175
Gerbner, G., 147
Gettinger, S., 120, 136
Gove, W., R., 175
Greenberg, S., 103
Greene, B. T., 136
Greenfeld, L. A., 120
Gropper, B., 136
Gross, L., 147

Haber, F., 215
Haenszel, N. M., 192
Hagan, F. E., 210
Hansen, A., 169
Harlow, N., 121
Hawkins, G., 120
Heck, J., 33, 38
Helwig, J. T., 42
Heslin, A. S., 192
Hindelang, M. J., 79, 81, 90, 94, 195, 220
Hirsch, P. M., 147
Hirschi, T., 81, 220
History of measurement in criminology, 16, 209-11
  "crime control" perspective and, 215-217
  evaluation of research projects, 214-15
  government agencies, creation of, 213-14
  government funding, 214
  NCS, 81, 98-99
  political aspects, 213-14
  President's Commission on Law Enforcement recommendations, 211-13
  progress made through research, 219-21
  self-report studies, development of, 220-21
  statistics program of LEAA, 216-19
  Supplementary Homicide Reports, 178
  Survey of Inmates and Census of Prisons, 122-24
  UCR, 22-23, 49-51
Holsti, O. R., 28

Homicide data sets, 175. *See also* National Center for Health Statistics homicide data set; Supplementary Homicide Reports
Hoover, J. E., 26
Hughes, M., 175

Imputation (estimation of crimes unreported by local police), 22, 42-44
  methodology of, 44-45
  results of, 46-47
Incident-based reporting of crime, 54-55. *See also* National Incident-Based Reporting System
Integration of research and statistics with operational data bases, 232-33
Intergovernmental component of statistical programs, 6
International Association of Chiefs of Police (IACP), 23, 49, 50, 62, 69, 74
International Classification of Diseases (ICD), 188-89, 191
Inter-University Consortium for Political and Social Research (ICPSR), 33, 78, 102
Israel, R. A., 192

Jacobson, Alvin, 38
James, G., 192
John D. and Catherine T. MacArthur Foundation, 210, 220
Johnson, B. P., 136
Jones, C., 160

Kennedy, S. D., 27, 187
Kent, D. P., 173
Kincaid, S. C., 58
Kindley, K., 187
Kitsuse, J. I., 32, 220
Klebba, A. J., 192
Klein, M. W., 215
Kluger, S., 160
Kryder, M. H., 170
Kuhfeld, W. F., 173

Langworthy, R. H., 192, 193, 198, 199, 200, 202
Laub, J. H., 85
LaVange, L., 107
Law Enforcement Assistance Administration (LEAA), 25, 119, 227

creation of, 213-14
statistics program, 216-19
Lehnen, R. G., 91
Lejins, P. P., 52, 177
Lentzner, H. R., 88
Little, R. J. A., 184
Loftin, C., 186, 187
Longitudinal data in social sciences, 106-8, 117
Lynch, J. P., 96, 102, 103, 104, 106, 108, 113, 114, 117

McCown, R., 159
McGowan, B., 135
McInerney, W., 93
Mainframe computers, 167-69, 170
Maltz, M. D., 24, 26
Marshall, T., 160
Martin, E., 102
Martin, M. E., 147
Masamura, W. T., 135
Mattison, B. F., 192
Mead, B., 23
Microcomputers for handling large data bases, 15, 157-58, 173
  baud rate and, 168
  data extraction, 171
  data types supported by data base software, 161, 163
  files of a data base, 160-61
  future developments, 169-70, 173
  limiting factors, 158-60
  mainframes, data transfers with, 167-69, 170
  "microspy" concerns, 167
  NCS data base, 161, 165
  on-line storage capabilities, 158-59
  printing capabilities, 159
  processing speeds, 159-60
  software requirements
    Data Interchange Format, 163-64
    data management and storage, 162-64
    file sharing, multi-user, 167
    indexing ability, 163
    recovery of data, 165, 166, 167
    report generation capabilities, 164
    restructuring ability, 163
    security of data base, 166-67
    statistical analyses, 165-66
    user interface, 163, 164-65

  spreadsheets, 172
  statistical analyses, 165-66, 172-73
  structure and linking of related files, 161-62
  UCR data base, 170-73
Miller, B. A., 138
Miller, R. E., 138
Miller, W. E., 148
Minor-Harper, S., 120
Montilla, R., 121
Moriyama, I. M., 192
Morris, N., 120
Multiple national indicators of crime, need for, 6, 16

National Academy of Sciences (NAS), 82, 97
National Advisory Committee on Criminal Justice Standards and Goals, 214, 217
National Archive of Criminal Justice Data, 15, 75, 78, 79, 94, 121, 123, 129, 148, 154, 233
National Center for Health Statistics (NCHS), Technical Appendix, 188, 191, 192
National Center for Health Statistics (NCHS) homicide data set, 15, 175-76, 188
  assessment of, 193-94
  classification categories, 188-89, 190
  criticisms of, 192-93, 194
  data collection and reporting tasks, 203-4
  data set variables, 189, 191
  initial reports of homicides, lack of research on, 203
  intersystem comparisons. See SHR, agreement with below
  intrasystem comparisons of data, 191-93
  quality and completeness of data, 203
  SHR, agreement with
    conclusions regarding, 201-2
    national comparisons, 194-98
    state and city comparisons, 198-201
National Commission of Law Observance and Enforcement (Wickersham Commission), 23, 211
National Commission of the Causes and Prevention of Violence, 177
National Crime Information Center (NCIC), 72
National Crime Survey (NCS), 10, 12-13, 75-76, 219
  accuracy of data, 109
  assaultive crimes, problems in measurement of, 90-91

Index

base rates, 82-83
changes over the years, 94-96
characteristics of data set, 78-80
City Surveys, 94, 98, 99
Commercial Survey, 94, 98, 99
confidentiality rules, 92
contextual information about crimes, 89
core and supplement format, 110-11, 117-18
Crime Panel, 98-99
crimes covered, 80
definitions of crimes, 84-85
descriptive information, 111
discrete crimes, measurement of, 85
evaluations of, 11-12, 97
explanatory information, 109-11
future developments, 225-26
geographical disaggregation of data, 91-93
hierarchical file structure, 78-79
history of, 81, 98-99
interview procedure, 77, 86-87, 94-95, 99
limitations of, 87-94
local area data, 114-15
location codes, 111-12
longitudinal file, 106-8, 117
measurement of crime with, 80-87
methodology of, 11, 76-78
microcomputers for handling data, 161, 165
omitted information, 11, 82, 88-90
panel design, 91, 99
persons covered, 79-80
phenomenon being measured, problems created by, 83-86
police services, information on, 113-14
process information, 89-90
property codes, 112
questionnaires used for, 90, 95-96
respondent knowledge of crime and, 83-84
sample size, limits on, 92, 95
sampling procedures, 76-77, 81-83, 95, 99
scope of, 79, 108
secondary analysis of data, 150, 153-55
series victimizations, approach to, 85-86, 88-89
telephone interviews, 77, 94-95
timeliness problem, 93-94
UCR, compatibility with, 65-66
UCR Redesign and, 25
underreporting by victims, 86-87
"victimless" crimes and, 85
victim-offender relationship data, 112-13
Victim Risk Supplement, 102-3, 111
Washington Metropolitan Area Survey, 103-6
NCS Redesign effort, 5, 97-98, 224-25
analyses of redesigned program, 233-34
by-products of, 102-8
consortium to undertake, 100
implementation of, 101
long-term changes, 115-18
near-term changes, 108-15
school crime supplement, 234
strategy of, 100-102
National Criminal Justice Information and Statistics Service (NCJISS), 119, 213, 216
National Incident-Based Reporting System (NIBRS), 54-55, 223-24
advantages over summary-reporting systems, 55-56
classification at agency level, 57
complications arising from, 56-57
implementation of, 57-62
Level I component, 57-59
Level II component, 59-60, 70-71
offenses reported, list of, 60-62
National Institute of Justice (NIJ), 213, 220
data archiving, 147
DUF and, 231
funding of projects, 13-14
NCS Redesign, 111, 118
National Institute of Mental Health (NIMH), 214
National Institute on Alcohol Abuse and Alcoholism (NIAAA), 135
National Office of Vital Statistics, 188
National Prisoner Statistics (NPS) Program, 119. *See also* Survey of Inmates and Census of Prisons
National Sheriff's Association (NSA), 69
National Survey of Crime Severity (NSCS), 219
NCHS. *See* National Center for Health Statistics homicide data set
NCS. *See* National Crime Survey
Nelson, J. F., 91
Nesbitt, C., 120
"New criminology," 16, 216
1984 Census of State Adult Correctional Facilities (1987), 123
Norris, S. L., 187

O'Brien, R. M., 175
Offender-Based Transaction Statistics (OBTS) programs, 65, 66
Office of Justice Programs, 213
Office of Juvenile Justice and Delinquency Prevention (OJJDP), 213, 232
Office of Management and Budget (OMB), 178, 195
Office of Victims of Crime (OVC), 213
Omnibus Crime Control and Safe Streets Act of 1968, 213
Owens, M. E. B., III, 79, 90, 97

Paez, A. L., 95
Palmer, T., 121
Patton, R. E., 192
Penick, B. K. E., 79, 90, 97
Peterson, J., 114
Pierce, G. L., 33, 38, 39
Piercy, D., 138
Poggio, E. C., 27, 28, 31, 32, 46, 52, 187
Police homicides, research on, 198-201
Police reporting of crimes, 26-27
Police service, information on, 113-14
Pollich, J. M., 136
Population Density in State Prisons (1986), 123
Pound, Roscoe, 229
President's Commission on Law Enforcement and the Administration of Justice, 81, 211-13, 214
Prevalence of Imprisonment, The (1985), 122
Prisoners and Alcohol (1983), 122
Prisoners and Drugs (1983), 122
Prison population, increase in, 120
Prisons and Prisoners (1982), 122, 123
Profile of State Prison Inmates (1979), 122
Profile of State Prison Inmates (1986), 123
Program Plan for Statistics, 220
Prosecution of Felony Arrests, 226
Prosecutor management information systems (PROMIS), 226

Raymond, M. R., 184
Recidivism models, 221
Reiss, A. J., Jr., 26, 32, 81, 82, 91, 98, 106, 109
Research Triangle Institute (RTI), 104
Riedel, M., 38, 181, 182, 184, 196, 200, 201
Robison, S. M., 31, 177

Rohe, W. M., 103
Rosch, W. L., 165
Roth, J. A., 221
Rubin, D. B., 184

SAS Institute, 41
Savitz, L. D., 177
Schneider, V. W., 46, 147, 152
Schrotel, S. R., 52
SEARCH (System for Electronic Analysis and Retrieval of Criminal Histories) Group, 57
Secondary analysis of data, 13-15, 145-46, 155
    administrative goals, 147-48
    archives, importance of, 147, 151
    benefits of, 145, 155
    data sharing for, 147, 149-51
    definition of, 145
    documentation for, 14-15, 149, 152, 153
    of National Jail Census, 152
    of NCS data, 150, 153-55
    principles of, 146-48
    problems of, 148-51
    scientific goals, 146-47
    technical obstacles, 149-51
    time savings through, 148
    of UCR data, 152-53.
    See also Microcomputers for handling large data bases
Seidman, D., 31
Self-report studies, 220-21
Sellin, T., 80, 175, 177
"Sellin dictum," 175
Sentencing outcomes, data base on, 227
Series victimizations, 85-86, 88-89
Shenk, F., 93
Sherman, L. W., 192, 193, 198, 199, 200, 202
Sherman, M., 120
Shinnar, R., 221
SHR. *See* Supplementary Homicide Reports
Shulman, H. M., 24, 26
Singer, S., 219
Skogan, W. G., 24, 25, 26, 29, 86, 87, 89, 91, 112
Skolnick, J. H., 26
Smith, William French, 226
South Carolina Law Enforcement Division (SLED), 70
Sparks, R. F., 87
Speckart, G., 136
Spritzer, R., 215

SPSS Inc., 41
Stanton, A., 135
State offender-based transaction statistics (OBTS), 227-28
Stone, M. D., 168
Straf, M. L., 147
Sullivan, R., 137
Supplementary Homicide Reports (SHR), 15, 54, 175-76
   classification categories, validity of, 186-87
   as computer-readable data, 36-37, 39
   data collection and reporting tasks, 203-4
   handbook and coding guides, 178-80
   history of, 178
   initial reports of homicides, lack of research on, 203
   intersystem comparisons. *See* NCHS, agreement with *below*
   intrasystem comparisons of data, 180-87
   missing cases and values, 184-86, 187
   NCHS, agreement with
     conclusions regarding, 201-2
     national comparisons, 194-98
     state and city comparisons, 198-201
     police reports, agreement with, 180-84
   responsiveness to requests and criticisms, 204
   revision of, 180
   underreporting of homicides, 187
Survey of Inmates and Census of Prisons, 10, 13, 119, 140-41
   criminal characteristics data, 130-31
     adjudication history, 133
     current offenses, 131-32
     pre-trial experience, 133
     prior criminal record, 134
     victim-offender relationship, 132
   data collection, 127, 128-29
   facility characteristics data, 129-30
   history of, 122-24
   limitations of data sets, 137-38
   methodology of Census, 11, 124-27
   methodology of Survey, 11, 128-29
   noncriminal characteristics data, 130
     alcohol and drug use, 135-36
     demographic characteristics, 134
     military service, 135
     prison activities, 136
     socioeconomic characteristics, 134-35
   objectives of, 120-22
   pre-testing instruments, 128
   sample selection, 128
   secondary analysis of data, 152
   simultaneous conducting of Surveys and Censuses, 123-24
   universe of facilities, definition of, 124-27
   utility of data sets, 138-40, 141
Survey of Inmates of State Correctional Facilities, 1974: Advance Report (1976), 122

Taub, R., 103
Taylor, B., 108, 118
Taylor, G., 103
Teilmann, K. S., 215
Theory-driven data collection efforts, 232
Time requirements of statistical programs, 230-31
Tracking of cases and persons accused of criminality, data base for, 226
Tracy, P., 219
Tully, E. J., 53
Turner, A. G., 25, 87, 90-91, 95
"Two language" problem in statistical research, 231

UCR. *See* Uniform Crime Reporting Program
Uniform Crime Reporting Handbook, 24, 26
Uniform Crime Reporting (UCR) Program, 10, 12, 47-48
   administration of, 74
   administrative and statistical data, differentiation of, 72-73
   auditing of data. *See* quality control *below*
   changes over the years, 51
   changing nature of crime and, 53
   classification of crimes by "coders," 27-28, 29-30
   as comprehensive part of systemic outlook of criminal justice, 73
   Crime Index, 23, 32, 50, 52; shortcomings of, 68
   critiques of, 51-53
   evaluations of, 11-12, 28, 52, 53-54
   future developments, 225-26
   history of, 22-23, 49-51
   homicide data, 176-78. *See also* Supplementary Homicide Reports
   interpretation of data, 32
   jurisdictional variation and comparability, 30-31

methodology of, 11, 27-31
microcomputers for handling data, 170-73
missing data, 11
misuse of data, 22
NCS, compatibility with, 65-66
operational definitions, 27, 28-30, 176
publications, 24, 66-67
quality control, 24
   current procedures, 62-63
   proposed changes, 63-65
secondary analysis of data, 152-53
state UCR programs, 52, 69-71
statistical sampling, use of, 52
summary reporting system, 25-27, 54-55
types of data collected, 24
usefulness of, 32-33, 71-73
user services, 67-68.
See also Computer-readable UCR data
UCR Redesign effort, 5, 21-22, 25, 31, 54
   analyses of redesigned program, 234
   compatibility with other crime data sources, 65-66
   Crime Index and, 68
   guidelines for redesigned program, 70
   implementation at state level, 71
   NCS and, 25
   quality control, 63-65
   testing of new system, 69-71
   users' attitudes toward, 69
   user services and publications, 66-68.
   See also National Incident-Based Reporting System
U. S. Department of Justice, 43, 216, 218, 221

Vandalism, 104
Veterans in prison, data on, 122, 135
Victimization surveys. *See* National Crime Survey
"Victimless" crimes, 85
Victim-offender relationships, data on, 112-13, 132, 182, 183, 185
Victim Risk Supplement (VRS), 102-3, 111
Visher, C., 221
Von Hirsch, A., 120, 133

Walker, S., 213-14
Washington Metropolitan Area Survey (WMAS), 103-4
   advantages of, 104
   disadvantages of, 105-6
   findings, 104-5
   screening procedures, 105
Watters, J. K., 136
Webster, William, 71-72
Weis, J. G., 81, 220
Welte, J. W., 138
Wheeler, S., 32
Whitaker, C. J., 96, 102
Wiersema, B., 46, 152, 187
Williams, J. R., 103
Williams, K. R., 185, 186, 187
Williams, T., 169, 170
Wilson, O. W., 31
Wolfgang, M. E., 24, 26, 29, 32, 96, 176, 177, 219
Woltman, H. F., 95
World Health Organization, 189

Young, F. W., 173

Zahn, M. A., 38, 180, 181, 182, 196, 200, 201
Zalba, S., 135